PIONEER ROOTS

PIONEER ROOTS

A Window to The Past

Mary Kay Krogman

ISBN-13: 978-1546761808

DEDICATION

This collection is dedicated to our ancestors,
both known and unknown.

Their life choices, traditions and decisions
allowed us to be where we are today.

Table of Contents

Photos and Documents

OVERVIEW

All efforts were taken to ensure accuracy; however, even after years of research, mistakes will be found. Researchers need to verify any information taken from this work. The main purpose of this collection is to share stories and family history with my beautiful grandchildren.

Joe's enthusiasm, encouragement and assistance made this project possible

Much appreciation to the innumerable individuals who, over the years, have shared or confirmed information, stories, research, and photos.

The project remains a work in process.

Chapter 1

The Voyage

In the blink of an eye Angelina's life had been turned upside down. The death of her husband had forced her into the role of a widow with three young children to support. There was little money and no close family, but there was a powerful force behind the widow. Angelina had an ardent desire to provide a better future for her children, and from this desire emerged a plan. Despite the risks, Angelina followed her instincts and chose to emigrate from Luxembourg to America. All the while, she was praying this wouldn't be the biggest mistake of her life.

It was 1866 when they left their homeland. The family of four traveled into the unknown with little more than a frayed shoestring budget and each other.

Angelina is just one of many capable risk-takers we will meet on the following pages. Our ancestors were faced with an array of difficult decisions as they considered the opportunities America might provide. Remaining near family and friends was a powerful reason to stay, but these were times when existing situations provided so little economic opportunity it seemed their only choice was to leave. We will meet families that immigrated following catastrophic crop failures, others that couldn't afford the increasing price of land, and for many young men, emigrating was a way to avoid conscription into the Prussian or German Army for up to six years. Whatever their reasons, they all had dreams of improving their status in life, and these decisions became much easier if a family member or close friends were already established in the New World.

Ocean travel was a dangerous endeavor in the 18th century and there were few rules to deter reckless behavior in the transportation industry and, of course, profits were a priority. Each successive decade offered new and better regulations providing increased safety. By the 1830's, when Theodore Niemann immigrated there were upgraded regulations concerning quality of food. By the 1840's when Henry Niemann, the Schultes, Riebolds and Krafts arrived, new regulations requiring exterior ship lights helped reduce night time collisions, and now there were even more rules relating to food and sanitation. This decade also saw the introduction of passenger steamships, however, the budgets of most travelers didn't allow for such an extravagance.

Today, a seven or eight hour flight from Germany to New York, with several children does not sound like an easy task. If we turn the clock back 150 to 200 years, an average voyage for an early sailing ship between these destinations was eight weeks! A large ship with perfect conditions might arrive in four weeks while small ships with a stormy problematic voyage were known to take up to a grueling twenty weeks. The latter was known to result in a staggering percentage of casualties during the crossing.

Most passengers traveled in steerage where their only lighting consisted of dingy oil lamps that were limited for use during calm seas only. Space was cramped, often just a bit over five feet in height requiring most adults to duck down when they walked. Bunks or berths were wooden 'shelves' about 6' x 3' stacked two or three high, each berth was meant to accommodate two passengers.

Except for food, nothing was supplied. Passengers were expected to provide their own bedding as well as cooking and eating utensils. During the first weeks, food was at its best, but then spoilage began to appear. You would hope that rotting food was disposed of, but that wasn't the case; the smelly spoiling provisions were simply included with daily rations. If seas were quiet passengers were allowed to cook their meals, usually soup or stew, they took special care not to let their pot tip over as waves rocked the ship for there would be no additional food until the next day.

During good weather, passengers spent as much time as possible on deck for fresh air and sunshine. If the seas were stormy, passengers were required to stay below deck, sometimes being locked there, not even allowed to go up on deck to use toilet facilities. When storms lingered, pails they used for toilets might topple over during a big wave. A stench that was bad on a calm voyage was almost unbearable during a storm. There was little or no light in steerage when the doors were closed because lamps were not allowed due to fire danger. Sea sickness which faded away after a few days returned during stormy weather along with an increase in disease.

We owe a huge Thank You to all of our ancestors who made the life changing decision to begin anew in a distant country. They made the trip safely and at some point in time, not all, but most of the individuals covered in these pages came to reside in Iowa or Missouri.

1837

Niemann Brothers

Galena, Illinois

Saloons of nineteenth century Germany were multi purpose gathering places. Not only did they offer the favorite local ale, but they also served as popular centers for the exchange of news and gossip. During a time in Germany, when emigration was rampant and locals received letters from America, the letter recipients often took the opportunity to become the center of attention. With correspondence in hand, they visited their local saloon and a crowd would gather to hear the letter read out loud. Residents were better informed about the happenings in German settlements across America than they were about their own country. They learned about plentiful land and good crop prices along with the opening of German schools and churches. On the other hand, they also learned not to blindly accept exaggerated stories shared by American labor recruiters in search of workers.

Seduced by the prospect of becoming a landowner, Theodore Niemann boarded the *S.S. Augusta and McLine* at Bremen, Germany on September 23rd, 1837. He was likely wondering what adventures his letters home would include. The ship arrived in New Orleans on November 20, 1837, other passengers from Ankum, Germany included the peasant family of John Herman Reiling, his wife Catharine Adelheid, three daughters Catharine [Mary] Adelheid age 16, Mary Ellen 5, Marie 10 and one son Arnold age 15. The family brought with them six boxes of possessions. In the springtime, after the Mississippi River became navigable, Theodore Niemann and the Reilings boarded a steamboat and traveled north to Galena. It is interesting to note Arnold Reiling later became the first mayor of Bellevue, Iowa.

Their arrival was during a tumultuous time in America, Martin Van Buren, the country's first American born president, had been inaugurated as the eighth president the previous March and only two months into his term New York banks began to fail. America was entering a major recession and unemployment was skyrocketing. Some areas of the country, especially in the east were experiencing a 25% unemployment rate.

Surely they had been informed of the economic crisis spreading across the country. However, amidst all the job losses and bank closings there was an exception, Galena,[1] Illinois. By good planning or amazing luck, it was fortunate for Theodore, that Galena was his destination.

Upon his arrival, Theodore was able to find work immediately by laboring in Galena's lead smelting works. His arrival corresponded to a phenomenal annual growth period of Galena's lead production. The local lead mines were producing the majority of the country's lead needs; consequently there was a plentiful supply of jobs available in mining and smelting as well as other local businesses. These opportunities were a strong lure for cash strapped immigrants. The year 1845 showed shipments of 54 million pounds of lead, the most lead shipped in any given year.

---

[1] Galena was named for the lead sulfide mineral of that name.

During this time the population of Galena was hovering around 14,000 residents, the population fell by over 10,000 people by the early 1900's.

In 1838 a ferry was established between Sand Prairie, Jo Daviess County, Illinois and Bellevue, Iowa, allowing pioneers to safely cross the Mississippi. Being a hard worker and a saver, it took Theodore less than a year to secure his first land patent. He had his eye on a plot of land across the river in Jackson County, Iowa. The timing of his acquisition corresponded with Iowa becoming a territory, opening new opportunities for land acquisition.

Jackson County had been receiving a trickle of settlers since 1833 and there were scattered settlers around the county when Theodore first began working his land. With the lack of roads and an abundance of trees and brush, a traveler might pass through the entire county thinking it was uninhabited unless he happened to encounter another traveler or stumble across a settler's cabin.

Theodore immediately began clearing land, soon building a log cabin. Over the years his holdings grew to over 600 acres. As he was preparing the land, Theodore continued to make regular treks across the river back to Galena. No longer in need of employment the lure to Galena was still strong; the lingering attraction being the large contingent of German settlers from the Hanover area. Visiting Galena provided an immediate sense of home and community with fellow Germans.

Theodore married Adeline Reiling, in Galena, Illinois on July 8, 1839. Adeline was a neighbor from his home town in Germany and had sailed to America on the same voyage as Theodore.

A few years after Theodore's arrival, his younger brother Henry followed. As his brother and many Hannover natives did, it is likely Henry took the Bremen, Germany to New Orleans, Louisiana route. Once in Galena, Henry's progress wasn't quite as dramatic as his brother's; he was splitting his time between the smelting works in Galena and assisting his brother clear land in Jackson County, Iowa.

Mirroring his brother's habits, Henry didn't mind traveling back and forth across the great Mississippi river, his home was on the Iowa side but his love was in Illinois. It was in Galena where he met Anna Maria Elizabeth Schulte, another native of Hanover, Germany. On April 28, 1846 John Henry Niemann and Anna Maria Elizabeth Schulte were married in Galena, Illinois. The couple immediately made their home on Henry's tract of unimproved prairie land across the river. *[continued at Farmers and Stone Masons]*

Anna Maria "Elizabeth" Schulte was born January 30, 1825 to Theodore Schulte and Maria "Elizabeth" (Heimann) Schulte, both parents were of German heritage and both born around 1796. Theodore and Elizabeth immigrated with daughters Frances and Anna Maria Elizabeth in 1844; if additional family members were among the group they have not been identified at this time. The Schulte's owned a small farm near Galena in Jo Daviess County, Illinois. To help with the arduous work they employed a hired hand to assist with the farm work.

Their younger daughter Frances married Henry Tobin a German immigrant. The Tobin couple began their married life in rural Galena on a farm, sharing their residence with Frances and Elizabeth's parents. The Tobin's had nine children, Theodore, Elizabeth, Henry and Bernard were born in Illinois and, Mary, Louisa, Joseph, Maggie and Edward were born in Wabasha County, Minnesota.

When the Tobins relocated to Wabasha County, Minnesota, they were accompanied by Theodore and Elizabeth Schulte who both lived into their 7th decade and are buried in Wabasha County.

1842

Francis Xavier Riebold

Franklin County, Missouri

Finding a needle in a haystack may provide better odds of success than locating an old immigration record. If your ancestor arrived pre-1845, and you have limited information, chances of finding the ship manifest you're seeking can be nearly impossible. If legible, surname spellings have unexpected variations, or if you're searching for an individual traveling alone, the researcher may find the surname they are looking for but only a single initial for the first name. Riebold immigration records fall into this category and confirmed immigration facts continue to be elusive.

To date we know that Francis Xavier Riebold emigrated from Germany in the early 1840's, with a destination of Franklin County Missouri.

Francis Xavier became a naturalized American on March 28, 1848. His naturalization document states ". . . upon the testimony of Albert and Gert Goebel two respectable citizens of the United States for five years that the said Xavier Riebold has resided within and under the jurisdiction of the United States for five years and one year immediately vesting this present application in the State of Missouri." With this he renounced all allegiance and fidelity to Austria.

During a similar time frame his younger brother Anselm also settled in Missouri.

In 1845 their sister Mary Antonia immigrated with her husband Leo Kohler, a fellow German, along with their three boys. Mary's husband Leo however died within a few short months, at which time the widow and her boys joined the household of her sister Cordula, her husband Ambrose Friedman and their daughter. The following year, in 1846, the widow Mary Antonia moved a few miles west and joined her brothers on Francis

Xavier's farm in Franklin County. It was here she met Judge Anton Yerger whom she married the following year.

Census records show that 1847 brought another sister to America, Mary Anna immigrated with her husband Xavier Arbeiter and family, they bought a farm in St. John's Township, Franklin County, Missouri.

And finally, according to census records, in 1854, Meinard Reibold sailed across the Atlantic and joined his siblings.

This is supposition, mostly from census and naturalization records, but it appears that six members of the Riebold family immigrated to America, three single brothers and three married sisters with families. These six siblings all settled in Missouri, specifically Jefferson and Franklin Counties. Even with this volume of information, their immigrations records continue to remain undiscovered. *[continued at Overcoming Adversity]*

1847

Nemmers Family

Jackson County, Iowa

July 1847 marked the arrival of Nicholas Nemmers and his family in Jackson County, Iowa. They chose Prairie Springs Township as their new home and immediately began building a small cabin. The location was near Tete des Morts which was later renamed Saint Donatus. Their farm was a few miles north of the Niemann families in Spruce Creek and just west of the Haxmeier brothers.

The Nemmers emigration followed the potato blight crisis in northern Europe. Although this famine was by far the most severe in Ireland, other Northern European countries such as Belgium, Germany and France also experienced famine related deaths, food shortages and economic upheaval. Many families were forced to make life changing decisions to stabilize their future.

Their situation was entirely different from the Niemann's, rather than two young brothers venturing out on their own, three generations of the Nemmers family traveled as a group, settling in Jackson County. After the decision was made to leave their homeland, families still faced tough choices. With limited luggage space, family heirlooms often remained behind. Farmers brought seeds, Nicholas being a carpenter brought his most practical tools and the lady of the house often brought heirloom dishes and a favorite tablecloth.

This family of immigrants included the patriarch, sixty-four year old Nicholas, his wife Catherine and three children, son Michael Sr., and daughters Caroline and Susanne. There was also the family of his son Nicholas and his very pregnant wife Maria Catherina (Freymann) with their three children Catharine, Michael P. and Nicholas D. Another daughter

Catherine and her family would follow a few years later. *[continued at Farmers and Stone Masons]*

1850
Manders Family
Jackson County, Iowa

The prize for most unique former home would have to go to Mathias and Elizabeth Manders. Their home in Sandweiler had a historical beginning as an abbey; it was then taken over by the French during the French Revolution in the 1790s. In 1820, twenty years after the revolution ended, the French government sold it to Mathias. The abbey was the Manders home for almost thirty years until the late 1840's when a downturn in the economy forced Mathias to sell his farm to the bank.[2] Today Sandweiler, Luxembourg is best known for a World War II German War Cemetery that contains almost 11,000 fallen German soldiers that died during the Battle of the Bulge.

The S. S. Sea Lion arrived in New Orleans June 10, 1850. Passengers included two families emigrating from the small farming settlement of Sandweiler, Luxembourg. Mathias and Elizabeth (Hentgen) Manders emigrated with their nine children, Marie, age 26; Peter, age 24; John Peter, age 21; Mathias, age 19; Marie, age 17; Michael, age 15; Elizabeth, age 13; Eva, age 11 and Sebastian age 9. The other family was Mathias' first cousin John Peter Capesius, Jr., his wife and their six children.

Once in New Orleans, they secured passage on a steamboat, spending the subsequent weeks making their way up the crowded Mississippi river with a destination of Jackson County, Iowa. As the steamboat approached Iowa, the scenery they enjoyed was riveting, the view changed with every mile and the scenes were all beautiful and unique. They saw wildlife, lumber mills, manufacturing plants, farms, blowing and drifting sand, Native Americans, tree covered islands of various sizes, and an assortment of towns. If they went as far as Dubuque they could peer up at an incredible variety of bluffs and rock formations. In Mark Twain's words, after passing Rock Island, "We move up the river – always through enchanting scenery, there being no other kind on the Upper Mississippi." [3]

One of the first national events that occurred after their arrival in Iowa was the swearing in of Millard Fillmore as president of the United States

[2] Betty (Manders) Jaeger, a descendant of Mathias, with the assistance of professional genealogist Jean Ensch of Luxembourg, researched the history of the Manders farm in Luxembourg.

[3] Life on the Mississippi by Mark Twain, page 412, Copyright 1883 by Samuel L. Clemens.

and California became the 31st state later that year.

Mathias and his family weren't the first Manders family from Luxembourg to arrive in Jackson County, Iowa. Mathias' nephew, Jean Pierre Manders, a son of Pierre and Marguerite (Schummer) Manders, were the first. Jean Pierre married Johanna Abend in Luxembourg during the year 1847, they had a baby girl named Anne in 1848 and left for America early in 1849.

During this period of ocean travel there was still fear of tragedy befalling a ship. Drunkenness among officers, excessive loads and defective construction were just a few causes of shipwrecks. Even with a growing list of rules and regulations, the early to mid-nineteenth century still counted an annual loss of 15 to 20 ships, and this didn't take into account that the number of deaths from disease still far exceeded the loss of life by sinking ships.

The young couple's voyage turned out to be a heartbreaking one and their excitement of new opportunities lost its sparkle when their precious young daughter was stricken with a severe case of measles and died at sea on May 24, 1849. Jean Pierre and Johanna traveled alone to Jackson County, Iowa where they spent a couple years farming just south of Dubuque. They had a second daughter in 1850; she was named Anne, in honor of her lost sister. Soon after her birth they moved to central Iowa, eventually settling in Dallas County.

It is reasonable to assume that after arriving in Jackson County, nephew Jean Pierre corresponded with Mathias, sharing the geography and development of the locale. The similarities to their home country and the growing collection of Luxembourgers certainly made Jackson County an attractive destination for Luxembourgers, especially stone masons. With family already in the area Mathias and his family had a link to home and a likely home-away-from-home as they built their own house. *[continued at Farmers and Stone Masons]*

1852

Zahner Family

Louisville, Kentucky

"Brother will betray brother" was a bible verse Ludwig Zahner never imagined would apply to him. The betrayal left a devoted family man in the depths of despair with a strong belief he let his family down.

The story behind this family may have been lost forever, had it not been for Ludwig's son, Maximillian Zahner. Max was a hard working German immigrant farmer, he not only wrote an in depth story of his past for his immediate family, he also wrote a story from the perspective of his half-brother William Ignasse Zahner. When presenting the story to his nephew he added this notation "I composed the family history according to your father's case and if I left out anything of which he knows that I may have forgotten, he can tell you where to insert it."

The story written by Maximillian Zahner is an impressive piece of work, especially considering the fact that English wasn't his first language and his education ended at age fourteen, possibly earlier. In all likelihood, someone else put his words to paper, but his dates and facts have been researched and found to be accurate. This story begins with the title "The Family History of William Zahner" and Max proceeds to tell the family history in detail, beginning with William's great-grandparents.

The great grandfather of William and Max was Franz Zahner, he left Switzerland with his family around 1785 and settled in the small German village of Liel, near the Rhine River. Here Franz went to work in one of the iron ore mines which were an important part of the local economy through the early 19th century.

In 1797 Franz passed away, leaving his oldest son, sixteen year old Ludwig as the sole source of support for the family. The young man was up to the task, it wasn't an easy road, but he managed to keep food on the table and maintained a small house for his mother and siblings. Four years later, he learned it was time to serve his country's military. Generally the individual supporting a family was given an exemption, but as with everything else in his life Ludwig had to fight for the right to remain at home. He won the fight and continued his duty to support his family.

Ludwig was a likeable young man, popular in his community where he married a local girl by the name of Anna Spitz. They raised their family in Liel where Ludwig became the mayor, a position he held for twenty years. He later became the town's revenue collector, apparently for another twenty years, bringing his retirement age to about 70 years.

There were five children in Ludwig and Anna's family, the middle child Ludwig Louis Zahner was born on June 8, 1809. Ludwig Louis was a multi talented individual having learned the talents of cabinet maker, mechanic, millwright and miller. He polished his talents by traveling to different regions learning the best methods of the trade, spending time in areas of Switzerland and Germany with a goal of perfection; he was a focused and talented young man. Ludwig was prepared for and likely expecting a smooth successful life, but fate would intervene every step of the way, dashing each plan the man ever made.

At the age of 28 Ludwig Louis Zahner married a native of Liel, Josepha Lang, daughter of Johannes and Ludovika (Zimmerman) Lang. Their only child was Maximillian, he was still very young when his mother, Josepha died of a tumor at the young age of twenty four years.

Three years after the death of his first wife, on February 2, of 1841, Ludwig married Frederika Meier who tragically died after the birth of their first child who was named Fredrick Louis. Ludwig was unable to handle an infant and young child on his own; consequently four months later, in June of 1842 he married Louisa Boehler. This marriage resulted in seven children, three living past infancy.

Trying to provide a better life for his family, the Zahner family moved to a nearby town named Hausen, where Ludwig rented a gristmill. In addition to being able to mill the grain, his talents extended to fixing and repairing the working parts. Ludwig was confident he would be successful. After three years and no glimmer of success, Ludwig abandoned the idea and moved back to Liel. Just as it looked like brighter days were around the corner, 1846 and 1847 had disastrous crop failures resulting in a diminished food supply and no jobs. To make matters worse the economic upheaval was followed by the German Revolution. This was a revolt of citizens that were tired of censorship, crushing taxation and poor working conditions. The revolt failed and conditions didn't change.

The family continued to struggle but they were hanging on. Improvement of their situation was always just out of reach. As the boys were getting older they could see the day approaching when the German Army would conscript them for service.

Following is William's story as told by his half brother Max:

"If we had known what hardships awaited us, our Father would have never undertaken to go to a new country, not knowing its language nor the manner of business carried on there. As there was an undesirable prospect that we boys would be compelled to serve in the army when we became of age, and as we was hoping to better our situation in general, so we started for the United States in the month of September 1852 to the great sorrow of all our relations in Germany.

"On the 28th day of September 1852 we went aboard a sail vessel named "Globe" in the seaport of Havre de Gare in France. After an extremely stormy voyage we landed in New Orleans on the 20th day of November 1852, a weary time of 53 days. After eleven days of steam boating up the Mississippi and Ohio Rivers we arrived at Louisville, Kentucky on the 1st day of December 1852.

"As my Uncle Anton Zahner had immigrated with his family to this country two years previous, and settled in Louisville, Kentucky, we also stopped at that place, and as it was in winter time, it was difficult to find some employment. But brother Max found some employment in a slaughterhouse where he had to rinse the slaughtered hogs until he took sick from being wet from head to foot all day in extremely cold weather."

The passenger manifest for "The Globe" shows Ludwig age 42 and Louise age 33 arriving with children Max, Fritz, Marie, and Willhelm. At this point Ludwig Zahner expected his luck to change, in his mind he had hit bottom and there was only one direction to go. Unfortunately for

Ludwig, this is where the phrase "from bad to worse" comes into play. Max's story continues . . .

"At the time we arrived at Louisville, we had enough money left above the expense of the long journey to buy a good farm. That money belonging to my brothers, Max and Frederick, to which they had fallen heir from their respective mothers. Said money was given in Father's care by the authorities at Court to invest the same in real estate for the respective heirs, in this Country. As it was not my Father's custom to be idle and as he did not succeed in getting a situation shortly after our arrival, he was induced by his brother, Anton, and the friends of the latter to enter into a partnership business at gardening near the City of Louisville. After our Father had expended all our money in the business, he found that he had been deceived by his brother in regard to the means of the latter, who made my father believe that he would pay back his share as soon as he could collect his money which he had loaned out; it was discovered, however, that Uncle had no outstanding money, which of course resulted in considerable dissatisfaction between the partners, and after a whole season of hard labor on our part, my Father was compelled to sell his share at a great loss for us, as from all the money invested besides the labor, we saved out of that wreck only seventy-five dollars.

This was not a very promising beginning for the Zahner family. After placing their faith and their money in the hands of someone they trusted, almost all was lost. *[continued at Overcoming Adversity]*

1853

Flammang Family

Dubuque, Iowa

The call went out in Luxembourg for German speaking priests. For J.P. and Elizabeth Flammang their excitement and pride exceeded the sadness they felt as their first-born son John Michael responded. Even if John Michael had known his father would leave his earthly bounds in less than a year, it is doubtful his plans would have changed. During a time when religious calling took priority over all else, his parents, more than likely, encouraged him to go.

It was 1853 when John Michael Flammang, a seminary student, emigrated from his homeland. His education to that point included a diploma from his local high school as well as initial coursework at a Luxembourg seminary. After arriving in America, Bishop Loras sent him to the Mount Saint Bernard Seminary in Key West, Iowa to complete his training. John Michael Flammang was ordained by Bishop Loras on April 18, 1854 at the old St. Raphael's Cathedral in Dubuque, Iowa.

Shortly after his ordination, he was sent to Saint Kunigunde in

Davenport, later spending some time at the parishes in Muscatine and Old Mission in Festina, Iowa. Finally he would be sent to a struggling Saint Donatus parish that would link many of the Jackson County settlers included on these pages.

While in Davenport, Father Flammang's brother John Nicholas "Nick" Flammang immigrated, traveling to Davenport and taking on a job as a farm hand. After his brother's departure from Davenport, Nick went south to Saint Louis where he spent the next few years, he then returned to Iowa and continued his labors as a farm hand working in western Dubuque County.

Annie Flammang, a sister to John Michael and John Nicholas, was a young woman who never imagined her brother's calling would have such a dramatic effect on her own life. Had we known the man, most of us would classify him as a workaholic. His mind was filled with plans and ideas and the man was desperate to bring them to fruition. It wasn't long before he realized he was in desperate need of a dependable housekeeper in a part of the country where there was a shortage of women. To fill this need, Reverend Flammang asked his parents to allow his younger sister Annie to join him in America. J. P. and Elizabeth Flammang were devout Catholic farmers in Koerich, Luxembourg; they strove to provide the best religious education for their children and when their first-born son John Michael became a priest they were proud beyond words. They agreed to his request and Annie joined her brother in America.

It was at Saint Donatus that Annie began to have serious trouble dealing with her homesickness. She was accustomed to an active household filled with family and loved ones, but here, day or night, she was always alone. Her brother's first priority was the revival of his parishioner's dedication to their faith, and he was not about to allow distractions to interfere.

If Annie had known a person could experience such loneliness and despair, she would have begged to remain at home, but it was too late for regrets. She needed to face the reality of being trapped in a foreign land while her brother was immersed in his work. Annie did have one thing going for her, the young woman still had her faith. She cried, she prayed, she pleaded with God to make it possible to return to her family. However, deep down she knew she was hoping for the impossible, praying for a miracle.

Many adjectives can be used to describe Reverend J. Michael Flammang, dedicated, devout, demanding and unyielding to name a few. Solely focused on his calling, many classified him as a zealot, but surprisingly he did have the compassion to notice his sister was suffering and even more surprising, he allowed her to return to their family in Luxembourg. Annie's prayers had been answered!

Annie returned to the Flammang home town of Koerich which itself carries a long and interesting history. The town's people, especially the farmers endured difficult times during the 19th century. Henri Mauer's Koerich pages on his website www.mauerhenri.com help the reader understand why so many of its residents emigrated. Even though the country became independent in 1839, the citizens of Koerich saw little if any change. After the French invasion, land was re-distributed to municipalities and local people including farmers. It should have created a new life for many of the farmers, but a conniving nobleman found a way around the new law. At that time Koerich and the surrounding land were owned by nobleman Georg von Pfortsheim. According to Henri Mauer's research, Pfortsheim "gave up his title as nobleman and became "Citizen Pfortsheim" farmer of Colpach. Since he wasn't noble anymore, his possessions weren't confiscated, and the farmers of Koerich stayed his leaseholders."[4] This inequity was passed from generation to generation until finally in 1934 one of the Pfortsheim descendants lost his holdings due to financial issues.

After a devastatingly poor harvest in 1847, the farmers of Luxembourg were struggling to maintain a decent standard of living. Between 1850 and 1860 there were approximately 6,000 Luxembourgers that immigrated to America. Many of Koerich's residents were included in that number.

Annie returned home to her mother Elizabeth (Greten) Flammang, who was now a widow and worried about her sons in America. Her second son Nikolas operated the home farm in Koerich and would be better off with fewer mouths to feed. One of Elizabeth's daughters had just joined a Luxembourg convent, Elizabeth felt there was no longer a need for her to remain in Koerich, but the need for her help in America was great. To fill that need she made the decision to spend her remaining days in America helping her beloved son J. Michael, and Elizabeth was accompanied by four of her daughters.

Annie, who even after learning to expect the unexpected, never imagined she would leave Luxembourg a second time. In 1863 she was on a ship with her mother and three of her sisters, heading back to the land she had been so thankful to leave behind. *[continued at Farmers and Stone Masons]*

1854

William Herrig

Jackson County, Iowa

A very accomplished family, Herrig ancestors lived in the small village of Wormeldange, Luxembourg for generations, dating back as far as the early 1700's. Dominic Herrig, son of John, was born in 1722. Dominic's son

[4] http://www.mauerhenry.com/koerichenglish.html

Mathias, was born in 1765. He supported his family through his work as a stone mason and bricklayer. Mathias was married to Johanetta Punnel in Wormeldange on December 26, 1792. Their family grew to five children, Mathias, Magdalena and Michael, Margaretha and Johann.

The 19th century brought the growth of the wine industry along the beautiful Moselle River. In the Wormeldange area, the soil along the river is permeated with slate, some areas holding no topsoil at all, just a layer of heat retaining slate which quickly releases the excess waters of heavy rain. These conditions are not ideal for most agricultural crops, but Riesling grapes can thrive, especially if they are grown on the slopes facing the river where they not only benefit from direct sunlight but reflections of the river water.[5] It was this growing industry in which the middle child, Michael Herrig, became interested. Census data reveals he was a wine maker and farmer. In addition to a small vineyard he likely raised a few small farm animals such as goats and chickens.

Michael married Catherine Thill at the age of 26 on February 21, 1827. They had a family of seven children, William, born in 1828; Anna Maria, born in 1831; Mathias Michael, 1834; Anna, 1836; John born August 15, 1840; Peter 1843 and John Peter 1846.

Michael's younger brother Johann or John, son of Mathias and Johanetta, appears to be the first of this family to emigrate from Luxembourg. John married Susanna Bauer February 17, 1830 in Wormeldange where they had a family of nine, possibly ten children, seven of which survived to make the journey across the ocean.

The exact circumstances that compelled the John Herrig family to leave their native Wormeldange and settle in rural Ohio are not known. John and family arrived in America July 7, 1854 on the *S. S. Julie*, sailing from Antwerp to New York. According to the manifest, John was 44 years old and immigrated with his wife Susanna 45, and their children Catharina 22, Mathias 18, Peter 14, John 11, Maria 8, Michel 6 and 11 month old Elizabeth.

John's nephews, the Jackson County Iowa Herrig brothers, were well educated residents of Wormeldingen Luxembourg. The first of the boys to venture to America was William, the oldest. Arriving in 1854, the same year as his uncle. Until William's name is identified on a ship manifest we won't be sure who arrived first, William or his uncle John, or they may have traveled together.

Three years after William immigrated, his brothers John and Mathias arrived. The youngest, John Peter, didn't set foot on American soil until 1868. *[continued at Dreams Realized]*

---

[5]Information from *The Encyclopedic Atlas of Wine,* C. Fallis, editor pages 258-259 Global Book Publishing 2006

1856
Ostwald Family
Dubuque, Iowa

"All kinds of domestic suffering [illnesses] had [rather] brought him down, so that for him it became tight [economically]; alone here he could still [nevertheless] become ruined [financially]."[6] Tom Steichen translated the information concerning Michael Ostwald from an 1856 Hegensdorf community chronicle for Tom Larson's family research. The chronicle offered no further detail concerning the nature of the illness or who was stricken, but we do know that four of their nine children, all born in Hegensdorf, had died before the Ostwald family immigrated to America.

Michael Ostwald, born September of 1798 was a master mason by trade as well as a respected builder in Hegensdorf, Germany. In 1826 he married Anna Marie Gerken the oldest daughter of Johannes Heinrich Gerken and Maria Catharina Stratmann. The Gerken lineage has been extensively researched by Tom Larson, an Iowa native. He has traced Anna Marie Gerken's family back to the marriage of Heinrich Gerken and Clara Anna Fumen in 1711. Mr. Larson also has a website where he shares his research, assisting scores of researchers with their "brick walls."

The Gerken family oral history includes descriptions of Anna Marie's father's service in Napoleon Bonaparte's army. This oral history, if true, says that Johannes Heinrich Gerken, born October 4, 1773 was a member of Napoleon's personal body guard unit. Most believe that he was in Napoleon's army, but there is doubt that a Prussian would have been a member of his personal body guard unit. But then again, maybe so.

Beside hard times and a bleak future, the family was drawn to America by the success of Michael's brother-in-law. The ship manifest of their voyage to America lists the Ostwalds as Michael age 55, Marie age 51, Caroline 22, Marie 21, Therese and Herman's ages are not legible. They arrived in New Orleans, Louisiana on April 29, 1856 on the ship New Orleans; their luggage consisted of only four boxes. *[continued at Overcoming Adversity]*

1857
Hoffmann Family
Jackson County, Iowa

The Hoffmann family used reconnaissance in their decision making

[6] The Gerken-Larson Heritage, a Family History researched and written by Tom Larson, has been available at his website located at rootsweb.com.

process. Once the scout, in this case Michael (b. 1835) had reported on the conditions, the family made their final decision; their decision was to join their scout in America.

A leading member of his community, Michael Hoffmann (b. 1805) was a successful cartwright and shop owner, he was also a horse dealer and trainer. Michael was born March 15, 1805 in Kehlen, to Michael Hoffmann, Sr. and Anna Maria Michels. He married Catherine Glaesener January 21, 1834, Catherine was also a native of Kehlen. The Hoffmann family consisted of seven children, Michael, Mary, Michael John (John M.), Franz, Angeline, Nicholas and John. The children had received a top level education in their homeland, arriving in America as a bi-lingual family speaking French and German.

Their first born child, Michael (b. 1835) learned the wagon-maker trade as an apprentice under his father's guidance. In 1857 the younger Michael left for America to scope out the possibilities, he settled in Tete des Morts township, Jackson County, Iowa. Partnering with Nicholas Kirchen and Jacob Bengnet, Michael Hoffmann operated a wagon-maker business.

Michael arrived at a very unsettling time in Jackson County history, the normally peaceful, "mind your own business" inhabitants of the county had become fed up with their justice system. There was the case of a brutal wife murderer, William Barger who was preparing for his third murder trial, he was now claiming insanity. Then there was a German farmer who was murdered by his hired hand and his body thrown into a thresher. The final straw was the discovery, in a wooded area, of another Jackson County murder victim. The locals were angry and scared, it took little convincing to assemble a sizeable vigilance committee. Not long after the committee was formed, two men had been lynched; one of them being William Barger. A local paper commented "In the name of God and humanity don't let Jackson county become a disgrace to the State."

The lawless events from 1857 didn't slow the influx of immigrants. Four years after Michael's arrival in Iowa, on May 3, 1861, his parents, Michael and Catherine with his five younger siblings ages 9 to 24 left Europe from the French port of La Havre and sailed for America, arriving in New York June 6, 1861 on the ship S. S. Vanguara. The passenger list showed Michael, age 57; Catherine, age 54; Maria, age 24; Michael, age 21; Francois, age 20; Angeline, age 16 and Nicholas, age 9.

From New York the Hoffmann family traveled to Iowa by rail. The Hoffmann's had a major advantage over many of their fellow immigrants, they arrived with a life savings, estimated between $2000 and $2500, more than enough to get them started in the new world. A few months after arriving in Jackson County, Michael, Sr. invested about half his savings on 190 acres of partially improved farmland, located in Prairie Springs Township, purchasing the land from John Moes. Next he invested in a few head of livestock and in a matter of months had made a complete transformation from European wagon-maker to American farmer. *[continued at Farmers and Stone Masons]*

1863

Meysenburg Family

Cascade, Iowa

Another Sandweiler family that embarked on a voyage to America was the Meysenburg family. Nicholas Meysenburg and Catharina Thekes were parents to ten children. Only five of their children survived to adulthood and wife and mother, Catharina died in 1859, a few days after giving birth to their tenth child.

In hopes of discovering new opportunities for their family, the oldest son Peter Nicholas (P.N.) acted as the family scout and immigrated in 1863, landing in New York and traveling directly to the Cascade area in eastern Iowa where he joined an existing settlement of Luxembourgers and there he engaged in farming.

After the positive reports sent by his son P. N., a year later the elder Peter Nicholas (Nicholas), emigrated with the remainder of his family, three daughters, 22 year old Suzanne, 24 year old Mary and 26 year old Anna, and one son, fourteen year old John Baptiste. The family arrived in New York on the S.S. Goschen in June of 1864 in the midst of the Civil War. They went directly to eastern Iowa to join Peter Nicholas.

The youngest Meysenburg daughter Suzanne, after being in America less than three months was joined with Mathias Manders, Jr. in the bonds of Holy Matrimony, their date of marriage was September 14, 1864. They had both grown up in Sandweiler, the families had attended the same church but Suzanne was 8 years old when the Manders family emigrated, she likely had a much better memory of Mathias' younger brother Sebastian than she did of her new husband Mathias. The young couple made their home at the Manders homestead with Mathias Sr. and Elizabeth, in the house built in 1850 by the Manders' stone masons.

The remainder of the Meysenburg family spent the next few years farming in Cascade, Iowa but they weren't completely satisfied with their situation. As their adventuresome spirit re-awakened, the Meysenburg family made plans to search for greener pastures. Their goal was to find the perfect area to establish a farm. P. N. was married on January 19, 1869, to Miss Mary B. Dehner and before long the family began their trek southwest in search of their dream homestead. There were six pioneers, P. N. and his bride along with his father Nicholas, sisters Mary and Anna and younger brother John. Initially they settled at a location near Topeka Kansas.

Kansas had been a part of the Union since 1861, but it didn't take long for the family to realize this was not what they were looking for. The climate was too warm, and the location wasn't to their liking, so they packed up and continued to Nebraska. A biography of P. N. tells us "Upon reaching the Platte valley, July 3, 1869, he decided to locate there and lost no time in preparing a habitation and notifying his friends of the location of his new home, and many of them joined him later."[7]

Peter Nicholas Meysenburg bought land for $2.50 per acre "he is now the proprietor of one thousand and six hundred acres of land that will compare favorably in value and fertility to the best in Butler county"[8].

John Meysenburg, born August 29, 1849, was the youngest member of the family to settle in Butler County. John married a native of his hometown, Susan Reisdorf, who was born to Peter and Anna (nee Simon) Reisdorf. His biography conveys that he was "a member of the county board for six years and still serving. He has always been careful of the interests of the people, serving them in such a manner as to insure the confidence and respect of all who were his daily associates, in business, social, and religious matters. Was a prominent member of the Catholic church, and one of its first adherents at the foundation of it in this county.

"He is now the possessor of seven hundred and forty acres of land, well improved, has a comfortable home, fine barns well stocked, and is highly esteemed for the thrift and good judgment he has shown in his management of his own affairs, as well as those of the county. In politics, he is a free silver democrat, and has filled a number of township offices."[9]

1866
Angelina Welter-Philipps and Children
Jackson County, Iowa

The words Luxembourger, sister, mother, widow, strong, decisive, immigrant, day laborer, and Iowan all describe Angelina Philipps. She was born in 1825 and grew up in a rural Luxembourger community. Her father Nicolas Philipps, was born March 22, 1780 and died September 24, 1843 when she was eighteen years of age. Her mother Catherine Molitor who was born October 24, 1776 died three years after her husband on September 11, 1846. Angelina's remaining family were two older brothers, Jean Pierre and Johan who both lived with their families in nearby, Graulinster, Grevenmacher, Luxembourg.

At the age of thirty-one, Angelina married Nicholas Welter, a forty-four year old widower with no children. The couple had three children, Peter

---

[7] Memorial and Biographical Record, George A. Ogle & Co. Chicago, 1899.
[8] Ibid.
[9] Ibid.

was born in 1857, Katharina in 1859 and Catherine in 1861. After the birth of their second daughter, Angelina's older brothers Jean Pierre Phillips and John P. both immigrated to America with their families. John Peter bought land and settled with his family just north of La Motte, Iowa; it wasn't long before he was thriving in his new home, brother John P. bought land nearby in southern Dubuque County and like his brother, his new life was bringing him success.

In 1865, Angelina's life took a sudden turn with the death of her husband Nicholas; he died leaving her with three young children and a future without promise. Her brothers were doing well in America, maybe she should follow in their footsteps. She wasn't excited about the prospect of traveling alone with children, but the benefits of providing her three children with more opportunity seemed worth the risk. The following year Angelina decided it was now or never and she made the bold move of disposing most of her possessions and purchased tickets to sail to America. The Welter family said their good-byes to friends and neighbors and set off for the train station.

Angelina wasn't wealthy and traveling to America wasn't cheap, everything had a cost, transportation to the port, the cost of food and depending on when the train arrived at the port they might need overnight accommodations. Angelina was sure she had thought of everything. She followed instructions and took the advice of people with travel experience, but to her dismay, once she arrived at the port and the passengers were preparing to board the ship, they were informed the ship had been quarantined.

Now there was yet another decision to make, but this turned out to be an easy one. She no longer had a home to return to, and then if they returned home, their funds would be depleted. Angelina accepted the shipping line's offer of an alternate ship in spite of the risk. The replacement ship was much smaller and the voyage would take longer. The sea would feel rougher and the conditions on the ship more crowded and less sanitary with disease more likely. But for Angelina, there was no turning back.

On the voyage, Angelina befriended a young mother caring for an ailing child. The ship's food supply was running low, and some of the food that was being offered was suffering from spoilage. Following suggestions of friends and neighbors, Angelina had brought three large bags of dried bread for her and her children. She was a compassionate woman, always concerned for the welfare of others and there was no hesitation, she shared her bread with the young mother and child.

The journey was a long one, it took over two months. The sea was rough and conditions were wretched, but when they arrived in America, the baby's condition had improved, and Angelina's new life was about to begin.

The journey from the port to Iowa was most likely by rail which had become the most affordable and was by far the fastest method of travel. *[Continued at Dreams Realized].*

* * *

Author's Note: Relationship confusion isn't limited to couples. Relationship confusion can also be applied to researchers attempting to understand family relationships of various levels of cousins. First cousins, second cousins, first cousins once removed, first cousins twice removed, what does it all mean? It may sound confusing, but it's not as complicated as it might seem.

First cousins are easy to understand, they are the children of your aunts and uncles and you all share the same grandparents. Second cousins are simply the next generation, any children of first cousins are second cousins to each other and all share the same great-grandparents. Third cousins share the same great-great grandparents, and on and on.

Adding the word removed is simply looking at cousins not in your generations; adding the word once refers to one generation forward or one generation back, twice would be two generations forward or back.

For example first cousin once removed would be your parents' first cousin or your first cousin's child, first cousin twice removed is your grandparent's first cousin or your first cousin's grandchild, thrice removed and you move on to great-grand, etc. Second cousin once removed is the parent's second cousin or your second cousin's child and second cousin twice removed would be your grandparent's second cousin or your second cousin's grandchild and so on.

1868

Krogmann Families

Iowa, Kansas, Minnesota, South Dakota

The Krogmann family had different generations emigrate at different times, settling in different parts of Iowa, some of their children dispersed around the Midwest. To aid in identifying family connections of those that immigrated, the following is a brief summary of information collected to date.

Generation I

Herman Heinrich Krogmann, born November 17, 1763 Steinfeld, Vechta Oldenburg, Germany, died December 6, 1842 in Steinfeld, Vechta, Oldenburg, Germany. He married Anna Maria Osterhus, who was born

July 25, 1762 in Steinfeld, Vechta, Oldenburg, Germany, she died September 16, 1822. Two of their sons, Herman Heinrich and Franz Ferdinand emigrated from Germany.

Generation II

Immigrated 1878 – The older of the two boys mentioned above, Herman Heinrich Krogmann was born November 26, 1798 in Steinfeld, Vechta, Oldenburg, Germany, he immigrated as a widower with his son's family, Carl Anton Krogmann (b. 1831) and wife Maria Agnes Rosebaum. They made their home in a settlement of northern Germans near Petersburg in Delaware County, Iowa.

Immigrated 1873 – Franz Ferdinand Krogmann was born October 8, 1801 in Steinfeld, Vechta, Oldenburg, Germany, like his older brother, he immigrated as a widower with his son's family Herman Heinrich Krogmann (b. 1834) and Maria Agnes Nieberding. This Krogmann family initially made their home near Clinton, Clinton County, Iowa. You'll notice a repeat of the name Herman Heinrich where Franz's son carries the same name as Franz's brother, one settling in Clinton, the other in Petersburg.

Generation III

Immigrated 1878 – Carl Anton Krogmann, (b. 1831) son of Herman Heinrich (b. 1798) immigrated with his wife, children and his father, Herman Heinrich.

Immigrated 1868 – Gerhard Herman Krogmann (b. 1825) son of Herman Heinrich (b. 1798) immigrated with his wife and children, arriving on April 22, 1868 on the S. S. Berlin. They traveled from Bremen to Baltimore, settling in Petersburg, then Dyersville, Iowa.

Immigrated 1873 - Herman Heinrich Krogmann (b. 1834) son of Franz Ferdinand (b. 1801) immigrated on the sailing ship S. S. Argonaut from Bremen to New York, arriving June 18, 1873. Passengers included his wife and eight children, Lena Nieberding, an aunt of Mrs. Krogmann, Grandpa Nieberding, and Grandpa Franz Heinrich Krogmann. There were also friends from their home town that joined the group.

Generation IV

Immigrated 1868 – Children of Gerhard Heinrich Krogmann (b. 1825) arrived with their parents initially settled in Delaware County, Iowa. Maria Anna located near Dubuque, Iowa, Francisca Carolina went to Nemaha, Kansas, Catharina Josephine moved to nearby Dyersville, while their brother Franz Heinrich located at New Hampton, Iowa.

Immigrated 1873 – Children of Herman Heinrich Krogmann (b. 1834) arrived with their parents, initially settling in Clinton County, Iowa - Maria Josephina, Maria Elisabeth, Maria Anna, Johann Heinrich, Clemens, Franz

Thomas, Joseph and Bernard.

Immigrated 1878 – Children of Carl Anton Krogmann arrived with their parents, initially settling in Delaware County, Iowa. One of the boys, Herman Henry raised his family in Lismore, Minnesota, three others, Franz, Anton and Margaret eventually settled in Ashton, Iowa.

Immigrated 1882 – Johann Heinrich Krogmann, grandson of Franz Ferdinand Krogmann (b. 1801), arrived alone, his parents Johnann Heinrich Krogmann and Maria Catharina Olberding remained in Germany. Henry first traveled to Clinton where his Grandfather was living with his uncle Herman, from there he joined other Krogmanns in Sioux County, Iowa and finally settled in Remsen, Iowa.

Johann Heinrich is a first cousin to the children of Herman Heinrich (b. 1834); they share Franz Ferdinand as their grandfather. Johann Heinrich's relationship to children of Carl Anton and Gerhard Heinrich, listed in this generation, is that of second cousin. His grandfather is Franz Ferdinand, a brother to Herman Heinrich, they share a great-grandfather.

Immigrated 1880 – Franz Henrich Krogmann (b. 1861) is another grandson of Franz Ferdinand (b. 1801) arrived around 1880. His parents were Franz Henrich Krogmann and Maria Catharina Berding. Right now it is unknown if his father remained in Germany or emigrated, his mother died in Germany. Franz eventually came to reside in White River, South Dakota.

1868

Cutting travel time by 75% over the span of twenty years almost sounds like science fiction; in this case it is reality. Voyages during the 1840's and 1850's often took two months or more. By the late 1860's and early 1870's, as the older sailing ships were being retired steamships took their place. Ancestors who traveled by steamer regularly arrived at their destination in two weeks or less! The result is a "savings" of 75% of their travel time! Budget restraints kept many families from experiencing the new steam ships since there were still less expensive options. The 1890's welcomed voyages that were often less than a week.

1868

Gerhard Heinrich Krogmann and
Franz Henrich Olberding Families

Delaware County, Iowa

The voyage from Bremen to Baltimore took twenty one days. They left the port of Bremen on the ship Berlin on April 1, 1868 and arrived in Baltimore April 22, 1868. Gerhard Heinrich Krogmann was in America!

That we are aware of he was the first of this Krogmann branch to set foot on American soil. Gerhard was the son of Herman Henrich (b. 1798) and a first cousin once removed to Remsen's Henry Krogman, Sr. Others from his family that came to Delaware County at a later date included his brother Carl Anton and family who emigrated with their father Herman Heinrich (b. 1798).

On the same voyage were numerous familiar names; Osterhus, Nieberding, Fortman and Olberding. One of the Olberding families was Franz Henrich Olberding, born April 14, 1815 in Holthausen, located near Steinfeld. Franz was an uncle of Henry Krogman, Sr. He emigrated with his family including his wife Catharina Gertrud Froehle and their children. When Franz and Catharine were married June 2, 1852, witnesses to the event were Gerhard Heinrich Krogmann, who they were traveling with and Johann Henrich Krogmann, who was Henry Sr.'s father.

Sorrowfully this is another voyage where we encounter a burial at sea. The Olberding family's baby daughter, Johanna Catharine, born May of 1867 died at sea on April 15, 1868. Henry Krogmann, Sr.'s mother was Johanna's godmother. *[continued at Dreams Realized]*

Other Olberding families that immigrated were a second cousin to Franz Henrich. Herman Heinrich Olberding was born August 12, 1824 married to Maria Bernardina Olberding on January 18, 1849. His family settled in Carroll County, Iowa. Their seven children, Bernard, Clemens August, Herman Henrich, Heinrich F., Maria Anna, Carolina Bernardina and Catharina Josephine all remained in the Carroll County area.

Another second cousin, Johan Henrich Olberding, born November 7, 1821 married Mary Agnes Kruse, she died in 1873. Ten years after her death Johan immigrated and settled in Nemaha County, Kansas with their four children. Johan Henrich bought land in Clear Creek Township, he farmed his land until 1900 when he passed away.

The children that immigrated: Maria Josephine, Maria Anna (married a Mr. Kohake), Herman Henrich (b. 1859) married Mary Agnes Schafer May 22, 1888; and Franz August (b. 1866) married Agnes Rose Tangeman January 3, 1894.

A family biography of Franz August includes information of his youth when he worked as a farm hand earning fifteen to twenty dollars per month. He was an avid saver and by the age of twenty-seven he had saved enough to purchase an unimproved half section in Richmond Township.

1873

Herman Heinrich Krogmann Family

Delaware County, Iowa

Letters from America were beckoning. The next to immigrate was

Herman Heinrich Krogmann, first cousin to Gerhard, uncle to Remsen's Henry, Sr.

Herman Heinrich was born to Franz Ferdinand Krogmann and Maria Engel Suennenberg on June 1834 in Oldenburg, Germany. Herman emigrated with his family, including his wife Maria Agnes Neiberding and eight children Josephina, Elisabeth, Johanna, Heinrich, Franz, Clemens, Joseph and Bernhard and his father Franz Ferdinand, his father-in-law and his wife's aunt. They left the Bremen Port on the S. S. Argonaut and arrived in New York on June 18, 1873. The six week voyage was said to be rough and stormy, ship hands performing daring tasks fixing and adjusting the sails. During the voyage, Maria Agnes Neiberding's father passed away, and like the Manders baby previously mentioned, he was buried at sea.

Herman's destination was Lyons, Iowa, located in Clinton County, they had friends from the homeland and heard of land opportunities. Herman purchased a farm from Michael Muldoon. *[continued at Dreams Realized]*

1878

Carl Anton Krogmann Family

Delaware County, Iowa

June 19, 1878 at the port in Bremen, Germany, Carl Anton Krogmann, along with his wife Mary Agnes Rosenbaum, their children and his father Herman Henrich (b. 1798), boarded the Schiff Baltimore. They arrived at Baltimore, Maryland on July 8, 1878, and went directly to Petersburg, Iowa where his brother Gerhard had settled.

1882

John Henry Krogmann

Clinton County, Iowa

Every few years another Krogmann took the voyage to America. This time it was Johann Heinrich "Henry, Sr." Krogmann, who was born November 29, 1861 in Steinfeld, Oldenburg, Germany, the son of Johann Heinrich Krogmann, Sr. and Maria Catharina Olberding.

Henry's background was unique; he came from two distinct social classes. His paternal ancestors and cousins had economic reasons for immigrating. His paternal grandparents, Franz Ferdinand Krogmann and Maria Engel Suennenberg, were married July 13, 1824; they were described as "Heuerling," a term used for centuries to describe a tenant farmer of northwest Germany.

In a nutshell, a heuerling's life was not easy; they signed an agreement describing what was required of them in return for the use of a tiny plot of land. Depending on the landowner, requirements included anything from cooking and cleaning for the landowner, to working his land. Housing was sub-standard and heuerling could afford very few farm animals. Because they had so little, they were meticulous in their care of the land, keeping weeds under control and timing their harvest to collect the absolute best crops. They often took off-season jobs that were quite a distance from their home just to make ends meet.

Unfortunately, once their plot was cleaned up and the land was producing a good crop, the landowner would take that land for himself and assign his least productive plot to his tenant farmer. It is understandable why so many heuerling immigrated to America in the mid to late 1800's, Henry's uncle and grandfather were among that number.

On the other side of Henry, Sr.'s family were Herm Henrich Olberding and Maria Elisabeth Fortmann, his maternal grandparents. Married August 1, 1809, Herm and Maria were described as "Eigener" in Holthausen, Germany.

Eigener was a social class described as a non-first-born farmer's son who settled on the outskirts of the village and later acquired additional land and finally full rights to use the common pastureland along with other privileges. Family land was often inherited by the oldest son only, and his younger brothers would become hired workers, hence a separate social class for non-first-born sons who eventually became landowners.

Following is the translated version of Henry's parents' marriage record:

1851

Married February 19

Proclamations made on January 26, February 2 and 9

Johann Henrich Krogmann, born September 22, 1828, legitimate son of Franz Ferdinand Krogmann and Maria Engel Suennenberg, Heuerleute in Holthausen.

Maria Catharina Olberding born November 10, 1818, legitimate daughter of Herm Henrich Olberding and Maria Elisabeth Fortman, Eigener in Holthausen.

The Newlyweds intend to live as Eigener in Holthausen.

Witnesses: Johann Friederich Wilhelm Ahlers, brother-in-law of the groom Franz Henrich Olberding, brother of the bride.

Because Henry's father became a landowner upon marriage, and Henry was the only son to survive to adulthood, he was in-line to become a future landowner. This however, wasn't enough to keep him from leaving his native country. Although no actual record has been discovered for Henry Krogmann's first trip to America, due to the possibility that none exists, we do have the stories he loved to share with his grandchildren, who passed them on to their children.

As the story was told by Henry himself, he arrived in America, a penniless teenager. He emigrated to avoid Germany's military requirement. He had a problem with the "Kaiser's Tyranny" and anticipated an upcoming war. At the time military service was fluctuating between three to six years and the recruitment trend was gravitating to younger men and boys. While on active duty, recruits were not allowed to marry, start a business or purchase property. They were essentially putting their lives on hold for their military and Henry wanted no part of it. His emotions on the subject were still apparent decades later when discussing the topic with family and friends, he had no qualms about openly declaring how much he despised the "Kaiser" and his ill treatment of German citizens.

Henry was a great story teller and as his granddaughter Florence remembered, he loved to tell stories of his trip to America. He described his experiences of being a teenage stowaway, how he made his way onto the ship and moved around the deck by hiding behind the flared skirts of mothers with children. Continuously alert and watchful, Henry always tried to make it appear he was with one family or another. Getting caught could mean working off the cost of the ticket or even worse, being sent back home. He was a discerning young man and apparently made it to his destination of Baltimore without being discovered.

Baltimore was an optimal location for an impoverished German immigrant to come ashore. Local employers were always in search of for new workers, young healthy immigrants were sometimes hired before they even left the docks. Needing money for train fare across the country, Henry took a job in one of over twenty breweries that were operating in Baltimore in the last half of the 19th century. Most of them had been established by German immigrants, and were ideal employers for recent German arrivals.

The wage for working at a brewery was good; he would have earned around two dollars per day. A room in a boarding house cost about 75 cents per day, so if Henry was frugal with his earnings, it would have taken about two months to save for train fare to the Midwest where he joined his grandfather Franz, a widower who arrived in Clinton, Iowa in 1873 with his son Herman Heinrich (Remsen Henry's uncle) and family.

Assuming Henry did in fact first arrive as a teenager, we also need to assume he returned to the land of his birth when his mother became ill, she passed away around 1879. Not having completed his military service, Henry had no choice but to keep a low profile so as not to be discovered by German Officials. For his return trip to America, Henry had funds to purchase a ticket for third class passage, (steerage), the price for a one way fare was in the twenty to thirty dollar range.

On this second trip to America, a ship manifest shows that Henry traveled from Bremen to Baltimore on the *S.S. Ohio.* A steamer of Ohio's size could make the voyage from Germany to America in less than two weeks. Food on board an 1880's era steamship leaving from a German port was provided and generally consisted of bread, potatoes and meat; there were also pickles, coffee and tea with a few low quality fruits and vegetables included. Third class passengers had the 'leavings' of the first and second class galleys. Women and children of third class were given priority over men. Often passengers brought dried foods and hid them for later use. By the end of the voyage the little food that was offered was suffering from spoilage. Those who had money could purchase from the cantina. The *S.S. Ohio* arrived in Baltimore September 23, 1882, and this time Henry had the luxury of continuing his trip to Iowa without working in a local brewery. *[continued at Dreams Realized]*

1882

Stuntebeck Brothers

Delaware County, Iowa was the starting point for each

German inheritance laws varied by region, an area in southern Germany had laws requiring a farm be divided between each of the children, resulting in farms so small they could no longer support a family. Northern Germany was different, still there were problems. After the passing of the parents, all land rights were transferred to the oldest son. Needless to say, when looking at a long military requirement followed by few future opportunities, many younger brothers packed their bags and left for America. Living in Northern Germany, the three younger Stuntebeck brothers were among the group that had little hope of ever gaining land rights. They were adventurous young men, each making the journey to America alone when they reached their late teens. Their immigration took place during a time when our country was experiencing the heaviest influx of Germans it had ever seen.

For some, the decision to leave would later have consequences as revealed in a letter written by the Stuntebeck brothers' sister-in-law Anna to Leonard. The translated version tells us "In our deceased mother's will each of you was bequeathed 900 marks, that is a total of 2700 marks. Now many people are claiming that you, Heinrich and, Franz can't get the money because the government is taking it because of your military situation. What will come of this, we don't yet know but will have to wait and see. We want to send you the money as soon as possible if we can." Whether they ever received a part of their inheritance is unclear.

The boys began their life in America by working as farm hands in Petersburg, Iowa, eventually settling in three different states, Iowa, South Dakota and Wisconsin. The timing of the brothers' emigration was primarily to avoid German military service.

Their youth was spent on a farm near the community of Lehmden, in Oldenburg, Germany, not far from the Krogmann home in Steinfeld. The youngest brother Leonard told his children and grandchildren that his family raised cattle in his native land.

The boys' parents, Franz Anton Stuntebeck and Anna Maria Behne (Maria) were both born in Lehmden, Oldenburg, Germany, their marriage occurred June 27, 1860. According to their marriage certificate, the young couple began their married life as heuerleute or tenant farmers, living with the parents of the bride. Anton and Maria had five children, the oldest was Hermann August born April 18, 1861; Franz Heinrich was born February 28, 1863, he died three months later. Franz Ferdinand (Frank) was born April 15, 1865; Heinrich was born September 7, 1869 and Leonard, on May 18, 1872.

The head of the family, Franz Anton, departed this world June 15, 1874, leaving his wife with four boys ranging in age from two to thirteen years of age. As the oldest son, it now became August's responsibility to take over his father's farming responsibilities; this may have benefited him later with a military exemption. Military service was mandatory for young males in Germany, however the person working to support the family was almost always granted an exemption.

Being the oldest son, August could also look forward to preferential treatment when it came to inheritance of land or property rights. August remained in Germany; he was in line to take over his parents' property rights and would have been much more content with his circumstances than his brothers who were destined to become laborers if they remained.

The first of the brothers to emigrate was Frank, in 1882 when he was about seventeen years old. Considering the lack of modern communication services and transportation systems, pioneers kept their families and friends amazingly well informed. Frank's first stop was Petersburg, in Delaware County, Iowa. It was a German farming settlement where, Frank's Aunt Maria Catharina Stuntebeck and Uncle Ferdinand Bohlke had settled a few years before.

As new farms were established, young immigrants without funds had no trouble finding a job as a farm hand. Frugal workers saved as much of their earnings as possible, then set out for points west where their savings would buy more. Frank did his own version of this practice, he worked in Petersburg for three years, and about the time his brother Henry immigrated, Frank moved west to Plymouth County Iowa near Remsen. One of the stories Frank shared with his great-grandson Jack Krogman was that he traveled the two hundred seventeen mile distance riding in a lumber wagon over rutted and mud roads. The uncomfortable trip would not have been considered a hardship for a frugal young German enjoying the benefit of a cheap ride. Once in Remsen Frank continued his work as a farm hand, he was now working for his Aunt and Uncle, Ferdinand and Kate Bohlke who had relocated from Petersburg on June 14, 1885. The trip to their new home took them through the aftermath of a tornado that claimed victims in Cherokee, Plymouth and Woodbury counties. One of their disappointments was the destruction of St. Mary's Catholic Church in Remsen.

In 1885, Frank's younger brother Henry, who was more adventurous than most, began making his way to America when he was only fifteen years of age. Like his brother, Henry began his new life in Petersburg, possibly taking over Frank's old job. Henry wasn't quite the fanatical saver that his brother was; he carried the philosophy of experiencing life, and never saw a good reason to pass up an interesting opportunity. Henry was naturalized November 3, 1890 at Manchester, Iowa. His naturalization paperwork cited his arrival in the U. S. as March 31, 1885.

It was now 1890 and finally, Leonard's turn, he was around seventeen years of age when he landed on America's shores. There is an interesting story that Leonard shared with his granddaughter Jo in reference to the ship that brought him to America. Leonard felt blessed and was always grateful for the timing of his voyage; word reached him later, the ship that brought him to America had sunk three weeks after his arrival. The timing would denote the ship sank on its next voyage.

Like his brothers, Leonard spent time in Petersburg, for a while both Leonard and Henry were living in Delaware County. Leonard was naturalized in 1896. *[continued at Dreams Realized]*

1884

Koos Brothers

Jackson County, Iowa

Smallpox was a word that struck terror into the hearts of family, neighbors, even entire communities. When an outbreak visited Bilsdorf, Luxembourg in 1881, a vaccine had been available for quite some time but Luxembourg was home to pockets of cult-like worshipers of St. Barbara "where her followers steadfastly resisted vaccination for fear of angering her spirit."[10] Barbara is patron saint of anyone in danger of sudden death.

It was June 27, 1881, the weather was unseasonably hot and humid and sixteen year old Peter Koos was overcome with a sense of foreboding. His father, Nicholas, son of Franz Koos and Marguerite Muller, had died three years previous at the age of thirty-eight leaving his wife and seven young children to manage on their own. Peter was now the head of the family, his

---

[10] Deliberate Extinction: Whether to Destroy the Last Smallpox Virus. Georgetown University Law Center. www.scholarship.law.georgetown.edu.

father had been a farmer and Peter worked hard to fill his shoes. As the oldest, it was his duty to take on the responsibility of supporting the family, the upside of the responsibility was that it earned him the right to inherit his parents' land privileges but Peter's plans for the future were evaporating before his eyes. Yesterday his six year old brother Frank died of small pox, his mother and his brother Henry were still gravely ill.

Peter's fears weren't so much about contracting the virulent disease, even though it was a disease that was known to wipe out entire families. His deepest concerns were related to his mother's recovery. He worried what the future would hold for him and his 5 surviving brothers and sisters if she didn't pull through. A few days later on July 1, 1881, his worst fears became reality when his beloved mother Catherine succumbed. Catherine was born December 11, 1842 to Jacques and Catherine (Block) Reiland, she was thirty-eight years old. Catherine and Nicholas had a family of nine children, all born in Bilsdorf, Luxembourg.

(1). Of the nine children, first was Marguerite, born May 1, 1864, she became the wife of Christopher Scheck, they made their home in Belgium. Marguerite lived to September 2, 1940.

(2). Peter was born January 1, 1866. After the death of his mother, any plans Peter had gone up in smoke. As a young man of sixteen years he was too young to inherit his parents land rights, and without a home there was no way he could support what was left of his family. Relatives living in the Bilsdorf, Luxembourg area most likely agreed to take in a child or two but few families would have the ability or funds to raise all six children.

Young Peter worked at a gristmill on a small river near his home. The work was hard, his days were long. Saving may have been difficult if there were expectations that he assist in the support of his siblings. In 1919, Peter's son Peter Michael, having just finished his military service, visited the mill where his papa had worked as a youth.

Three years after his mother's death, 19 year old Peter Koos was bound for America on the steamship S. S. Westernland, the ship was recently built and had just returned from its maiden voyage. The young man was practically broke but through creative negotiating gained passage after securing a job as one of the ship's fireman, or better described as a steamship's coal shoveler. The job entailed back-breaking work but that presented no problem for Peter, he was eager for a fresh start and wherever he settled, financial success and independence were both prominent on Peter's list of goals.

The S. S. Westernland left Europe from Antwerp with a destination of New York's Castle Garden immigration center, Peter arrived March 22, 1884 and the manifest listed his destination as Chicago.

(3). Marie was born September 24, 1867; she married Dominick Gehenge on May 20, 1896.

(4). Nicholas was born September 17, 1870, his immigration occurred in 1890.

(5). Henry was born May 22, 1872, he survived his bout with smallpox, but carried the scars with him for the rest of his life. In 1887 Henry followed his brother Peter to America. He joined Peter Reiland in Chicago and unlike his brother, Henry was drawn to the thrills and challenges of working on water towers and he soon expanded his expertise to windmills. Eventually Henry joined his brother Peter in La Motte, Iowa.

(6). Anne was born September 7, 1874 and died November 24, 1874.

(7). Jacques, a twin, was born November 3, 1875, he died the following day.

(8). Francois was born November 3, 1875; he was a victim of small pox and died June 27, 1881.

(9). Joseph Frank was born March 1, 1878, he immigrated to America with his brother Nicholas, arriving at Castle Garden on February 27, 1890. The brothers were among the last immigrants to pass through the Castle Garden immigration station. The facility closed April 18, 1890 because overcrowding had become "intolerable, while corruption was rampant, with thieves descending upon the unsuspecting immigrants."[11] Arriving, with limited funds may have actually been in their favor. The adage "you can't squeeze blood from a turnip" comes to mind. *[continued at Dreams Realized]*

* * *

REMAIN OR RETURN?

For the most part, the immigrants on these pages remained in America, at this point of the research, only one instance of a related immigrant returning permanently to their native country has been documented. However if distant cousins had come to America and soon returned home, it is doubtful we would even be aware of it.

Records concerning emigrants from America weren't considered as important as the records for arrivals; consequently, returns were poorly documented. If they can be located, passport applications offer the researcher the opportunity to discover whether their ancestor applied for a passport to leave America but this only provides information from the application of someone needing a passport, not if they actually made a trip somewhere.

As travel became easier, in the late nineteenth and early twentieth century, travel back to visit relatives became more common, sometimes the American immigrant spent a year back home to visit friends and relatives.

[11] The Ellis Island Immigrant Cookbook by Tom Bernardin, New York, NY, August 2015.

There were also occasions the immigrant returned home to claim an inheritance. For Germans that hadn't fulfilled their military requirements this could be tricky, if caught they could be completing a few years in the military before allowed to return.

Professional researchers believe there were far more immigrants returning back to their native country than first thought, but when considering the immigrants discussed on these pages, ancestors that wanted to return couldn't afford the fare and those that could afford the trip preferred to remain in America.

S. S. Westernland - Transportation used by three Koos brothers.

Mill where Peter Koos worked before emigrating from Luxembourg.

Maria (Behne) Stuntebeck and sons Leonard? and August.

Verzeichniß

1851 im Kirchspiel Steinfeld Verlobten, Proclamirten und Copulir

Copulirt.	Proclamirt. Tage.	
Februar 19	Januar 26 Februar 2-9	Johann Henrich Krogmann geboren 1828 d. 27. Septbr ehelicher Sohn von Franz Ferdinand Krogmann und Maria Engel Sümmenberg, Heuerleute in Holthausen. Maria Catharina Olberding geboren 1818 d. 10. November eheliche Tochter von Herm Henrich Olberding und Maria Elisabeth Fortmann, Erben in Holthausen. Copulati wohnen als Erben in Holthausen. Zeugen: Johann Friderich Wilhelm Ahlers, Schwager des Bräutigams Franz Henrich Olberding, Bruder der Braut.
Februar		

1851 Marriage-Johann Henrich Krogmann, Maria Catharina Olberding.

Chapter 2

Farmers and Stone Masons

Plentiful Land! The dream of becoming a landowner was the enticement that drew many pioneers to the Midwest in the early nineteenth century. The Preemption Act of 1841 allowed a settler to stake a claim of up to 160 acres. After they had occupied the property for just over a year, they were given the option to purchase the land from the government prior to its availability to the public. There were laws against speculation, but those laws were seldom enforced.

Records of the Bureau of Land Management General Land Office suggest the land purchased by Henry Banks in Richland Township, Jackson County, may have been through a speculator. The speculator did hold a legitimate military warrant in his name for 160 acres, but in addition to his own warrant he made numerous claims, plus he redeemed military warrants for scores of other soldiers and their heirs, these warrants were redeemed not only in Jackson County, Iowa but in neighboring counties as well, all totaled, during the 1850's he held title to thousands of acres in Iowa alone. The result was that true pioneers couldn't stake a claim, if they didn't want to wait, they bought land that was for sale.

Most Iowa pioneers had a farming background and they were prepared for the hard work they would face. By the 1830's, settlers were crossing the Mississippi River, staking claims in the eastern counties of Iowa. For these pioneers, the road ahead for would-be-farmers wasn't for the faint of heart. Jackson County Iowa was covered with beautiful scenic landscapes and wildlife, but certainly not an ideal setting for immediate crop farming. The county was covered with mature trees, and the land near the river included bluffs, rocks and boulders along with a tangle of bushes and brush.

For a family daring enough to stake a claim on unimproved land, every able body from the household was put to work chopping, sawing, dragging or digging from sunrise to sunset. We'll meet families that dealt with a variety of circumstances ranging from land laden with rocks and trees to a family living on an island in the middle of a major river, they all met their challenges and they all had a resolute determination to succeed, most having little to invest besides their work ethic. They were well aware that every acre cleared added to profit for the upcoming year. Tree stumps were the biggest challenge. These stubborn protrusions were chopped, burned and if available, sometimes treated with saltpeter. Even after the most aggressive actions, portions of the stumps remained for a year or two with crops planted around them. Winter's ravages weakened the roots, sometimes to the point that a team of oxen could break the stump free of the earth.

Living off the plants and wildlife in Jackson County, Iowa was a definite advantage when trying to feed a family, but much of the land itself was far from being ready to cultivate. Clearing a few acres per year was an accomplishment, and according to Urbandale, Iowa's Living History Farms "Most farms in 1850 averaged 160 acres in size, with farmers cultivating anywhere from 25 to 40 acres."[12]

Farmers weren't the only settlers with the need to be frugal and vigilant; shop owners were also prudent, always incorporating a variety of products and services into their business. Successful shop owners understood their customer base was made up of cash strapped settlers and if they offered a limited range of products or services they would soon be out of business. The early years of settlement of a community offered little room for luxury, an example is seen when an 1854 news article in the first issue of Maquoketa's Sentinel newspaper made mention of the lack of a barber. A few weeks after the article appeared, a German barber arrived in town and opened a makeshift shop, his venture was short lived, due in part to unrealistic expectations. In a matter of weeks, the German was gone, leaving a note "I hope you will wonder that I left in such a hurry I was compelt to do so. If I can't earn my board her, I tink it is high time to leave this place, I have to go to a place where Men git Shavet, not where they Shave themselves like they do here . . . Tat is the reasons I left this misprable hole."[13]

During the mid 1800's an acre of well-tended oats or corn might produce 25 to 35 bushels per acre, wheat produced half that yield but the market price was double that of corn and oats. An acre of oats might produce 30 bushels, at a price of 20 cents per bushel; the farmer would collect around $6 per acre. That first year or two, when the farmer had only a few acres cleared, it wasn't unusual to clear less than $100. This windfall needed to last; there were no extravagances, no new clothes, no store bought toys. The money was spent on necessities, fifteen cents to replace a horseshoe, twenty cents for a pound of coffee, fifteen cents for a pound of

[12] Living History Farms - 1850 Pioneer Farm at www.lhf.org

[13] The Jackson Sentinel, Maquoketa, Iowa, 1854, reprinted in the 1934 anniversary issue.

sugar and if there was enough money, they may have invested in the innovative John Deere plow for ten to fifteen dollars.

Hogs and sheep were a reasonably priced investment at just a couple dollars each while beef ranged from $5 to $20 for a calf or a young cow, a pair of oxen was priced from $50 to $75 while a single young healthy horse might cost as much as $100 or more.

Horse thieves were severely punished, as seen on western television shows, hanging a horse thief was not uncommon. Severe punishment for theft of a horse dates back centuries, not only because of their value, but loss of a horse for transportation had a major impact on a family's life.

1839

Johnann Theodore Niemann (Theodore)
Jackson County, Iowa

In 1839 Theodore Niemann and his young bride, Mary Adeline Reiling took up residence in the rustic cabin Theodore built on his claim which began as 320 acres. They were surrounded by nature, with few and distant neighbors, the only sounds that disturbed the peaceful surroundings were the echos of an axe reverberating through the hills.

Their children were August (b. 1841, m. Anna Steichen), Theodore J. (b. 1843, m. Mary), Anton, Mary, Anna Elizabeth (b. 1849, m. Nicholas Rolling), Henry (b. 1852, m. Mary Walsh), Rosanna, Nicholas G. (b. 1856, m. Helena Marie Schaffer), Angeline, Julius, and Frances Johanna (b. 1868, m. William A. Welp).

In addition to his acreage in Jackson County, Theodore owned another 160 acres in Cherokee County, Iowa. It could be management of this property that lead son Henry to Marcus, Cherokee County, Iowa where he opened a hardware store. In 1920 Henry's household included his mother-in-law, Anna Duggan who was listed as 88 years old. Note that Duggan was Anna's maiden name, she was the widow of John Walsh.

1845

Haxmeier Family
Jackson County, Iowa

Have you ever considered changing your name? Immigrants often walked away from the port of entry with a new name. Sometimes it was simply a new spelling, other times it was an entirely new name; and sometimes it was a choice and others it was a rushed immigration official. A popular reason for an intentional name change was to blend into local culture, but changing a name from Lohenrich to Haxmeier doesn't seem to fall into this category. So why did these brothers change their name?

The Haxmeier family has been quite a challenging one to trace; we can be thankful to the tireless efforts of researchers like Rebecca Stewart who shared her discovery of the connection of Theodore Haxmeier/Hoxmeier to the Lohenrich surname. From her research, the reasoning for the name change appears to be linked to a translation of Lohenrich that bore a negative connotation.

In total, five sibling immigrants have been identified; all were children of Hermann Heinrich Lohenrich and Anna Griete Engel Rotgers Alf, the latter passed away April 5, 1839 and the former joined his wife on February 22, 1844. Five of their children, immigrated, none keeping the Lohenrich surname. Once in Iowa, four sons went by the name Haxmeier or Hoxmeier, and children that remained in the Jackson County Iowa area stuck with Haxmeier while those that ventured west used the version spelled Hoxmeier. Keep in mind when searching for a record on this family, there is a long list of spelling versions.

Like Theodore Niemann earlier and the Herrig brothers later, the Haxmeiers selected Jackson County properties in Tete des Morts Township in close proximity to each other. Records show, at one point in time each of the five siblings are documented as having lived in Jackson County, Iowa. It appears that at least three of the Haxmeier brothers immigrated soon after their father's death in 1844. Their sister Margaret arrived several years later with her family. Brother Harmon may also have been one of the late-comers.

The children of Hermann Heinrich Lohenrich and Anna Griete Engel Rotgers Alf that immigrated were:

(1). Gerhard Harmon Lohenrich Haxmeier was born July 7, 1808 in Leschede, Germany, his wife was Anna Margaretha. Little has been revealed about Harmon's early life, at one point he bought land near his brothers in Tete des Morts Township, Jackson County, Iowa, and by the 1870 census he and his wife had retired and were living with his younger brother Henry.

(2). Euphemia Margaretha Lohenrich was born March 21, 1812; she married Johann Theodore Ketteler in Germany on June 20, 1837. The year 1865 brought them to America with several, maybe all of their living children. On the 1870 census Margaret and Theodore and their youngest son were living in Tete des Morts township with an older son Theodore and his wife Helena.

(3). Johann "Theodore" (Lohenrich) Haxmeier was born January 7, 1814 in Hannover Germany, it was there he grew up and spent his early manhood. Theodore was around thirty years of age when immigrating to America, his destination was eastern Iowa where he began his life in the New World as a farm hand, he soon placed a claim on a plot of land in Jackson County, Iowa; he immediately began working the land and built a small log cabin.

On February 25, 1848, Theodore obtained three land patents totaling one hundred sixty acres in Tete des Morts Township, Jackson County, Iowa. Forty acres were added in 1852 and in 1853 there was another forty acre land patent plus two forty acre Military Warrants, one he acquired from a Corporal in the War of 1812 the other from a private in the Florida War. The total acreage reached at least three hundred and twenty acres.

Shortly after acquiring the initial Land Patents, Theodore was united in marriage to Caroline Nemmers , a native of Kehlen, Capellen, Luxembourg, Caroline was born December 26, 1827. She had immigrated with her parents John Nicholas, a carpenter, and Catherina (Weber) Nemmers, all natives of Luxembourg, coming to America as a family in 1847. Theodore and Caroline (Nemmers) Haxmeier's family of seven began with Henry P.

(i). Henry P. Haxmeier was born July 1849. On September 27, 1871 Elizabeth Maria Gilles became his wife; the couple had eleven children, all born in Jackson county. They were named Theodore, Frances, John C., Peter, Paul, Susan, Catherine, Christine, Margaret, Louise and Paul. Henry spent his entire eighty-one year life span in Jackson County.

Peter, and five of his siblings raised their families in Nebraska, the spelling of their surname was changed to Hoxmeier. Farming was their trade and they worked hard to achieve success.

Referring to one of Henry P.'s grandsons "Mr. Hoxmeier operates 770 acres in Harlan County. He cares for 30 Hereford stock cows, and produces dry-land corn and wheat.

"He farms with his father, Peter Hoxmeier. The father-and-son team has had a soil conservation plan on their farm and grassland ever since the Harlan district has been organized."[14]

(ii). Helena was born August 6, 1850; She was the first to leave home when she married John Herrig on October 24, 1868. John was a very attentive husband and father, if Helena wanted something, all she had to do was ask and John made it happen. The couple had fifteen children, Caroline, born August 30, 1869 married Anthony J. Till; Henry died as an infant; Anna, born September 1, 1873 married Peter Till; William Joseph born September 28, 1875 married Caroline Poll; John Matthew's birth occurred January 18, 1877, he married Mary Ellen Horan; Mary and Michael died during their first year; Theodore was born April 23, 1883, he married Christina Poll; George, born December 26, 1883, died during his first year; Margaret born June 2, 1885 married Joseph John Till; Helena born June 29, 1887 married Charles Hilbert; Christina born October 29, 1888 married Nicholas Leo Flammang; Joseph born January 15, 1890 married Helena Ties; Mathias was born January 15, 1890 and Anthony born April 15, 1893, married Regina Huilman.

---

[14] Omaha World Herald, Omaha, Nebraska, Monday October 12, 1959.

An explanation of the birth dates of Theodore and George is not available. George was born only eight months after Theodore, a doubtful option is that George was premature, another possibility is that one of the boys was adopted or one of the dates could be in error. The dates do match tombstone records, but tombstones can also be in error.

(iii). Mary was born in 1853. She was a teenager when she entered the Sisters of Notre Dame convent in Milwaukee on November 14, 1870 Mary became a novitiate (novice) on August 22, 1873 and was given the name Sister Mary Pulcheria, her excitement was short-lived as she died less than a month later, on September 20th. Sister Pulcheria is buried at the convent Cemetery in Elm Grove, Wisconsin.

(iv). Margaret was born in 1855. In September 1871, around the time of her brother Henry's marriage, Margaret joined her sister Mary at the Sisters of Notre Dame in Milwaukee. *[continued at Lead by Faith]*

(v). Anna's birth occurred on August 13, 1856; she married John Peter Herrig (brother to William) on October 18, 1874. Their eleven children were Elizabeth, William Peter, Mary, Henry, Michael died as an infant, Michael, Mathias, John Joseph (died as an infant), Nicholas, Thereasa and Leo.

The stress of modern times can lead people to yearn for days gone by. The appeal of a simple lifestyle can appear enviable on the surface, but peeling back the layers of the "simple life" can reveal conditions that are now considered archaic, even cruel.

Anna was a sensitive young woman who experienced more childhood loss than most. When she married John Peter Herrig at eighteen years of age her memories of youth were clouded by the loss of an older brother when she was a young girl; at twelve she lost her mother; at fifteen, her father and at seventeen her twenty year old sister. Even with this endless string of tragedies in her life, Anna was coping . . . right up to the point where she lost a child.

Grief and sadness engulfed her, add to that the possible condition of post-partum depression, and day to day activities became difficult; some days just getting out of bed in the morning was a challenge. The prevailing attitude toward a woman who was well provided for and had a loving family was "what more could she want?" If Anna had actually expressed her feelings she would have received little empathy when bringing up the loss of a child because the underlying feelings of the time were to "get over it" like other people did.

There was no sympathy or privacy for Anna's emotional state. The following newspaper article shows how little compassion was shown to our forebears experiencing emotional challenges. The front page of the Maquoketa, Iowa, Jackson Sentinel, read:

"Sheriff McCaffrey removed Mrs. Jno. P. Herrig from her home in Tete des Morts township to the State insane asylum at Independence last Saturday. She has been in a demented [depressed] condition since last December and her friends have hoped that she might recover, as she did when similarly afflicted sometime before this. She is a young woman 36 years of age and the mother of eight children, the youngest being 18 months old. Mr. Herrig is a well-to-do farmer with a wide acquaintance and highly respected. His friends sympathise with him in his trouble and hope for her early recovery. The unfortunate lady was accompanied by her sister-in-law and also her brother, Peter Kalmes."[15] Note, she did not have a brother or brother-in-law with this name.

Another article informs us that Jackson County had Commissioners of Insanity to make snap decisions as to the patient's fate. In Iowa, each county had a board of commissioners made up of three people, a respectable doctor, a lawyer and the circuit court clerk. These three people decided whether the person would go home or to the asylum.

Lucky for Iowans, the Independence facility was a forward thinking hospital, they kept meticulous records and their goal was to return patients home to their families, not to imprison them. Patients included individuals with depression, meningitis and epilepsy, along with sufferers of paralysis and rheumatism the family couldn't or would no longer care for.

The gardener at the Independence, Iowa Hospital for the Insane was Jonathan Bland,[16] he was a magician with flowers, flowering shrubs and plants. The results were a beautiful and relaxing atmosphere at the hospital where 300 acres of flowering paths could be enjoyed. Anna was treated for a second time and soon returned home to her family.

(vi). Johannes was born about 1859, he died as a child.

(vii). Michael T. Hoxmeier was born September 1862, on the 1880 census, the seventeen year old Michael T. was working as a farmhand for his uncle, Henry. By the time Michael was twenty he had relocated to Alton, Iowa where he went into business with his cousin Theodore, they opened a general store that was aptly named "Hoxmeier's Store," it grew into a thriving establishment. Michael was married in 1889 to Louise Eggspuehler and had four children. They remained in Alton until around 1912 when Michael sold his share of the business to his partner and moved his family to St. Paul, Minnesota.

Census records can be misleading and inaccurate but they can offer an abundance of information as they do here. In 1920, Michael and Louisa were in their late 50's, their four children, all professionals were still living with them, Michael was a general practice lawyer; Christine, a public school teacher and Roman and Simon who were both bookkeepers worked for a

---

[15] Jackson Sentinel, Maquoketa, Iowa, Thursday, August 13, 1891.

[16] Jonathan Bland's flower shop celebrated 100 years in business in 2015.

railroad and bank respectively.

* * *

It was the winter of 1869 when Theodore was suddenly thrust into the role of a widower, Caroline was only forty-two years of age. The oldest daughter, Helena had married the prior year leaving Theodore to press-on without the two women who had kept the household operating. There were five children at home, ranging from seven year old Michael to twenty year old Henry. The household responsibilities fell on the shoulders of Mary and Margaret, the two older girls.

Unlike many in similar circumstances, Theodore did not re-marry; the Haxmeier family, was growing up and they were moving forward. One by one, his children were leaving the nest, Mary and Margaret left for the Sisters of Notre Dame Convent.

After Henry's marriage the family remaining at the homestead was reduced to three members, Theodore, Anna and Michael. One would think the family had endured enough, yet the adversity continued. On November 30, 1871, less than three years after his wife passed away, Theodore followed his wife. He was just fifty-seven years old. Theodore is buried next to his wife and their son Johannes at the Catholic Cemetery in St. Donatus, Iowa.

If there was a bright spot to be found, the two remaining children were left with a debt free farm with two uncles farming within a mile radius. It is not clear exactly what happened to their living situation, the two children, in all probability moved in with a sibling or a neighboring uncle.

Considering the unexpected nature of Theodore's death it doesn't come as a surprise that he died intestate. His land remained in estate status for years after, the children having to fight for their birthright.

(4). Johann Gerhard Haxmeier was born September 29, 1816. Gerhard's immigration was also somewhere around the mid 1840's, Gerhard's first land patent was for 40 acres on section 30 of Tete des Morts township in Jackson County, Iowa, it was dated February 25, 1848.

(5). Johann Heinrich "Henry" Haxmeier, the youngest was born February 15, 1823, and like his brothers Theodore and Gerhard, Henry purchased a 40 acre land patent in section 30 of Tete des Morts Township on February 25, 1848. Around 1852 Henry married neighbor Susanne Nemmers, a sister to his brother's wife Caroline. He bought another 40 acre land patent on November 10, 1859. *[continued later with the Nemmers family]*

* * *

"Aging in place" has recently described as a new concept for retirees;

the Center for Disease Control describes aging in place as "the ability to live in one's own home and community safely, independently, and comfortably, regardless of age, income, or ability level." This new concept was the assumed course of action taken by many of our ancestors in the generations that preceded us.

For past generations, especially before WWII, when our ancestors reached their declining years they were still considered an important and valued part of society, they had cared for their children, now it was time for the children to return the favor. There were no worries of paying for long term care or planning how to pay for a retirement home. Homes were passed from generation to generation and once the infirmities of old age became an issue, they were likely still living in their longtime household with the child that took over the family business, or there was another relative prepared to assume the responsibility for their care.

Early American settlers' rules were flexible, but there were rules. For farm families, especially when the patriarch was still living, the parents generally remained on the Home Place. When there was only one surviving parent, the arrangements varied widely from family to family. Space available, congeniality of involved family members and financial resources all played a role. There were open-armed families that took in any family "stray" without complaint or issue. Although the patriarch felt it was his right to remain on the home place for the remainder of his life, a widow often left the home place and lived with a daughter.

Aged family members moving in with a younger generation were not limited to parents; Henry Haxmeier's house was one of those welcoming homes that was generous to a marked degree. As of the 1870 census, Henry Haxmeier's older brother Herman, age 62 and wife Margaret, age 71 were living with Henry and Susanna's family.

Herman's wife Margaret died August 19, 1878 and is buried in the St. Donatus Catholic Cemetery, Herman now a widower was still living with his brother Henry and family in 1880. Herman died November 25, 1886; he is buried beside his wife in St. Donatus.

Once Henry and his wife Susanna retired, they switched roles with their son John and his family. John was now operating the farm and Henry and Susanna helping out as they could. They celebrated their fiftieth wedding anniversary on the land they had lived on for their entire marriage. After all these years, they still had neighbors to whom they were related. One of Henry's nephews, Theodore Kettler was now farming next door on the land his brother Theodore once farmed. Henry died in 1903 and Susanna in 1907. Their burial took place at the Saint Donatus Catholic Cemetery.

1846

Henry Niemann and Elizabeth Schulte

Jackson County, Iowa

In 1832 the Sac and Fox Indians had been directed by President Andrew Jackson to leave areas east of the Mississippi and relocate on the Iowa side. A raid was mounted by Chief Black Hawk in Jo Davies County, Illinois, but the settlers erected a quick fort and the attempt was unsuccessful. This became the last Native American attack east of the Mississippi.

On the west side of the Mississippi, the Bellevue area was a seasonal home to the Sac and Fox Indians, one of their villages and their burial ground was located just south of the town. Remnants of the tribes remained until the late 1840s. Their location near Bellevue afforded them the conveniences of a general store, blacksmith and flour mill a few miles away. Businesses had been popping up since 1836 and the town was thriving.

After their marriage on April 28, 1846, Henry Niemann and Elizabeth Schulte began their life in a log cabin in Jackson County, Iowa, then a part of the Iowa Territory. The Homestead Act required their dwelling be at least ten feet by twelve feet. A glass window was also required, but that feature could be added another time.

Later that year, on December 28, 1846, Iowa became the 29th state. Some of the early settlers tell of Indians walking right into their cabins without knocking, startling the occupants but never threatening. Since the Niemann's lived in Fox and Sac territory, one wonders what encounters Henry and Elizabeth experienced. If there were visits from surprise guests, it's likely they offered food and hospitality.

On February 7, 1847 their first child, a daughter they named Mary Ann was born in their log cabin. The nearest church to have her baptized was the Cathedral in Dubuque, some twenty miles away. The journey to the Cathedral began with a trek through the woods that Henry was very familiar with. Once at the river, if running, Gordon's Ferry transported them, if frozen, their oxen and sled made the trip up the river. Either way, Elizabeth's family, living in Jo Daviess County, Illinois, were bubbling with excitement since they could share in the event.

In 1848 through a land patent, Henry acquired title to 78.70 acres of land on the northern edge of Bellevue Township, hence becoming an official neighbor to his brother Theodore.

Although Henry had already cleared several acres, he faced years of clearing land where nature had grown at will for centuries. Whenever possible Elizabeth was available to assist, she wasn't a robust woman but she was sturdy and fit and didn't hesitate to shoulder a share of the workload. Elizabeth reportedly built a retaining wall behind their home; the wall was built with flat stones and earth, it and was still standing proudly a hundred years later.

With just the two of them, a team or two of oxen would have been a necessity to pull a plow through the unbroken sod. Oxen were more economical than horses and the investment would have paid for itself in a relatively short amount of time. When funds were especially tight, the first year or two, it wasn't uncommon to share the cost of a team with family or neighbors. This practice reduced the initial investment of purchasing the animals and an ox-bow for each pair, with additional savings seen by feeding fewer animals through the winter.

Wildlife was abundant and if Henry was a good hunter, he had no problem feeding his family by fishing, trapping and hunting. Squirrel stew, roasted pigeon, dried venison, quail, catfish and trout provided nutrition without spending their savings. There was also a plentiful supply of herbs, fruit, berries and greens for Elizabeth to add flavor to a meal of wild game. Foraging in the woods could be more rewarding than traveling to the market; berries included grapes, raspberries, wild strawberries and blackberries. Farmers that owned land with patches of wild berries along an established road weren't guaranteed to enjoy the fruits of their land; it was often first-come, first-served. Berry pickers felt the bushes along the road were available for anyone passing by. Most berry pickers saw nothing wrong with stopping to gather the berries visible from the road, their basket brimming with juicy berries as they headed home. The disappointed landowner would need to make new plans for Sunday dessert.

The bountiful Jackson County wildlife made the news across the country shortly before the Niemann's arrived. Various articles spoke of a mind-boggling gathering of pigeons, three miles long and a half a mile wide. When leaving or returning from food gathering, the pigeons darkened the sky with their numbers; the noise was deafening to the point it silenced the report of a gunshot.

According to the Audubon Society, these passenger pigeons were North America's most abundant bird. Flock size went from hundreds of millions of birds in the mid 1800's to just dozens of birds in the late 1800's. The passenger pigeon, "researchers have agreed that the bird was hunted out of existence"[17] the last one died in captivity in 1914.

As the Niemann financial situation improved, the size of their farm expanded, in 1852 Henry acquired a second land patent for 37.99 acres; he also purchased an additional 95 acres bringing his holdings to just over 210 acres. During the expansion period, Henry built for Elizabeth one of the finest homes in the area; it was there that their seven children, first

---

[17] Audubon Magazine "Why the Passenger Pigeon Went Extinct" by Barry Yeoman, Published May-June 2014.

generation Americans, were raised.

(2). After Mary Ann's birth in 1847 their son John arrived February 1850. John married Katharine Sieverding and they farmed in the Bellevue area. John and Katherine's family consisted of four daughters, Elizabeth M., Mary G., Rosa C., and Regina A. The oldest and youngest, Elizabeth and Regina both lived to almost 100 years, three of the daughters remained single and Mary married Edward John Ernest a neighboring farmer; they added two grandsons to Henry and Elizabeth's family tree, Edward and Joseph.

(3). Elizabeth, was born about 1853. At the time of the 1885 Iowa census she was listed as single, a dressmaker, age 32. The following year she married German immigrant George Benninghouse, they soon relocated to Canada. This information is not verified but it is said their family consisted of three sons Joseph, Alphin and George.

(4). Margaret Elizabeth Niemann was born May 1854. When she was nineteen years old Margaret took a big step, she married John Anton Koob in Saint Donatus, the date was April 14, 1874. He was Luxembourg born, and a widower with four children. His first wife was Anna Maria Kettler, who died in 1873.

In addition to the four children from John's first marriage, they added eight children to their family, the first was John Anton born in Jackson County in 1875, then Louis A. and Alphonse A., both born in Dubuque County; Julius A., Rosa A., Margaret A., Emil A. and Mary A. were all born in Dakota City, Humboldt County, Iowa.

The Humboldt County area was experiencing a booming economy with the recent construction of a railroad, John took advantage of the growth and purchased a dry goods store, during their early residence there he also worked as postmaster.

(5). Henry Herman Niemann was born September 22, 1855. He remained at home, handling the farm until age 35 when he married Catherine Schultz, a native of the Bellevue area. Henry and Catharine relocated to Marcus in Cherokee County, Iowa where he opened a jewelry store that handled watch and jewelry repairs. Henry H. and Catharine had three children, Loretta, Helen and Raymond. Henry lived to the age of 86.

(6). Theodore joined the Niemann family in 1858. Like his brother Henry, Theodore moved west to Cherokee County, Iowa. He became a druggist and opened a drug store in Marcus, Iowa. In 1895, at the age of 37 he married Hope Walsh, their four children were, Theodore, Naomi M., Anna Ruth and John P. According to a 1914 history of Cherokee County, his business was destroyed by fire in 1911.

Theodore, Sr. died in 1918 at the age of 60 in Marcus, Iowa. His widow never remarried, she supported the family by taking in boarders and became postmaster of Marcus in 1919, a position she held for over ten years.

(7). The youngest was Joseph M. born in 1861, he remained single, spent his entire life in Jackson County on the farm in Bellevue Township. One by one his siblings grew up and left home until only Joseph was remained. He eventually purchased the home place. The 1915 Iowa Census shows him as retired at age fifty-three and renting out the farm which was valued at $18,000. Joseph eventually lost his vision to cataracts.

* * *

It was 1864 in Eastern Iowa, Henry and Elizabeth, two immigrants from Hannover, Germany had done well for themselves. They were raising a growing family, they owned a fertile farm and were respected by their friends and neighbors, but their fairy tale story was about to take a calamitous turn.

On March 30, 1864 Henry died of what descendants have described as "black-leg", which is actually a bovine disease. From that characterization a conclusion can be made that the probable cause of death was gas gangrene which can cause the affected area to swell and turn black, basically displaying symptoms in humans that are similar to the symptoms that black leg displays in cattle.

When Henry Niemann died, he left his 39 year old wife Elizabeth with seven children ranging in age from a 17 year old daughter Mary Ann, down to two year old Joseph.

Life for most pioneer women was much different than we saw on "Little House on the Prairie." Although an entertaining show it didn't always reflect the reality of pioneer living, entailing long hard days and plenty of "dirty jobs". Most pioneer women were hard working, caring for more than the home, acting as part of a team with their husband until the children were old enough to help. When tragedy entered their life they were well aware this was no time for indecision.

In the 19th century it was prevalent for pioneer widows and widowers, especially when small children were involved, to remarry within a year of the death of their spouse. A farm widow needed a hearty worker to tend the land, while a widower with small children needed a caring person to handle the day to day requirements of raising a family. In the case of pioneers this was a necessity.

Widowed women of the pioneer era had limited options. They could flounder in despair, find a new husband to take on the farming responsibilities or step up and try to manage on their own. Elizabeth chose the latter option. Her brother-in-law lived on the neighboring farm, and she had two children approaching adulthood that would share the workload. She was lucky to be in a financial position to hire a farm hand to help out, a practice that continued for many years.

Elizabeth Niemann outlived her husband by forty years; she spent those years on the farm they had worked together for almost twenty years. By the 1900 Federal Census, Elizabeth was 75 years of age, living with her son Joseph who was single. At that point in time their household included a 31 year old farm hand, Jacob Becker as well as a seventeen year old servant girl Rosa Jager. Other information we learn from the census was that Elizabeth could read, write and speak English.

Ten years later, on the 1910 census, Elizabeth was still aging in place, still living with her youngest son Joseph. They no longer had a live-in farm hand but there was a seventeen year old servant girl named Clara Van Danaker listed as a member of their household. This census attests that Elizabeth's predominant language was German and she could not write but considering the number of years Elizabeth lived in America and the fact she raised seven children, a logical presumption here is that she could in fact speak English, but she was getting up in years and may have reverted to speaking with her son in her native tongue. A census taker not familiar with the family may have answered the question by observation, not thinking it was necessary to ask.

Elizabeth lived to her 86th year, passing away August 16, 1911; she is buried in St. Nicholas Cemetery beside her husband Henry. Elizabeth and her husband were one of three couples that donated the land for Saint Nicholas cemetery fifty-six years earlier. Two gravestones mark their last resting place, one is a worn stone with a German inscription showing the name Heinrich Niemann and informing the visitor his hometown was Ankum Hannover and that he was the husband of Elizabeth Schulte. Beside the worn stone is a more modern one with an English inscription marking both their graves.

Elizabeth was able to age in place, and this practice was continued through the next generation as Joseph's vision began to fail. No longer able to carry on the day to day farming, he rented the farm to Frank J. Ernst, a brother-in-law of his niece Mary Niemann. At the time of the 1920 census, Joseph still resided on the farm where he was born but he was now a boarder with the Frank and Rose Ernst family.

Joseph lived to the age of 73; he left the farm to his nieces and nephews after his death, but the farm wasn't immediately sold. A year later, one of his nephews, Nicholas Flammang, a son of Joseph's oldest sister, moved there with his family and lived on the old Niemann homestead for the next couple years.

The Flammang family had relocated from Nebraska after a harrowing escape from the Republican River flood of 1935. The farm was eventually sold at which time the Flammang family relocated to the Saint Donatus area.

1848

John Nicholas (Nicholas) Nemmers and Catherine Weber

Tete des Morts Township, Jackson County, Iowa

The average size of a living room in a small house today is 256 square feet. A pioneer's log cabin ranged from 10' x 10' or 100 square feet to a more permanent structure of 16' x 16' or 256 square feet. The temporary cabin built by the Nemmers clan after their arrival in Iowa was probably on the smaller side, 10' x 12' with a loft for sleeping. Nicholas was an accomplished carpenter, a trade he continued after arriving in Jackson County, his age may have slowed him down, but his expertise would have been invaluable.

Nicholas and Catherine along with their son Michael and younger daughters Caroline and Susanne were all living with their son Nicholas, Jr., his wife Mary and their growing family. When landing on American shores Nicholas and Mary already had three children and John was born three to four months after their arrival in Jackson County. That brings the total number of residents to eleven!

Wow! Can you imagine that many people living in an area the size of your living room? It's hard to comprehend. How could they manage with so little privacy? Thinking back to their journey across the ocean, over a month living with strangers, absolutely no privacy, using a chamber pot positioned in the corner of a communal bedroom, eating without a table and no bathing opportunities suddenly makes living in a single room, with only your loved ones, sound like a dream come true.

The family lived this way for a couple years before building a more commodious permanent home with two rooms and a loft, which served as home for fifteen years before a traditional Luxembourg stone mason's type structure was built.

When imagining the standard of living of the mid 1800's, a common reaction today might be to cringe at the thought of using an outhouse. When that's the only private option available, it's an option to be thankful for. Think about the positive features of an outhouse, it offers total privacy - unless, of course, you are using a multiple hole (seat) outhouse. You might ask why anyone would build a multiple hole outhouse, the answer is, they had a reason for everything. Outhouse holes were generally different sizes, children (and probably moms too) were scared of falling in, a smaller hole provided safety and peace of mind. For the ultimate in luxury, sometimes they were different heights or even had an adjustable step for the younger folks.

Jackson County, Iowa had a terrain that any adventurous young lad would love! As with many farms along the river, there were caverns, gaps and hollow areas in the bluffs, the Nemmers farm was no exception. From

Rev. Nemmers stories, there was "one cavern in the cliffs of his father's farm, which the boys called the 'Indian House.' Here the smoke blackened cliff showed where the Red Men had made their camp fire and cooked their venison and smoked their pipes before the white men came and drove them away from their native hills."[18]

(1). Nicholas was the oldest child of John Nicholas and Catherine Nemmers, he was born February 12, 1816 in Dondelange, Luxembourg, his marriage to Maria Catherina Freymann occurred in Kehlen, Luxembourg on February 17, 1841. Of their nine children, three were born in Luxembourg, Catharine, married William Herrig, Michael P., married Catherina Marks and Nicholas D., married Anna Kaiser. Their first American born child, John joined the family shortly after arriving in Iowa, on October 16, 1847. Next was Carl who married Margaret Even; Mary; Peter Sr. married Margaret Keiser; Susan married Jacob Mangrich and John Peter Sr. married Margaret Mangrich.

A grandson of Peter Sr. and Margaret (Keiser) Nemmers, Clayton F. Nemmers, was a member of Admiral Richard Evelyn Byrd's Antarctic expedition. The expedition was formed to train personnel and test equipment for the United States Navy Antarctic Developments Project. This was the largest exercise ever undertaken in Antarctica. During this expedition, which involved thirteen ships and 4,700 men, they mapped over one third of the continent. The purpose of the expedition was two-fold, it kept the soldiers engaged after the war and "The military rationale behind the operation was to acquire polar logistical experience, since U. S. forces might have to fight a war against the Soviet Union in the far north."[19] Clay was a crew member of the USS Currituck, a seaplane carrier, and an integral part of the expedition.

(2). Catherine, the oldest daughter was born around 1820 in Luxembourg, it was there she married John Kleitsch. About the time of her father Nicholas's death, Catherine, her husband and children Michael, Mary, Catherine, Eliza and John had immigrated to America. By 1860 they were settled onto a small farm in Tete Des Morts Township near her brother and mother. At this point they had added two American born children, Angeline and Susan to their family and in 1864 Margaret joined the family. During the 1860's, it appears the family relocated to Linn County, Iowa.

The 1880 census shows Catherine was suffering from dropsy, it also lists their 23 year old daughter Angeline Ellen as a victim of paralysis. There are no other records to support this statement; she may have been a polio

---

[18] The Progress Review (La PorteCity, Iowa), Sunday, December 4, 1949.

[19] The Seventh Continent, Antarctica in a Resource Age by Deborah Shapley, 1985.

victim with mild symptoms that faded with time. She married Albert Buehler in her thirties; they became the parents of seven children.

(3). Peter Nemmers, died at birth, November 24, 1820.

(4). Michael was born in Luxembourg in 1821. Several years after arriving in America, Anna Even became his wife, they were married in Saint Donatus. Michael and Anna purchased land and farmed in neighboring Prairie Springs Township, Jackson County, Iowa. Their children were Nicholas B., John married Mary Anne Schiltz, Michael, Jr. married Barbara Plein, Theodore married Anna Herrig, George Sr. married Margaret Frantzen, Mathias married Anna Margaret Schiltz and Henry married Mary Kascht.

* * *

Nearly every aspect of farming was difficult for settlers and human nature has most of us on a continuous quest for an easier way to perform our work. Of course there were many things that were difficult or even impossible to improve, but there are always routines that offer room for improvement. During the winter, there was little to fill the hours, there was no radio or television and books were scarce and expensive. Women had no trouble filling their idle hours just caring for the children, the home and keeping everyone fed. Men would look for ways to get ready for spring, fixing and improving their tools for the upcoming season.

Michael Nemmers, Sr. saw room for improvement in his existing planting tools and instead of sitting around wishing for a better tool, he decided to take action and invented a new and improved hand corn planter, Michael submitted his plans to the United States Patent office in May, after the winter doldrums, and on November 25, 1873 he was awarded patent number 144919.

This invention, simply put, had a height of about two to three feet, with a similar appearance to other hand corn planters. This one allowed the user to select a setting for the number of seeds released each time, a revolving disk held the seeds in place. The unit included protections to prevent seeds from getting stuck or going sideways, a plunger carried the seed into the ground and when the plunger was pulled back the dirt was cleaned off in preparation for the next seeds.

There were scores of patented hand planters which made mass production an unlikely prospect, but there were probably various versions of his invention in the hands of relatives and local friends. With the advent of tractors and the farm implements that followed, the outdated, innovative planter was in all likelihood tossed into a corner, never to be used again.

(i). The oldest of Michael's children, Nicholas B. Nemmers was born March 15, 1852, he was always moving, never idle, one of those people that could handle several projects in progress at any given time. Once reaching his late teens, Nicholas attended Pio Nono College in Saint Francis, Wisconsin he studied music and earned his degree in 1874.

The first years after college were spent teaching at the local Luxembourg Independent School in Prairie Springs Township, La Motte, Iowa. N. B. married Elizabeth Manders, daughter of Civil War veteran John Peter Manders on July 5, 1876. In 1882 he left teaching behind and purchased a general store in La Motte.

Nicholas B. Nemmers was also a local politician and leader. The variety of positions he held included Town Council member for the town of La Motte, Mayor of La Motte, Postmaster for La Motte, Prairie Springs Township Treasurer, school board member, assessor and was an Iowa State Representative for two terms or four years from 1890 to 1893.

In addition to all of his extra-curricular activities N. B. operated the store until his death February 3, 1923 at which time his wife Elizabeth took over. Elizabeth was mentioned in the "Centennial Edition" of Jackson Sentinel Newspaper. In a write-up about the town of La Motte, the article states "The oldest resident of LaMotte is Mrs. N. B. Nemmers, who purchased her home in 1882."[20] The same article mentions that she is the owner of one of the oldest buildings in the town, although it doesn't inform us which building that might be. Apparently, the building was the birthplace of a little person named Major Noble George Washington Winner, born July 12, 1869. His parents moved to Linn County, Iowa and he joined Barnum & Bailey Circus when he was eighteen years old.

At the time of this article Elizabeth was still running the family business. She continued on this path, as her husband did, until her death on December 8, 1945. The 1940 census lists four daughters and a son living at home. Kate, age 62 was a telephone operator that had worked 72 hours the prior week, Margaret a dressmaker, Theresa worked locally as a maid, Henry was a farm hand and Mary the youngest at age 40, was a teacher. After Elizabeth's death, three of their daughters handled the store for the next twenty years. The Nemmers store was a central part of the small town for well over eighty years.

(5). Caroline Nemmers was born December 26, 1827 in Kehlen, Luxembourg. After arriving in America, Caroline was living in a crowded Nemmers cabin. On an adjacent property, lived a bachelor by the name of Theodore Haxmeier. The year after arriving in America, on September 25, 1848 Caroline married Theodore Haxmeier in Dubuque County, Iowa. The couple had seven children. *[see the Haxmeier Family.]*

(6). The youngest, Susanne Nemmers was born May of 1831, like her sister Caroline, she married a neighbor. Henry Haxmeier was a brother to

---

[20] The Jackson Sentinel, Maquoketa, Iowa, Centennial Edition, June 1938.

Theodore, and owned land next door; in 1853 Susanne and Henry were married; they raised a family of seven children, all born in Jackson County, Iowa. They were raised on a farm but most of the children left farming behind:

(i). Theodore Hoxmeier born July 21, 1854 was married to Maria Krier January 16, 1878 by Rev. Flammang. Their family consisted of fourteen children, Claire, Henry, Susanna, Michael T., Margaret, Nicholas, Dominic, Anthony, Katherine, Maria, Bernard and Clara. The family's home was in Alton, Sioux County, Iowa, where Theodore owned a general merchandise store.

(ii). George L. Haxmeier born September 20, 1856 in Saint Donatus. He became a Roman Catholic priest and eventually a Monsingnior.

(iii). Catherina Hoxmeier, born in September 6, 1858, married Dominic Krier January 16, 1878. Their eight children were Henry, Nicholas, Johanna, George, Lena, Anna, Christina and Anthony. They raised their family in the Edgerton, South Dakota area. On the 1900 census, Dominic owned a general merchandise store, their oldest son farmed, Nicholas and George worked in the store, Johanna was a milliner and the younger children were in school.

(iv). Michael H. Haxmeier was born in 1861, married Margaret Even November 21, 1888. Their children were Joseph who died at age two and Anna Christina (b. 1890, m. Amos Klein). Michael died in 1898 in Sioux County, Iowa, his wife Margaret then spent some time in South Dakota with her brother Nicholas, a hotelier in South Dakota before returning to Alton, Iowa where she raised her daughter.

(v). Helena Hoxmeier was born July 23, 1863; she married Anton Goebel and their children were Maria, George and Clara. Anton had a farming background but opened a clothing store in Alton. He left Lena a widow around 1908 when their children were young. Their daughter Maria became a teacher and son George took over the clothing store at a young age, he sold the store in 1913 and relocated to Saint Louis. Lena moved to Los Angeles, California in retirement.

(vi). John Hoxmeier was born March 1866, he married Maria Arend in 1891, they remained on the home farm in Jackson County raising their six children, Rosa, Anna, Lena, George, Louis and Marcella.

(vii). Christina Mary Haxmeier was born March 16, 1870, she married Francis Niemeyer October 14, 1896. Their six children Maria Georgia, Norbert Henry, Leo Francis, Margaret Matilda, Helen Grace and Dolores Mary were raised in Elkader, Iowa, where Francis owned and operated a general store.

* * *

For the Nemmers family, the first death on American soil was in 1857 when the patriarch, Nicholas, passed away at the age of 74, the date was March 7, 1857. He is buried in the Saint Donatus Catholic Cemetery. At that time they were still living in in their two rooms with a loft, cabin.

After her husband's death, Catherine moved a few miles from her son's farm and joined her youngest daughter Susanne who had married German immigrant, Henry Haxmeier. The Haxmeier home was a welcoming one, Henry and Susanne had an open door policy to needy family members, they also took in boarders from time to time. The 1860 census shows their household included Henry, his wife Susanne along with children Theodore age 6, George age 3, and Catharine age 1; additional residents were Susanne's mother Catharine, a farm laborer named John Hegleson and a twenty-four year old Austrian merchant named Joseph Petsche.

Catherine lived for several years after her husband's death, the exact date of her passing isn't confirmed but could be as late as 1876. She is buried next to her husband in the Saint Donatus Catholic Cemetery, their gravestone is written in German and the text is quite worn and difficult to read, but an article written by Sister Mary Marcellinda OSF translates the inscription on the tombstone as follows:

"Here rests in God the respected (the German has "ehrsame") John Nicolaus Nemmers at the age of seventy-three years. He was born in Donde-Lingen, Luxembourg, and died March 7, 1857. May he rest in peace. Here rests also his devoted wife Catherina Weber, born in Donde-Lingen, Luxembourg, descended from (ancestor's names illegible on tomb stone). She died March 25, 1870. R.I.P."[21] However, if you see the stone in person, no matter what angle you look at the inscription, the year does not appear to be 1870, it looks more like a four digit year ending with 6.

1849

Andrew Schmidt and Elizabeth Bonnekesel

Tete des Morts Township, Jackson County, Iowa

"Heads of Death" or Tete des Morts Township was named by the French, long before Andrew Schmidt acquired a farm there. The gruesome name has ties to Jackson County, Iowa's Sac Indian history. The Sac and the Sioux were enemies and during one particularly bloody Sioux attack, the Sacs gained the upper hand killing their aggressors; the bodies were pushed over the bluff onto the creek bed below. Years later, French traders

---

[21] About The Nemmers Family by Sister Mary Marcellinda Kass OSF; as of December 2014 her article was included on the website http://www.adams-mckain.com.

discovered the skulls and bones of the Sioux along the creek's edge. Taking in the sight, the traders didn't hesitate in naming the area "tetes des morts." Early on there were calls to change the name, including Rev. Flammang, of Saint Donatus Catholic Church. The name of the town soon changed to match the church, but the township and the creek still bear the name Tete des Morts. In spite of the name, it is still one of the most picturesque locations in Iowa.

Not long after the Niemanns were settling into their home just north of Bellevue, Andrew Schmidt was emigrating from Lengerich in Northern Germany. Like the Niemanns he was a native the Hannover area, and like the Niemanns he located north of the town of Bellevue, his land was in Tete des Morts Township, just south of Theodore Haxmeier's farm.

Andrew (Andres) Schmidt was born November 3, 1817, son of Johann Bernard Schmidt and Catharine Aleio Eilman. Andrew landed in New York October 22, 1846, and was naturalized July 6, 1857 in Maquoketa. He married Anna Maria Elisabeth Bonnekesel around 1849, she was from the Hannover area and was the daughter of Johannes Heinrich Lambert Bonnekesel and Maria Aleio Kuter.

Nine children were born to Andrew and Elisabeth, all born and raised in Tete des Morte Township, Jackson County, Iowa.

(1). Andrew was born June 6, 1850, he married Mary Schiltz on November 26, 1872. Their nine children were Rosena, John Peter, Susan Lucy, Helen, Elizabeth, Maria Mae, Lucinda Barbara, K. Dorothy and Lester. Andrew died in Bellevue, Iowa, May 2, 1926.

(2). Anna Mae Elizabeth was born September 27, 1853, she married John Louis Ernst November 26, 1872. They became the parents of seven children, Edward John, John C., Conrad F., Frederick L., Anton Henry, Frank J. and Elizabeth Anne.

(3). Catherine was born July 5, 1854, her marriage to Frank Stein took place around 1874 and the couple had eight children, Theodore Frank, Annie Mary Caroline, Mary Elizabeth, Joseph William, Caroline M., Frank Theodore, William Anthony and Kathryn.

(4). Lucetta Elizabeth was born July 9, 1856, she married John P. Franzen around 1883, their family of six was raised in Springbrook. The children were Mary Magdalene, John William, William, Peter John, Elizabeth Marie and Mary Christina.

(5). William Frederick was born October 23, 1858; he married Mary Kettman April 7, 1884 at Spruce Creek, Iowa. They lived in Scott County Iowa and retired to South Dakota. Their children were George, William B., Ralph John, Bernard, John and Theresa.

(6).Edward C. was born December 4, 1859, he married Justina Augusta Linneberg on October 4, 1883 at Saint Donatus. Their children were Frederick William, Elizabeth Theresa, Frank Henry and Mary Eva.

(7). Christina Caroline was born March 1866. At nineteen years of age, on January 11, 1886 she was married to John Henry Krogmann. Initially they settled in Sioux County, and then a few years later they relocated to Remsen, Iowa. They were the parents of John Henry, born October 11, 1888 and Elizabeth born in 1892, who died as an infant.

Henry and Lena also took in an Orphan Train child with the name of Catherine Keller.

(8). Mary Elizabeth was born in 1868; she married August Brinker in 1889 at Bellevue, Jackson County, Iowa. Their children were Henry, Benjamin and Anna. Their home was located in South Dakota.

(9). Henry was born May 23, 1869, he was married to Anna Bregenzer April 3, 1894 at St. Joseph's Catholic Church in Bellevue, Iowa. Their eleven children were born in Canada; Anna Mary, Theresa Susanna, John Henry, Mathias, Elizabeth Mary Anna, Mary Margaret, Josephine Mary, Pauline Anna Mary, Andrew, Catherine Mary and Edward Pius.

1850

Mathias Manders and Elizabeth Hentgen

Prairie Springs Township, Jackson County, Iowa

Timing is everything. The Manders family arrived in Jackson County, Iowa July of 1850 with hopes of establishing a family farming operation. At their arrival, the current year's crop was well under way. Once the crop was harvested, a number of farmers were sure to sell their property and move on to greener pastures.

Mathias had time to explore the area and learn about possible opportunities. For a family of stones masons, a property laden with rocks, bluffs and stones was preferable, and they found the perfect parcel just north of Saint Donatus. Four months after arriving in New Orleans, on October twenty-fourth Mathias purchased one hundred sixty acres from Gerhard Budde for $562.00.

Prairie Springs township had quite varied terrain, "the highest points have an elevation of 1190 feet above the sea, while at the middle of this township in the valley of Morts creek the altitude is only 740 feet."[22] This valley that the locals called "down in the holler" is where Mathias built his house. Much of the interesting and varied landscape of Jackson County could be seen within the borders of the Mathias Manders homestead.

Up the hillside from where they would build were bluffs and outcroppings, and a countless number of loose stones scattered about. A spring bubbled from the hillside and coursed through the property flowing

[22] Iowa Geological Survey, Annual Report 1905. Frank A. Wilder, Ph. D., State Geologist, T. E. Savage, Assistant State Geologist.

into Tete des Morts Creek. The stream provided easy access to water for oxen, horses and livestock. There was a variety of wildlife available for a quick meal and for a little excitement there were plenty of rattlesnakes. Having spent many hours exploring the hills of the farm in the 1960's, I can attest to its scenic and peaceful atmosphere, as well as the rattlesnakes!

Most of an emigrant's belongings had to be left behind, with limited luggage space they had to choose wisely. Being a family of stone masons, Mathias and his adult sons brought their most useful tools; Elizabeth brought her favorite cookware and they would have also included seed collected from their Sandweiler garden and crops.

Stone masons have been around almost as long as farmers, their building materials are often freely available. There are many early stone structures we all recognize and have long been tourist attractions, such as the Egyptian pyramids, the Taj Mahal, the statues on Easter Island, Stonehenge and many more. Medievel stonemasons endured a seven year apprenticeship and they became experts at fabricating flat surfaces, which is the basis of stone masonry.

The durability of the Luxembourger stone mason's work is evident around the town of Saint Donatus. A 1929 article in a Miami newspaper focused on a community "where the wheels of progress have not ground away nature's beauty" and when describing the expertise of the Luxembourger stone masons "Few modern architects could match the craftsmanship which was employed in erecting the buildings. They are of heavy stone, covered with smooth cinder stucco composition. The proportions of the facades and the designs formed by perfectly arranged doors and windows give the buildings a remarkable degree of unity."[23] These same buildings are still standing today, still in excellent shape, in fact the entire town has been place on the National Register of Historic Places.

Having their favorite chisels, mallets and kevels at hand, a trained stone mason had the ability to build a house, and with the expertise of the Manders stone mason crew they had the manpower to complete the task quickly and efficiently.

Every able body in the family labored at clearing stones and brush from what would become their cropland, the stones were sorted by size and shape as a lumber yard would organize boards. This collection of stones and rocks would be the materials used to build the new Manders home. Quality stones too large to transport were chiseled to size on site before being delivered to the construction area. Their final masterpiece was a two story structure. The first floor contained two rooms, there was a steep narrow stairway leading to the second floor with two bedrooms, and there was even a cramped stairway leading to the attic which was outfitted with

---

[23] Miami Herald, Miami, Florida, July 28, 1929.

two small windows.

The house enjoyed a long life, from the Manders family, to Mathias, Jr.'s family, then his daughter Rose and her husband Theodore Weiseler who added a clapboard addition. Electricity was added in 1960, unfortunately the historic home was torn down in the 1980's.

On March 1, 1852 Mathias added a forty acre plot of land to his holdings by taking advantage of a land grant.

By 1860 Mathias and his sons had improved 40 acres of land, the remaining 160 was hilly, rocky and covered with timber including hickory and oak. After Mathias, Sr. passed away in 1869 at the age of 73, forty acres of partially improved land was sold and the farm was back to the original 160 acres.

After another ten years, in 1880, under the management of Mathias, Jr. another 40 acres had been improved, leaving only 40 acres of timber and 40 acres unimproved. According to the farm census, in 1880 Mathias had five horses and a collection of livestock consisting of nine cows, four steers and seventeen hogs. It was typical of farmers to dabble in a variety of farming categories, not only for food for their own family but failure in one area wouldn't wipe out the business, plus there was opportunity for continuous cash flow.

* * *

Mathias Manders and Elizabeth Hentgen were married in Sandweiler, Luxembourg January 9, 1823. They were the parents of nine children.

(1). Marie Manders the oldest, was born November 17, 1823 in Sandweiler. On April 12, 1852, Maria married George Hottua, a blacksmith in Dubuque, Iowa, he was a Luxembourger born in 1823. Their three children were born in Dubuque County, Elizabeth in 1856 and twins Mary and Mathias were born in 1857. Misfortune visited Maria August 7, 1861 when her husband George passed way. He left her a house in Dubuque and 160 acres of land in Minnesota.

After George's death, Maria married George Van Dillon in Dubuque, Iowa. Reported in the 1865 census they had relocated to the farm in Minnesota, a daughter Eva was born to them around 1865. Maria spent her later years living with her daughter Elizabeth and son-in-law Peter Eltgroth. Maria died on November 22, 1882 in Caledonia, Houston County, Minnesota, it is there she is buried.

(2). Peter Manders, the oldest son was born December 29, 1825; he immigrated in 1850 and became naturalized in Maquoketa, Iowa during the month of May 1858. Rosalie Capesius became his wife. Their family grew to nine children, Hilarius, born in 1855, Mary 1859, Matthew in 1861. Matthew was still an infant when Peter left for Civil War military service *[see*

Military Service chapter]. Children born after he returned were Pauline in 1864, Michael 1866, Sebastian 1868, Joseph 1872, Elisabeth 1875 and Annie 1876, the two youngest dying as infants and Rosalie left her husband a widower after Annie's birth.

Peter lived on his farm (aging in place) until after his ninetieth birthday when he moved in with his daughter Mary (Manders) Olinger, who lived nearby. Peter lived to be 95 years old!

In March of 1922 an unfathomable tragedy visited Peter's family. Two of his grandchildren, first cousins to each other were discovered dead with gunshot wounds to their heads. Newspapers engaged in tabloid journalism to report the tragedy. The event captured frontpage headlines across the state. An Illinois paper had this to say:

"GIRL, 15, AND COUSIN, 22, FOUND DEAD

"Dubuque, March 31.-The bodies of Veronica Manders, 15, and her cousin, Erich Manders, 22, were found in a field with bullet holes in their heads.

"Both were last seen Wednesday. Veronica attended church at St. Catherine's with Mary Manders, her cousin and sister of Erich. They walked home together. Veronica left Mary at her home and started a short cut through her Uncle Hillary Manders' farm to her own home, a half mile away. After noon, Peter, a brother of Erich, found the body of Veronica lying on her face. It was believed death was due to a hemorrhage until the coroner discovered a bullet wound in the back of the head where the girl's hair covered it.

"Meanwhile, Erich was missing. His body was found in a field. It is believed to be a case of murder and suicide.

"According to relatives there was nothing known to them of any love affair between the two cousins. Veronica was the daughter of Joseph Manders and Erich was the fourth son of Hillary Manders, Joseph's brother.

"It is considered possible that Erich may have shot his cousin accidentally and then killed himself through grief or fear of the consequences.[24]

Very few papers even mentioned the latter option; they couldn't seem to think beyond the splashy version. Not knowing the cousins, a conclusion is more of a guess, but the accidental shooting version fits better with the actual circumstances, especially since Veronica was cutting through her uncle's property.

(3). The second son, John Peter Manders born in 1828 married

---

[24] Newspaper article from the Rockford Republic, Rockford, Illinois Friday, March 31, 1922.

Catherine Hentges when he was about 30. The couple remained in the St. Donatus area; they had eleven children, Elizabeth, Mathias, Catherine, Peter, Susan, Peter C., Henry, Theresa, John, Anna, and Mary.

From 1867 to 1869 he held the official position of county supervisor. John Peter lived to the age of 81.

(4). Their fourth child was Mathias Manders, he was born September 5, 1830. At the age of 20 he made the choice to immigrate to America with his family rather than complete his military service, he is listed as a deserter on Luxembourg's militia service rolls. He was named for militia service in the 1849 call-up, and has since been "stricken from the rolls as a deserter."

According to Luxembourg military history, during the 1830's the required military service was 5 years in length, one year of continuous duty and three months during each of the next four years. By 1846 there was a required increase in the size of the militia by about 20% but there was no mention of a change in service requirements, Mathias was called up for duty in 1849 so his first year was satisfied but the requirement for four additional years of three months per year had yet to be fulfilled.

Susanne Meysenburg was the third of ten children born to Pierre Nicholas Meysenburg and Catharina Thekes in Sandweiler, Luxembourg. Her date of birth was April 10, 1842. She married Mathias months after arriving in Iowa and the couple made their home near St. Donatus. They joined Mathias' parents in the house built by the Manders stone masons in 1850.

Mathias and Suzanne had five children, Nicholas, Katherine, Rose, Peter Donatus and in 1872 their fifth child was born. The infant died January 19, 1872 and Suzanne died four days later . . . an event eerily similar to the death of her mother except Suzanne was only twenty-nine years of age.

Mathias was unable to handle the farm and care for the children on his own, his father had passed away a few years earlier and his mother was getting up in years. Mathias was the only man in the household, his oldest son was just seven years old. To ease the burden, Mathias took his youngest son, Peter Donatus to Bellevue to be cared for by his widowed sister-in-law, Elizabeth (Capesius-Manders) Lucke, who had recently remarried.

As we have seen before, it wasn't unusual for a grieving spouse to remarry the year following a loss, such was the case with Mathias. Later that year he married a widow named Elizabeth Gluden. Elizabeth's past is quite elusive, but her obituary refers to two daughters, Annie Steins of Chicago and Mary Lehman of Worthington, Minnesota. This sounds like a mountain of information which should lead to Elizabeth's past, but her daughters Mary and Annie have been just as difficult to trace as their mother.

After the marriage, Peter Donatus returned home to rejoin his family and become acquainted with his step-mother. From the many memories passed along by the Manders family, although no one could replace the children's mother, everyone agreed that Elizabeth was a loving, dedicated mother that cared for the children as if they were her own.

(i). Mathias and Suzanne's oldest son Nicholas Manders, who was born in 1865 died at the age of 20 of appendicitis.

(ii). Katherine Manders was born February 24, 1867 and married Luxembourger Henry Piitz February 12, 1890. They moved to a farm in Butler County, Nebraska in 1891 and there raised three children, Mathew born December 1890 in Iowa, John born February 1892 in Nebraska and Rosa born January 1896 in Nebraska. Note that the branch of Henry Piitz's family that remained in Iowa only used one "i" in the spelling of their name.

(iii). Rose Manders, born in 1868 married Theodore Wieseler in January of 1894. Rose and Theodore had ten children; their nine daughters were Magdalena, Clara, Margerite, Cleta, Veronica, Mary, Catherine, Anna and Suzie and their son was named John.

(iv). Peter Donatus Manders, the youngest of Mathias Jr.'s surviving children was born in 1870, he married Margaret Schartz and they raised their family on a farm in Jackson County, Iowa.

(5). Marie Manders was born September 29, 1930 in Sandweiler, Luxembourg. In Bellevue, Iowa, April 15, 1851 she was joined in Holy Wedlock to Carl Thimmesch, a Luxembourger born in 1825. They had thirteen children, only eleven are named here. The first four, Mathias (b. 1852, m. Elizabeth Dauwen), John Peter (b. 1856, m. Catherine Palen), Peter (b. 1858, m. Mary Rohn) and Michael H. (b. 1861, m. Elizabeth Wagner 1885), were born in Dubuque County, Iowa. Carl and Mary then moved to a farm in Dakota County, Minnesota for a short time before moving to Freeburg, Minnesota where seven children were born, Mary Ann (b. 1862, m. Nich Hoscheit 1885), Marian (b. 1865, m. Nicholas Hosch 1885), Nicholas (b. 1869, m. Mary Freilinger 1896), Theodore (b. 1872), Theresa Mary (b. 1874), Mathias Peter (b. 1876, m. Kate Hoffmann ~1901), Lavina (b. ~1877). Carl lived to age 87, passing away in 1913 and Mary, who was active to the end, lived to an impressive 101 years, leaving this world on December 10, 1931. They are both buried at Calvary Cemetery in Caledonia, Minnesota.

(6). Michael Manders, born July 4, 1834 was Mathias and Elizabeth's sixth child; he lived with his parents until 1861 when he joined his sister Eva and her family in Crooked Creek Township, Houston County, Minnesota.

August 17, 1862 he enlisted as a Private in the Minnesota Infantry, during the next three years he was promoted to Corporal and was mustered out August 19, 1865. After the war he returned to Minnesota and again lived with the Fisch family. On October 5, 1869 he married Anna Katherine Schmitz, they farmed in the Minnesota Lake area of Faribault County, Minnesota. Michael and Anna had five children, Nicholas George, Eva, Christina, Elizabeth and Maria.

Michael was postmaster for the Freeborn Post Office in Houston County in the late 1860's, the position carried a $24 salary.

Michael died in 1915 at the age of 80, his wife survived him by twenty years. *[more about Michael at the Military Service chapter]*

(7). Elizabeth born in 1837 married Peter Kass, son of John Kass and Annie Krier, September 26, 1860. They made their home in the town of Bellevue, Iowa where Peter was initially a blacksmith, later he became a cattle trader and by 1900 he was a "capitalist." Census records show he retired by 1910. Their family consisted of five children, Elizabeth, Mary, John Baptiste, Anna and Theresa.

(i). Their oldest daughter, Elizabeth Kass was a dressmaker, she married Michael C. Evans, on April 22, 1883. Michael owned a general store, first in Kingsley, Iowa and then in Marcus, Iowa, the same location three Niemann's had business interests. They were blessed with eight children, Odie N., Julian P., Gilbert W., Camilla, Esther, Lloyd, Arthur C. and Edmund.

(ii). Mary Kass was born in 1863, on July 29, 1891 she drowned in the Mississippi river near her home in Bellevue. She hadn't been well, couldn't sleep at night and would get up and walk outside. If she didn't come back in 15 minutes her dad would go and look for her. This time he couldn't find her. A fisherman found her the next day, on the shores of the Mississippi.

(iii). John Baptiste "Batty" Kass married Katie Schiltz, he trained for the pharmacist occupation and opened a drug store in Wayne, Nebraska. They had a daughter Edna who died at age 19 a couple months after her marriage. John had died when Edna was just a tot.

(iv). Anna Kass lived to age 61.

(v). The youngest, Theresa Kass died in Remsen, Iowa. Longevity is abundant in this family, she was 99 years old.

As many of her siblings, Elizabeth (Manders) Kass also lived a long life, she died at the age of 82, and is buried next to her husband at St. Joseph's Catholic Cemetery in Bellevue, Iowa.

(8). Eva Manders, the eighth child and youngest daughter was born April 11, 1839. She married Theodore Fisch in September of 1859. They moved to Houston County, Minnesota and raised a family of ten children, Nicholas J., Mary, Mathias, Elizabeth, John Peter, John Peter, Anna K., Mary Catherine, Mary M. and Michael L. Eva lived to be 94!

(9). Sebastian Manders, the youngest was born March 26, 1841 to Mathias and Elizabeth (Hentgen) Manders, he was nine years of age in 1850 when the family arrived in America. On January 26, 1867 in Jo Davies County, Illinois, Sebastian married Elizabeth Capesius, the daughter of Peter Capesius and Suzanne Anna Gonner. The young couple made their home in the river town of Bellevue, Jackson County, Iowa. In 1869 their family was just getting started, daughter Annie was two years old and baby Peter was born that fall. Sebastian and Elizabeth had high hopes for the future.

Family stories suggest the highly contagious disease of infantile paralysis (polio) struck the family, with the first victim being five month old Peter who died February 28, 1870, his father Sebastian followed six month later, on September 2, 1870. Two year old Annie was a survivor but was now unable to use her legs; the situation left Elizabeth in a very oppressive situation; no money, no income and a daughter that needed special care. Since they weren't farmers, there wasn't a plot of land to generate income and Elizabeth was frantic to find a way to care for herself and her daughter. Sebastian's sister, Elizabeth (Manders) Kass, who also lived in Bellevue, proposed an idea that seemed to be a perfect solution. What could possibly go wrong?

To support her penniless family after her husband's death, the widow Elizabeth Manders became a live-in housekeeper and nanny at the home of Joseph Lucke, who also lived in Bellevue. Joseph was a recent widower and local shoe merchant, he was also a next door neighbor to Elizabeth's sister-in-law Mrs. Elizabeth Kass. There were five children in his family, Anna, Joseph, William, Clara and Frank, all under the age of 12, in addition to caring for these five children she cared for her disabled daughter, and was temporarily taking care of her recently widowed brother-in-law's toddler, Peter Donatus Manders.

Elizabeth was a busy young woman, she didn't mind the hectic pace, and it kept her thoughts off the personal tragedies that invaded her mind during idle moments. All parties involved were benefiting from the new arrangement; but, all good things seem to end, in this case it was the local Catholic Priest that intervened. His instructions to Elizabeth were to marry the man of the house or get out. Elizabeth feared she would be out on the streets with her three year old daughter, destitute with no prospects for their future.

Joseph and Elizabeth were married July 30, 1872, two years later their family began to grow, first Henry was born in 1874, Susan in 1875; John was born in 1876; Elisabeth in 1877, Nellie in 1879, Mary in 1882, Leo in 1886 and finally Emma in 1888. Their blended family consisted of fourteen children.

Annie Manders, though confined to a wheelchair was widely known for her sewing and handiwork expertise. She was especially adept at creating delicate doilies.

* * *

The parents, Mathias Senior and Elizabeth Manders, spent their senior years on their farm near St. Donatus, in 1863 he sold his farm to his third son Mathias who was still single at that time. Mathias Senior died June 13, 1869 and his wife Elizabeth (Hengen) died April 10, 1875. They are both buried at the St. Donatus Catholic Cemetery.

1858

Hoffmann Family

Prairie Springs Township, Jackson County, Iowa

Two ancient Roman roads intersected near the community of Kehlen, Luxembourg. What is now a quiet village has a history that dates back to the Gallo-Roman period when Roman soldiers marched through the area. Nearby excavations of Celtic tombs has added to the history of the surrounding area. By the 1800's, the Romans were long gone and Kehlen had become a small picturesque farming community.

The Hoffmann's left Kehlen with their eyes open to a new opportunity and a desire to find a community that will remind them of home. Now a resident of Prairie Springs Township, Michael Hoffmann, Sr. was the owner of 190 acres of land and a small collection of livestock. With two of his adult sons, Michael John and Frank, they continued the efforts of clearing land and increasing cropland acerage on their sizeable farm.

The first years in America, when Michael and Catherine Hoffmann were laboring on their new farm, their son John Michael was the work-horse. Nine years after settling in Jackson County, John Michael married Anna Wagoner January 11, 1870 in St. Donatus. The two couples, representing two generations remained together on the home farm. Michael, Sr. initially insisted on maintaining control over his new farming occupation but eventually agreed to turn the reins over to his son John Michael.

Michael and Catherine spent their later years surrounded by ten grandchildren, six boys and four girls. The patriarch passed away on February 4, 1893 and his wife Catherine enjoyed another six years with her grandchildren, passing away on October 31, 1899.

(1). Son Michael Hoffmann, Jr., their first born as well as the family scout was already on his own as an established wagon maker in St. Donatus. Michael Jr. was born March 1, 1835 in Kehlen, Luxembourg, married Mary Heiter, February 6, 1867, soon relocating to Key West, Iowa where Michael continued his trade of wagon-making, the couple had a family of seven children, Susan, Nicholas, John, Frank, Peter, Michael and Anna.

The spring of 1885 brought major change as they relocated to South

Dakota where they established a farm just south of Emery. They enjoyed over twenty years in South Dakota before Michael's wife Mary died on April 9, 1906. A few years after Mary's death, Michael retired and moved to Bridgewater, South Dakota, with his daughter Susan. He died in Bridgewater on August 18, 1926 at the age of ninety-one.

(2). Mary Hoffmann was born November 25, 1836, in Kehlen, Capellen, Luxembourg. According to her official birth record "In the year one thousand eight hundred thirty-six, the twenty-sixth of the month of November, at ten o'clock in the morning, there appeared before me, the mayor and civil registrar of the town of Kehlen, canton of Luxembourg, in the province of Luxembourg, Michael Hoffmann from Kehlen, thirty-one year old cartwright residing in this town, who declared to me that a female child had been born in Kehlen yesterday at five o'clock in the evening, from his marriage to Catherine Gloesener, twenty-eight years old, with no occupation, and that he intended to name her Marie."[25] In addition to Michael, there were two witnesses to his declaration, Nicolas Hoffman a twenty-eight year old day laborer and Peter Welter a thirty-three year old school teacher, all residents of Kehlen and each signing the document.

Two years after arriving in Jackson County, on November 26, 1863 she was married to Henry Banks by Rev. J. Michael Flammang in Saint Donatus.

Henry was born to Nicholas Banck and Elisabeth Kuhn on April 8, 1836, his place of birth was Kehlen, Capellen, Luxembourg, a community with a population of around 3,100 in 1850. Living in a small community, we can speculate that Mary and Henry were acquainted in their native country, and going a step further, this might be what drew the young man to leave his family and immigrate to America.

Henry owned an 80 acre farm in Richland Township, it was located in an area that was described as one of the most desirable prairie sites of Jackson county, the location was just south of La Motte. Their first home was a 16 x 14 square foot one room stone and log cabin with a loft. The home was located on a rocky knoll towards the bottom of the hill. Less than fifty feet distant, flowed a crystal clear stream, Farmer's Creek. The distance to water was quite convenient for wash day and other househould needs.

On March 13, 1865, Henry doubled the size of his farm, adding 80 acres, paying $300.00 cash to William Reed for the land. Henry was a talented farmer, by 1870 his land was valued at $3,000, he had a total of 160 acres of which 100 acres were improved, 40 remained wooded and 20 acres were pasture and non-crop usage. In addition to land, there were four horses and livestock consisting of three cows, eight head of cattle and ten

---

[25] Birth record of Mary Hoffmann, professionally translated by Ann Sherwin.

swine.

The Banks' became the parents of four daughters.

(i). Katherine Banks was born November 4, 1864; she was married to Nicholas Kayser December 29, 1885. Nicholas was the son of Nicholas Kayser and Elizabeth Koos, born August 29, 1857 in Bilsdorf Luxembourg. They were the parents of ten children, Peter, John Baptist, Felix, Virgie, Mary Christena, Agnes Virginia, Frank, Cecilia, Lucy and Christina. Their family was raised in Hanson County, South Dakota. Katherine died January 23, 1942 and her husband died later the same year on October 5, 1942.

(ii). Mary Banks was born around 1865; she died in 1882 during her teen years.

(iii). Margaret Banks was born March 23, 1867; she married Peter Koos in a double marriage ceremony with her sister Katherine on December 29, 1885. Peter and Maggie had ten children.

(iv). Anna Banks was born June 5, 1869; she married Henry Koos, brother to Peter on February 17, 1897. They had two children, John Joseph married Loretta Clasen they had two sons and their son Leroy married Mary Kilburg and had four sons.

***

By 1870 Mary Hoffmann's brothers Michael John and Nicholas were managing the home farm. Nicholas planned on staying until his brother's marriage, then he would be free to make his mark on the world, farming wasn't in the picture. On January 11, 1870, a joyous family gathering took place when Michael John Hoffmann married Anna Wagoner, they planned to live at and operate the Hoffmann home place.

A few days after the marriage of Michael John and Anna, at the age of 33 Henry Banks died, leaving his wife Mary with a farm and four young daughters. The couple had only been married for seven years. Henry is buried at the Irish Catholic Cemetery of St. Theresa's, just outside of La Motte.

Mary's circumstances were assuredly better than that of many widows, her parents still lived in Jackson County. At this point Nicholas was the only single young man in the family, and he was obliged to put his life on hold for the good of his family. He moved in with his sister Mary and took the reins of the Banks farming operation.

Family legend says he eventually ran low on patience and was more than ready to continue with his life plans. He let it be known that it was time for Mary to move on with her life so he could begin his.

On February 8, 1871 Nicholas may have been more elated than his sister Mary when she became the wife of Jacob Marso. He was an immigrant from Luxembourg; Mary and Jacob Marso would add six children to Henry and Mary's four daughters. The children, all born in Richland Township, Jackson County, Iowa were Elizabeth (b. 1872), Michael (b. 1873), John J.

(b. 1875, m. Nina Jones 1903), Frank Joseph (b. 1877, m. Eliza Wilcox), Suzie (b. 1879, m. Leo Schroeder), Mary M. (b. 1882, m. James O'Donnell).

Mary (Hoffmann-Banks) Marso lived to the grand old age of ninety-two.

(3). Michael John Hoffmann, "John" was born June 14, 1839 in Kehlen. After living in Jackson County, Iowa for almost nine years he married Anna Wagoner on January 11, 1870, the marriage ceremony was performed by Rev. J. Michael Flammang. During the first two decades of their marriage they managed the Hoffmann homestead.

A trend we've seen with the Hoffmann men, they seemed inclined to make dramatic changes in their lives around their fifth or even sixth decade of life. John continued this tradition, although this change wasn't a dramatic one. In 1893 he and his wife bought a large farm near St. Donatus, near the Hoffmann homestead.

Michael John and Anna raised a large family, their children were Michael (b. 1871, m. Katherine Hentges), Nicholas (b. 1873, m. Anna Hingtgen), Jacob (b. 1875, m. Mary B. Pauly), John (b. 1877, m. Anna Weimerskirch), Frank (b. 1879, m. Elizabeth Gindt), Catherine (b. 1883, m. Nicholas Duschen), Peter (b. 1883, m. Rosalia Langenfeld), Anna (b. 1886, m. John Peter Polfer), Margaret (b. 1888, m. Joseph C. Pauly) and Theresa (b. 1892, m. Michael J. Fischels). Their longevity was impressive; eight of them lived to their 80's or 90's!

As the saying goes, Necessity is the Mother of Invention. This is often applicable to farmers. Many farmers created very useful inventions, making their lives easier, but few took the steps to make it official. One of Michael and Anna's grandsons, Walter P., a farmer in La Motte applied for a patent in 1950 for a Calf Feeding Device, and the patent was issued in 1953.

(4). Frank Hoffmann, born October 17, 1841, married Susanna Heiter in 1865; they became the parents of six children, Elizabeth, Nicholas, Michael, Nicholas, John and Margaret. Susanna passed away and in 1880 Frank married Anna Hingtgen and eight more children were added to the mix, those children were Elizabeth, Frank, Maria, Theodore, Katherine, Peter, Joseph and Frances.

Frank was a successful farmer in Mosalem Township, Dubuque, Iowa (border of Jackson County) near St. Catharine and not far from the farm his father purchased upon arriving in Iowa. Frank and Anna enjoyed many years of married life, Anna lived to December 20, 1930 and just a week later, Frank joined his wife.

(5). Angeline Hoffmann was born January 5, 1846; she married Peter Entringer in St. Donatus on June 4, 1868. Peter was also born in Luxembourg, he had immigrated and settled in La Motte in 1856. The couple worked on a farm located near La Motte where their ten children were born, eight of which grew to adulthood. Their children were Michael, Albert, Frank, Rosa, Susie, Charles, Lucy, Mary, Annie and Peter.

(6). Nicholas A. Hoffmann was born November 26, 1849, in Kehlen, Luxembourg. He was living with his parents, ready to venture west when his brother-in-law Henry Banks died. Nicholas who was single at the time, came to his sister's rescue, operating her farm for the next year until she re-married. Almost immediately after his sister's marriage, N. A. Hoffmann followed the throngs to Nebraska, then continued on to Colorado. Once there he set up and operated a small general store. Less than a year later he cashed in his investment, returning to his parents' home in Iowa where he began teaching at the country school.

On February 1, 1875 Nicholas Hoffmann married Elizabeth Mueller, Iowa born and raised. He worked as a teacher until 1883 when the family moved to La Motte where Nicholas bought a general merchandise business from John Wilson and Sons. During the late 19th and early 20th centuries, general stores used a practice of offering premiums to their customers. Premiums were offered for anything from buying a certain box of cereal, to paying your bill to spending a certain amount. These premiums came in the form of toys, dishes and other knickknacks. Among Nicholas' more popular premiums were bowls and plates. Many residents of the La Motte area were sure to have a plentiful supply of dishes with the following imprint on the bottom:

Hoffmann's Store
"The Tireless Toiler For Trade"
LA MOTTE, IOWA

A public spirited man, he was selected postmaster for the town of La Motte, a position he held for many years, a span only broken by the terms of Nicholas Nemmers. Nicholas Hoffman continued his connection with the local school system by spending eighteen years as President of the Board of Education for the local school district.

The couple had six sons and one daughter, Michael was born 1875, Katherine 1877, John M. born in 1879 married Mary A. Lucke, Peter 1882, Frank 1886, Joseph M. 1892 and Aloysius J. 1898. All the children were born in Jackson County.

Nicholas died October 21, 1927 at the age of seventy-seven. Eleven years later, his wife Elizabeth was mentioned in the "Centennial Edition" of the local paper. In a write-up about the town of La Motte, after listing the oldest resident as Mrs. N. B. Nemmers, the article continues "Mrs. N. A. Hoffmann ranks second, having purchased her property in 1883."[26]

---

[26] The Jackson Sentinel, Maquoketa, Iowa, Centennial Edition, June 1938.

1860

John Nicholas Flammang

Tete des Morts Township, Jackson County, Iowa

West of the Mississippi, the 1850s offered a copius supply of farmhand positions. Wages may have been as high as twelve to fifteen dollars per month, including room and board. For the past five years Nick had been working as a farm hand, he began near Davenport in 1855 and then moved on to Saint Louis. By July of 1860 Nicholas had returned to Iowa, and was working as a farm laborer in Liberty Township of Dubuque County. Nick was working for Anton Pfeffer a semi-retired farmer in a household that consisted of Anton along with a son-in-law, Ernest Goebel, daughter Catherine and grandson Henry.

His brother Michael was overwhelmed in the building up of his parish and was in dire need of dependable help. Nicholas left his job as a farm hand and contracted as a carpenter on the Saint Donatus parish building projects.

Included in Rev. Michael's responsibilities was Spruce Creek's satellite parish of Saint Nicholas. This may have been the link that drew John Nicholas Flammang and Mary Ann Niemann together. Building projects were completed, Nick was back to working as a farm hand. In the 1860's during harvest season, farm hands could earn over two dollars per day plus board by working for local farmers in need of help.

In 1864 one of Reverend Flammang's parishioners was dealing with a tragedy. Henry Niemann had died, leaving his wife Elizabeth with seven children the oldest was a pretty young seventeen year old by the name of Mary Ann. This leaves us to wonder if Nick was one of the individuals lending a hand and finding love in the process.

Nicholas Flammang and Mary Ann Niemann were married November 21, 1866. The couple made their home on a farm in Tete Des Morts, Township near St. Donatus they raised a family of thirteen children. It is said they could see the St. Donatus church spire from their farm.

(1). Their first child Michael Flammang was born in 1867, he died as an infant.

(2). Elizabeth Flammang was born on the Feast of All Saints Day, November 1, 1868, and considering the family background her career choice is not a big surprise. She joined the Sisters of Notre Dame. *[continued at Lead by Faith]*

(3). Alois Francis Flammang was born May 9, 1870, he grew up on the family farm and enjoyed farming. As he was approaching adulthood Alois took a fancy to one of the neighbor girls, the problem was, there was a bit of a feud going on between their parents. The discord wasn't exactly at the level of the Hatfield's and McCoy's but both young people knew there was to be no contact between the two families. They were forced to sneak out to see each other. Once their relationship approached the point where they decided to take the big step to the altar, they were still too scared to tell their parents.

At church one Sunday they asked one of their friends, Margaret Schartz, mentioned in another part of this book, to come to the house and help with the preparations. Margaret was happy to help but her church shoes weren't meant for walking on frozen wintry gravel roads, and her sore feet were a memory she wouldn't soon forget. Even more memorable was the stress and anticipation surrounding her friends; the young sweethearts were getting married and their parents were yet to be informed! Alois Flammang married Anna Loewen in St. Donatus, Iowa on Monday, February 12, 1894.

The happy couple had ten children, all born in Orleans, Nebraska and they all grew to adulthood and all had families of their own. The children were Nicholas Alois (b. 1896, m. Ruth Fuller), John (b. 1898, m. Anna Consbrook), Josephine (b. 1900, m. Julius Schmidt), Michael Joseph (b. 1902, m. Susan Regina Pittz), Clara (b. 1903, m. Frank Graf), Lawrence Leroy (b. 1905, m. Josephine Bertha Pittz), Leo (b. 1906, m. Viola, d. 1941), Philomena (b. 1908, m. Edward Hoffman), Elisabeth (b. 1913, m. Nicholas Clarence Hoffman) and Cecilia (b. 1917, m. Merle Howart).

Alois followed the Flammang occupation of farming in Harlan County, Nebraska. After over 30 years of farming, in 1926 he put his Orleans farm up for sale, the description being 160 acre farm, all level, well improved, 5 miles from Scottsbluff, 2 wells, 15 acres fine alfalfa, 35 acres pasture, 30 acres sweet clover, 14 acres wheat grass land, balance in cultivation. He spent many years in retirement, living to the age of 83, April 30, 1954.

(4). Joseph Flammang was born February 1872 and died June 1874.

(5). On June 20, 1874 Joseph Walter Flammang was born. At the age of twenty he left Iowa and went to Harlan County, Nebraska where he began building his farming operation. On October 26, 1897 he married Mary Ann Eltz in Adams County, Nebraska. They had nine children, Harry Lewis (b. 1898, m. Madeline Pond), Mary Margaret (b. 1899, m. Harold Baltes), Clarence Matthew (b. 1902, m. Mary Dunlay), Arthur (b. 1904), Agnes (b. 1907, m. Carl Brackman), Regina (b. 1909, m. James Schumacher), Louise (b. 1911, m. Jean Hammond), Alfred Lawrence (b. 1913, m. Edna Farmer), and Walter Joseph (b. 1915, m. Katie Irene Pierce).

Over the years his land holdings in Harlan County grew to 560 acres, there he raised purebred Poland China and Hampshire hogs along with Hereford cattle. Near Gering he owned an additional 250 acres of irrigated land. In addition he was Vice President of Stamford Bank; he was a member of the Knights of Columbus and a member of St. Mary's Catholic Church. Joseph Walter lived to the age of 87; he died December 15, 1961.

(6). John Peter Flammang was born February 20, 1876 and died in a tragic accident on September 13, 1897. John was riding in a buggy being pulled by a team of horses that became startled, sending the team galloping out of control, straddling a large tree with the buggy coming up the middle.

(7). Alphonse Clement Flammang was born February 6, 1878; at the age of 22 he purchased land near his brother's farm in Nebraska. On January 9, 1901 he married Christine Wolbers in Otter Creek, Iowa. They were blessed with twelve children. Three of them, Colette (b. 1901), Raymond (b. 1903) and Mary (b. 1910) died in infancy, and nine survived to adulthood, Eleanor (b. 1905, m. Sylvan Edward Grime), Bertha (b. 1907, m. Ford McCoy), Arthur (b. 1908, m. Josephine Oswald), Harold (b. 1912, m. Violet Perry), Genevieve (b. 1914, m. James Waldo), Alverna (b. 1916, m. Lawrence Synak), Joseph Bernard (b. 1918, m. Gloria Hanson), Magdalena (b. 1921, m. Alan Givens, and Mildred (b. 1923, m. William Ayers).

Alphonse and Christine began their life together in Harlan County, Nebraska on a small farm; they lived in a sod house. Over the years Alphonse purchased several farms in Harlan County, their 320 acre home farm was in Sappa Township and called the "Shady Grove Dairy and Stock Farm." Alphonse developed expertise in purebred Spotted Poland China hogs and from there moved on to Holstein dairy cattle. He didn't limit his involvement to farming, he was director of the Farmers Equity Co-op Creamery Association in Orleans for 19 years and was a bank director. (The same bank where his brother was vice president). He was a member of the Knights of Columbus and of Saint Mary's Catholic Church. In March of 1945 their farm was for sale and listed as 320 acres; 160 good alfalfa ground, 15 in alfalfa now, 240 under cultivation, 20 acres sweet clover; $12,000 improvements with modern barn, 36x108, farm elevator, capacity 10,000 bushels; 200-ton silo; tile chicken house; modern 8-room house, electric equipped. Milk sold to creamery. Terms.

After retirement Alphonse and Christine were able to spend more time enjoying their hobbies of reading and traveling. Alphonse lived to the age of 75, passing away April 13, 1953.

(8). George Clement Flammang was born March 1, 1880. As a young man, George began studying for the priesthood; all went well for a while, but after a time he began asking his parents for money on a regular basis, his parents kept sending money. Finally his parents, overtaken by suspicion, decided to visit their son and learned he had lost interest in a religious vocation and was spending the funds on dating and socializing with friends. Times haven't changed as much as we think!

George then followed his brothers to Nebraska and met Louise Mary "Lula" Lennemann, who was from a prominent farming family in Harlan County. They were married May 11, 1911. Their farm was the "Sunny Slope Ranch". George and Lula adopted twin daughters, Elizabeth Ann "Betty Ann" and Elizabeth Louise "Betty Lou." George was only 58 years old when he died on April 6, 1938.

(9). Rose Anna Flammang was born April 29, 1881, she attended school through eighth grade. Rose remained single, she moved with her parents to Dubuque and took care of them in their golden years. After their passing, Rose remained in Dubuque until about 1926 and then moved to Orleans, Nebraska where several of her brothers were farming. Rose became a housekeeper for Rev. John E. Hahn and his mother. She was still there as of the 1930 census.

It was in the 1930's that Rose learned she had cataracts like her mother and might eventually lose her sight. She felt lucky having access to new medical procedures that could improve her vision. What she didn't count on was the ineptitude of the local doctors. Rose had surgery on the eye with the cataract, it soon became infected, the infection spread and she ended up losing most of her eyesight in both eyes.

Rose spent some time with each of her siblings in the area, then moved to a small house in Orleans, at the time of the 1940 U. S. Census Rose was renting the same home. On March 8, 1958 at the age of 77, Rose passed away; she is buried with her parents in Dubuque, Iowa.

(10). Nicholas Leo Flammang was born November 22, 1882 in Saint Donatus, Iowa; like his older brothers, he bought farmland in Nebraska. Nicholas married Christina Herrig January 18, 1910 at St. Catherine's Church in Jackson County and Christina joined Nicholas in Nebraska. Their family of eleven consisted of three sons and eight daughters. About nine years after their marriage they purchased a different farm which they named "Spring Creek Ranch" located about a mile northwest of Orleans, Harlan County, Nebraska. The Chicago Burlington Quincy Railroad cut through the northeast corner of their farm and the Republican River flowed nearby.

Around 1930 their farm was visited by a tornado which destroyed their barn and removed a corner of the roof of their home. The barn was rebuilt and the house repaired, but during the Dust Bowl days, with water already scarce, one of their neighbors installed a powerful new irrigation system, draining the little water available to their own irrigation system, the dairy herd was suffering and a change was needed. The Flammang's sold their farm and rented one near Indianola, Nebraska near the Republican River, there was plenty of fertile soil and things were looking up. They had only been living there a matter of months when just after noon on Friday May 31, 1935 their lives would change forever.

The prior night, eastern Colorado and western Nebraska had been hit with high intensity storms; possibly as much as twenty-four inches of rain had fallen in an area that was already saturated with earlier downpours. A meandering river that was normally shallow and three to four hundred feet wide became "a raging torrential wall of water, as deep as 20 feet and as wide as two miles at some points, demolishing or obliterating everything in its path."[27] The Flammang farm was in its path. All of their farm equipment, buildings, their home and personal possessions were taken by the river, but through a miracle of timing they all survived the ordeal.

Thirty-five cows had survived the flood but the family needed to relocate, they moved to a small farm just across the border ten miles from Norton Kansas, but the dust bowl was still raging and it only took six months to determine the new location wasn't going to work, the beleaguered family then moved back across the border to Holland, Nebraska, and from there, the first week of April 1940 they returned to Iowa, renting a farm in Prairie Springs Township in Jackson County. The next nine years began by renting Joseph Niemann's farm for a couple years followed by a move to what used to be the Manders homestead.

In late 1949 Nicholas had purchased a farm near their current home between La Motte and Saint Donatus. Nick was hospitalized before the actual move to their new home took place. He died at Mercy Hospital in Dubuque, Iowa, never having an opportunity to live on the farm on which he planned to retire.

(11). Michael Joseph Flammang was born January 30, 1884; he lived with his parents until about 1913 when he joined his brothers in Nebraska. On his WWI draft registration card he is listed as a farmer working for himself, but there is an odd entry on the form "The registrant is acting under a Guardian, Joseph Flammang, Orleans, Nebr. – Guardian".

Michael returned to Dubuque after the death of his father then went off to California after the death of his mother. He spent many years working at the Los Angeles General Hospital as a kitchen helper, then a cook. Michael died January 15, 1964 in Los Angeles.

(12). The twelfth of the thirteen children was Henry R. Flammang, born July 17, 1887. He grew up on the family farm in Jackson County, Iowa and moved with his parents to Dubuque when they retired. Around 1910 he relocated to Dyersville, Iowa and opened a Jewelry and Music store which soon became a jewelry and clock repair store. He married Antoinette Strait on October 23, 1917. In the spring of 1924 he sold his jewelry store to Ray Steger, a Minneapolis jeweler that had previously lived in Dyersville. A few years later he bought the store back.

Years later, after his children became involved in the business, the store was re-named Flammang and Kramer. They had two children, one son and one daughter, his children took over the jewelry store after his death on June 13, 1968.

(13). Theodore Joseph Flammang, was born January 9, 1890. When he was in his later teen years Theodore's parents left the farm and moved to

---

[27] The Bureau of Reclamation, Republican River Flood History, Chapter IV.

Dubuque. For extra money he enjoyed gathering berries and nuts, then selling them at the open market in Dubuque. For reasons unknown, Theodore preferred to be called Joseph.

In 1908 Theodore graduated from the school of accounting at Dubuque College, he found a job as bookkeeper and sold real estate on the side. He had a girlfriend for a while, she was a devout Catholic and joined a convent, but their friendship continued through the decades, and when Theodore was in Iowa they would meet for a meal and conversation.

Anyone that remembers Theodore remembers a tremor that caused his head to shake. This disability dated back to his time in the service. On July 27, 1918 he joined the Army Corps of Engineers, one day in the barracks some of the soldiers were engaging in horseplay, one of them jumping onto Theodore's back from the top bunk, knocking him down. The collision caused permanent damage to nerves in his neck, causing the tremor that continued for the rest of his life. The injury prevented him from joining his fellow soldiers when they were sent overseas, and resulted in his discharge on January 23, 1919. A few days after his return home, his father Nicholas passed away.

The Flammang siblings were close, which is evidenced by the fact that after Alois and Joseph Walter took advantage of the cheap and plentiful land available in Nebraska, eventually they were joined in Nebraska by brothers Alphonse, Nicholas, George and Michael. Considering this, it's not surprising that when a real estate opportunity rose, there was interest from several of the brothers. One wonders why Nebraska farmers would suddenly develop an interest in distant real estate. A credible answer would be that the idea was sparked by Theodore's interest in real estate.

Some of the brothers were making dramatic changes to join in on this once-in-a-lifetime opportunity of a Florida land deal. Their adventure lasted about three years, after the adventure came to an end they all returned to their former homes in Nebraska and Iowa.

A detailed obituary about Theodore's life included a related story. It's one of those stories that begs for more details. The background begins with Florida's booming economy and real estate market in the 1920's. The rumors were that a short term land investments could quadruple in value in less than a year's time. The prospects were even more enticing than stock market returns, and the lure of a quick profit snagged four of the Flammang brothers.

Theodore's interest in real estate explains his participation, Joseph wasn't a farmer, so he may have joined the investment group. The venture took place about the time that Henry sold his Dyersville, Iowa jewelry store to a Minnesota businessman, so he was likely one of the investors, which leaves one of the Nebraska farmers as the fourth participant.

The brothers bought and developed land in the Miami area, including the Everglades, and the land where the Miami Airport now stands. By the time the brothers became involved, the real estate bubble was nearing its peak; there were many similarities to our more recent real estate debacle. It wasn't long before prices began to plummet and investors who mortgaged their properties were in dire straits. "The boom became a bust and so the four returned to their homes in Nebraska and Iowa in June of 1927. They were happy to salvage what little money they did by disposing of their properties. During their return trip by car they learned that a hurricane had destroyed the entire area which they had just sold."[28] *[continued at Lead by Faith]*

* * *

Nick and Mary Ann remained on their Saint Donatus farm until their retirement around 1907, when they moved to Dubuque with children Rose, Michael, Henry and Theodore, the four children still living at home, their new residence was located at 57 Ries Street.

During August of 1916 Nicholas and Mary Ann celebrated their golden wedding. The day began at 7 a.m. with a mass celebrated at church, their eight sons and two daughters all present. They were presented with "two magnificent rocking chairs" along with many good wishes.

Mary Ann developed cataracts and after time lost her eyesight. Nicholas died January 13, 1919 at 85 years of age and Mary Ann became ill a year after his death, she was sick about six months and passed away on May 18, 1920 at 73 years of age.

---

[28] Obituary for Brother Angeles Theodore Joseph Flammang written by *Quentin Duncan, O.Carm.*

166

CERTIFICATE, No. 5268

THE UNITED STATES OF AMERICA,

To all to whom these Presents shall come, Greeting:

WHEREAS Henry Niemann of Jackson county Iowa

has deposited in the GENERAL LAND OFFICE of the United States, a Certificate of the REGISTER OF THE LAND OFFICE at Dubuque whereby it appears that full payment has been made by the said Henry Niemann according to the provisions of the Act of Congress of the 24th of April, 1820, entitled "An Act making further provision for the sale of the Public Lands," for the East half of the North East fractional quarter of section four in Township eighty six North of Range four East of the fifth principal meridian in the District of lands subject to sale at Dubuque Iowa containing seventy eight acres and seventy hundredths of an acre

according to the official plat of the survey of the said Lands, returned to the General Land Office by the SURVEYOR GENERAL, which said tract has been purchased by the said Henry Niemann

NOW KNOW YE, That the UNITED STATES OF AMERICA, in consideration of the Premises, and in conformity with the several acts of Congress, in such case made and provided, HAVE GIVEN AND GRANTED, and by these presents DO GIVE AND GRANT, unto the said Henry Niemann

and to his heirs, the said tract above described: TO HAVE AND TO HOLD the same, together with all the rights, privileges, immunities, and appurtenances of whatsoever nature, thereunto belonging, unto the said Henry Niemann and to his heirs and assigns, forever.

In Testimony Whereof, I, James K Polk PRESIDENT OF THE UNITED STATES OF AMERICA, have caused these Letters to be made PATENT, and the SEAL of the GENERAL LAND OFFICE to be hereunto affixed.

GIVEN under my hand, at the CITY OF WASHINGTON, the first day of March in the year of our Lord one thousand eight hundred and forty eight and of the INDEPENDENCE OF THE UNITED STATES the seventy second.

BY THE PRESIDENT: James K Polk

By J K Stephens, asst Sec'y.

S. H. Laughlin RECORDER of the General Land Office.

A Henry Niemann Land Patent

Elizabeth (Hentgen) and Mathias Manders Sr.

Suzanna (Meysenburg) and Mathias Manders Jr.

Elizabeth (Gluden) and Mathias Manders Jr.

Peter D., Catherine and Rose Manders

Peter D. Manders & Margaret Schartz

Mathias, Michael, Peter, J. P. Manders

Mathias Manders

Theodore and Eva (Manders) Fisch

House Built by Mathias Manders-1850

Chapter 3

Overcoming Adversity

1849

Francis Xavier Riebold and Maria Louisa Kraft
Franklin County, Missouri

Imagine a Missouri farmer in the 1840's. Of all the visions that come to mind, few would conceptualize farming on a small island.

The location of Johannes Meis/Mees and his wife Louisa Kraft's Missouri farm was quite extraordinary, it was situated in St. John's Township on Saint John's Island in the middle of the Missouri River, and what's even more astounding is that they weren't alone! The Meis family was surrounded by fellow German immigrant farmers on a fertile island near Washington, Missouri. (Note: Some land documents refer to the island as Santa Fe Island).

There is evidence supporting the possibility that this island may have been home to white settlers since the very early 1800's. Lewis and Clark's journals for May 25, 1804, as they were traveling along the Missouri River, made a referral to passing the last settlement of whites on an island; it is thought that this may have been a reference to St. John's Island.

Forty-five years later, the Meis family was living on Saint John's Island, operating a productive farm and raising their daughter Mary. In April of 1849, John Meis passed away; he was buried at St. Francis Borgia Catholic Church on April 22, 1849.

Louisa (Kraft) Meis was in a distressing situation, there was no extended family to manage the farm, and her only child was too young to assist. She was surrounded by German neighbors, many of whom had their own problems. The Xavier Arbeiter family consisted of a widower with six children aged 5 through 18 and the Riebold household was a mixture of Francis Xavier, a farmer, his brother Anselm a woodchopper, their sister Mary Antonia, her new husband Judge Anton Yerger and three sons from her first marriage to Sebastian Kohler, who died shortly after immigrating. Note that neighbor Xavier Arbeiter's wife's maiden name was Marie Ann

Riebold, it is reasonable to conclude she had been a sister to Francis Xavier, Anselm and Mary Antonia.

Louisa knew if any profit was to be realized, crops must be planted shortly. Not long after her husband died, June 19, a legal agreement was signed that would eventually transfer John Meis land grant to Francis Xavier Riebold and the following day on June 20, 1849, Louisa was married to Francis Xavier Riebold by Reverend A. Eysvogels at Saint Francis Borgia Catholic Church.

At this point Louisa fully expected to return to a quiet country life as a farm wife but as events unfold, the quiet life was not in the stars for her. Francis Xavier had purchased a thirty five acre land grant on Santa Fe Island *or St. John's Island* (abutting Louisa's land) just prior to the time he and Louisa were married. Six months later, in January of 1850, he purchased an additional 100 acre land grant. Then in June of 1850 a 120 acre land grant of John Meis was transferred to his heirs. The total of their land holdings at that point was 255 acres.

On the 1850 U.S. Census (December) Louisa and Francis Xavier were living on Santa Fe Island, their household included Louisa's daughter Mary from her prior marriage, their newborn infant son the census lists as John and Francis Xavier's brother Anselm, the wood chopper, whose services were in continuous demand. Their neighbors were his sister's family consisting of Anthony Yerger, Mary Yerger, Sebastian Kohler, Leo Kohler and Xavier Kohler, also the Arbeiters, Xavier and children - Fred Fidel, Frances, Josephine, Flavius and Mary.

Francis and Louisa became the parents of five children, all born in Franklin County, Missouri.

(1.) The first child (named John in the 1850 U. S. Census) was Anselimis Riebold, born July 16, 1850 and baptized July 25, 1850. Little Anselmis was buried at St. Francis Borgia Catholic Cemetery on July 31, 1852.

(2.) Frances Antonia Riebold was born January 17, 1853 and married an enterprising inventor and resident of her mother's boarding house in 1871, William Zahner. *[more at the Zahner family]*

(3.) Francis Joseph Riebold was born in 1854. The little guy may have been sickly from birth; physician records show nineteen visits during July and August of 1854 to one of Francis Xavier's children, visits including medicine were $2.50 each. Francis Joseph died around September 11 and was buried at Saint Francis Borgia Catholic Cemetery on September 13, 1855.

(4.) Josephine Riebold born July 3, 1856; she married Henry Ziegelmeyer in Jackson County, Missouri on February 9, 1875. Their twelve children were Louisa Katherine, Mary, Marguerita, Catherine, Emma, Gretchen, Henrietta, Henry, Frances, Frank J., Otto S. and William who was born in 1891.

(5.) Margaret Catharine Riebold born April 19, 1858; she married Edmund Gustave Pueschel on August 12, 1874. Their child Otto William was born October 9, 1879.

A tranquil life was continually out of reach for Louisa. She lost her first husband John Meis and remarried. Next she endured the loss of two young sons; then on December 12, 1858, her family was blindsided with another crushing blow when her husband, Francis Xavier died. Although his cause of death is unknown, records of his physician show several occasions over the prior few years where a period of daily visits were made to care for him. The most recent occasion the doctor's records show daily visits to Francis Xavier from December 6th through 10th. Whether due to illness or injury, it appears his death was expected. Francis Xavier's last will and testament was prepared, on December 6th, the date of the first doctor visit.

Louisa Kraft-Meis Riebold was thirty-nine years old and for the second time in less than ten years had been thrust into the role of a widow. The timing being winter allowed a few months to prepare a plan before spring planting season arrived; the year 1859 was no doubt a difficult one for the family, but they had a live-in farm hand that was familiar with the details of the farming operation.

One of the neighbor boys Fidelis Arbeiter had been the Riebold's hired hand and had been living with the family "from the year 1853 to the year 1858 without any intermissions"[29]. This young man, a probable nephew of Francis Xavier's was now being launched into farm management.

Moving forward to the spring of their second year without Francis Xavier, the family was moving forward. On April 25th, 1860, Louisa's daughter Mary, according to the marriage record "still a minor, but with the consent of the mother" was married to Fidelis Arbeiter. Their marriage took place at Saint John Borgia Catholic Church. Nine children would bless this couple, namely Louisa, John, George Earnest, Edward, August Edmond, Tray, William Frederick, Joseph R. and Ben F. The first three children were born in Franklin County, Missouri; the last six were born in Kansas City, Missouri. Most of the children grew up and remained in the Kansas City area.

The two families, two women, a baby, three little girls and one young man worked the 255 acre farm[30]. There were scattered areas of untillable land; nevertheless, this was a substantial area for one man to handle.

Although the reasons are unknown, Louisa was planning a change. The

---

[29] Sworn Statement signed by Fidel Arbeiter on December 5, 1862.

[30] An 1861 probate document refers to the land holdings as 400 acres, Francis Xavier may have purchased an additional plot of 160 acres at some point in time.

woman had lost two hard working husbands while living on Saint John's Island; she may have seen a similar future for her daughters. The profusion of unpaid bills amounted to $1,238; there wasn't enough personal property to pay the bills without selling some of the real estate. This should not have presented a problem since Louisa had more land than she could handle, she could sell part and still have enough to live on.

That was the plus side, on the negative side we have a farm surrounded by an unpredictable river, there were regular springtime flooding issues and the isolation created by the river limited education, social and worship options. Louisa's hasty decisions of the past happened to turn out in her favor, but this time could be different.

On October 22, 1860, Louisa made an agreement with Frenchman John Henry Holls, it appears she sold her personal property to him for $1,000, this included furniture, farm equipment and livestock. She sold 220 acres to him for $1,500. The following day, October 23, 1860 she was married to Mr. Holls, by a Justice of the Peace in Pacific, Missouri. Mr. Holls was a Franklin County saloon keeper that rented out boarding rooms.

Louisa was well aware that by entering into a marriage she violated the terms of Francis Xavier's will, she was subsequently removed as executrix of the estate and replaced by a court appointed executor. It doesn't appear this had an effect on transactions, but there are almost 100 pages of documents relating to the will, probate proceedings, etc.

So many questions. What was she thinking? Did she just want to get off the island? Did Louisa move to town with her younger daughters and help out at the saloon? How long did this marriage last? Will any of these questions ever be answered? It probably didn't take long before the enormity of her marriage mistake was realized.

If the probate records of 400 acres were correct, there were still 180 acres remaining in the estate, plenty for Fidel and Mary to farm.

As of July 31st, 1863, they were still living on St. John's Island in Franklin County. Fidel's Civil War Draft registration lists him as a 32 year old married farmer.

Many of Louisa's life changing events were related to marriage, it appears she felt the need to be taken care of; consequently she kept placing herself in situations where she was dependent upon others.

That was about to change, Louisa was preparing to make the biggest decision of her life, cut all ties to Saint John's Island and start over.

With the proceeds from the personal property and land, Louisa hoped to buy a large house in the city where she could apply her skills of running a busy household. Saint Louis was just to the east, but both families, the Riebolds and the Arbeiters chose to travel across the state to Kansas City.

In the 1800's boarding houses typically housed young men migrating from the farm and looking for a job. Occasionally the young boarders were included in the church and political activities of the owners. Typical boarding-house keepers were unmarried middle class women who needed an income. Working women suffered loss of social status but a boarding-house carried less of a stigma than working away from their residence.

Looking forward to a steady income along with a new world of opportunities for her young daughters, Mrs. Louisa Riebold packed up her belongings in the early 1860's and with her four daughters, son-in-law and grandchildren, moved from rural Franklin County, Missouri across the state to bustling Kansas City confident she could succeed operating a boarding house. She didn't re-marry.

By 1870 Louisa's boarding house business was thriving, she had 9 boarders; one of them was a twenty-one year old tinsmith named William Zahner, we'll hear more about William later.

Next door to the boarding house lived Louisa's daughter Mary (Mees) Arbeiter with her husband Fidel and growing family. Fidel worked as a laborer and eventually would go to work as a porter for W. E. Zahner, one of his sons worked at the same company as a tinner.

1850

Julia Colliton and William Farrell

Vicksburg, Warren County, Mississippi

In 1850 almost half of the immigrants living in Vicksburg were Irish, and in Vicksburg, the Irish-Catholics had a better chance of acceptance and fitting in than those living in Illinois or New York. It was 1850 when Julia Colliton emigrated from Ireland to America. She may have traveled alone, but there is evidence that she landed in New Orleans with family, possibly a brother, their destination being the city of Vicksburg, Mississippi.

Julia Colliton or Colton was born August 27, 1829 in County Kildare, Ireland to Frank and Catherine Colliton. On May 31, 1855 Julia Colton married William Farrell in Warren County, Mississippi. William was a fellow Irish immigrant from County Kildare, and like his bride it is suspected he immigrated with family. The couple operated a small grocery store in Vicksburg.

A few months after their marriage, Vicksburg was in the midst of a yellow fever outbreak, it was a minor outbreak, the couple was lucky and they weren't affected. A very politically incorrect newspaper article mentioned a few words about the outbreak; "The fever at Vicksburg.-The Vicksburg Sentinel of the 8th instant mentions an increase of the yellow fever at that place, saying that "some of the better class of our citizens are being attacked with it, which we regard as the most alarming feature of the disease." Five deaths had occurred since its preceding issue."[31] Comparable comments in today's politically correct world would end with apologies, job loss and countless subscription cancellations.

The young couple had a daughter Mary Ann who was born between 1856 and 1858. Mary Ann had little if any time to get to know her father. Yellow fever was back in the city in 1858 and it was creating panic among the citizens. One article quoted a letter "dated Vicksburg, Miss., August 27th, 1858: - 'Our citizens are scattering in every direction to-day, in consequence of yellow fever among us. Its form is very malignant'."[32] It was during this outbreak, on September 4, 1858 that William succumbed to the disease.

Yellow Fever is a mosquito borne illness described as a hemorrhagic fever. It begins with flu-like symptoms of aches and fever, progressing quickly to liver and kidney failure. Its effects on the liver result in a severe jaundice or yellowing of the skin, hence the reason for the name Yellow Fever. The time span for the disease is in the neighborhood of two weeks.

After William's death, a capable Julia supported Mary Ann and herself by operating the grocery store left by her husband. She worked hard and the store prospered. Julia wanted the best for her daughter, first sending her to St. Francis Xavier Academy in Vicksburg. About the time of the Civil War Mary Ann was sent to Sisters of Mercy Convent in St. Louis. There is a possibility she was sent to Saint Louis for a better education, but a more likely reason was that Julia had Mary Ann's safety in mind when the decision was made.

After spending eight years as a widow, Julia re-married in 1866. Like her first husband, Edward O'Neil, was also an Irish immigrant; the couple had one son, Frank, in 1868.

Julia was a savvy woman, with a new baby and a husband, the expectation may have been that Julia would stay at home and tend to her family. There was a husband in her life now and he could take care of the business. Julia however didn't think it prudent to let someone else run her shop, she had worked through the war to keep her business in order. The self reliant mother and wife had no intention of turning her business over to anyone. According to the 1870 census, Julia was still in the grocery business; described as a grocer and her husband Edward was listed as a clerk.

After twelve years of marriage, Julia was left a widow for a second time, again during a Yellow Fever outbreak. This epidemic began July 1878 and ended in October after the first frost, Edward died October 25, 1878. The outbreak took nearly 20,000 lives, 1,000 of them were residents of

---

[31] Daily National Intelligencer of Washington D. C. Wednesday, September 19, 1835.

[32] The Sun, Pittsfield, Massachusetts, Thursday, September 9, 1858.

Vicksburg.

Julia was an expert in overcoming adversity, she was dealing with another mournful event in her life, but with an unfaltering determination, she moved forward. The financial aspects of her life were under control; the emotional side was more difficult. This time Julia didn't remarry.

1853

Zahner Family

Clark County, Indiana

"Our father now looked around for a place of refuge for the family and finally found such a place in an old log cabin on a neglected farm over in Indiana, were looking to the winter almost entirely without any means for a living. On the 14th day of January 1854 we was blessed with twin brothers, John and Louis, which of course did not improve our situation, but it was the will of God.

"Our condition had now arrived at such a degree of poverty that we had never experienced before, but it was still to come worse. The loss of our money and the following hardships created a constant grieve of our Father and he apparently grew weaker right along.

"On June 1st at the age of 16 years, my brother, Max found employment at building a railroad near by and some time in the month of August in the same year Father went to work there too, in order to earn a little money, when after sixteen days he broke down entirely and died three days thereafter, on the 10th day of September 1854, at the age of forty-five years, leaving his family without a home and about two hundred and fifty dollars in debt, which we had to borrow in order to buy provisions for the family and to make a start on a farm."[33]

The family now consisted of six people, Louisa, the mother of Mary, William and John, one of the twins having died around six months of age, and two of her step-sons Max and Fred.

(1). The oldest of the two step-sons was Maximillian Zahner, born May 13, 1838 to Ludwig Louis Zahner and Josepha Lang. His mother Josepha died when he was just a toddler. After the death of his father Max was just sixteen years old but familiar with working off the farm for others, he continued his efforts to help the family pay off their debts, then after his mother re-married, he felt he was better off completely on his own. He was an intelligent and industrious young man and was able to do a variety of jobs, along the way he learned the trade of cooper and even at his young age was asked by neighbors to teach their sons. He met Elizabeth Henbit

[33] An excerpt from pages 2 and 3 of a family history written by Uncle Max Zahner for his Nephew Eddie.

during this time and they were married on Valentine's Day of 1860.

The couple worked hard, buying a small farm, and overcoming many hardships along the way. They had a family of twelve children, Mary, Appollonia, Louis, John, William, Andrew, Maximillian, Joseph, Elizabeth, Josephine, Fredericka all born in Clark County, Indiana, and an adopted daughter, Marie. After the death of Elizabeth's parents, the family moved to a farm near Shawnee in Johnson County, Kansas where Max and Elizabeth continued to raise their family.

Max died August 26, 1920, three days after he lost the love of his life, Elizabeth Henbit.

(2). Fredrick Louis was born February 15, 1842 to Ludwig Louis Zahner and Fredericka Meier.

(3). Mary Eve Zahner was born June 1, 1846, her christening occurred June 7, 1846 and her history is still a work in process.

(4). William Zahner was born October 22, 1847 and Frances (Fannie) Riebold became his wife around 1871. They became parents of eight children between 1872 and 1894. The boys grew into hard working over-achievers while the girls "married well." Census records show that except for Alma and Louise, their children had the wherewithal to employ live-in servants in the 1920s and 1930s.

(i). William and Fannie's first child was Louise Frances Zahner, born in 1872. She married Benjemin Allen Cantrell, a farm boy, in 1895. In 1901 their daughter Lucille F. was born. By 1928 when Fannie died, Louise was living at her parents' home, it appears the family was in transition from their Missouri farm to Arkansas. The 1940 census shows them living in Crawford County, Arkansas.

(ii). Frank Louis Zahner, their oldest son was born November 4, 1875. He married Anna Catherine Slichter September 11, 1916. Their daughter was Genevieve Frances, born August 16, 1920. Frank spent his working years at Zahner Manufacturing. Genevieve married John Charmley on June 17, of 1950.

(iii). On July 20, 1878, Henry Fredrick Zahner was born. He later joined his father and brother at Zahner Manufacturing, eventually moving up to the position of manager. He married Marie Rosalia Bruening in 1903, their children included Bernard, Arthur and Victor. Henry died on July 20, 1940 in Kansas City and is buried at Calvary Cemetery in the family plot.

(iv). Edward Joseph Zahner was Born April 7, 1882, like his brothers, Edward also worked at Zahner Manufacturing. Edward married Edna Graf; the couple lived in the Kansas City area with their daughter Frances Jane until the 1920's when they relocated to Indiana where Edward was a manufacturer of metal trim. Edward died on September 21st of 1836 at La Porte, Indiana.

(v). Alma Zahner was born July 1, 1884. In 1905, Alma married Edward

Francis Mulligan of Vicksburg, Mississippi.

(vi). Margaret Zahner's birth date was August 10, 1886. She attended Creighton University Law School in Omaha, Nebraska, however there is no record indicating she actually practiced law. Margaret married David W. Newcomer, Jr. of D.W. Newcomer and Sons in Kansas City. Their children were David, and twins Jane and Warren.

(vii). Mary Frances Zahner was born September of 1888; she died around the age of 14.

(viii). Karl William Zahner, the youngest was born May 13, 1894, he joined the American Expeditionary Forces in 1917, his unit was based out of Ohio. Karl spent his service time in France, by the time he was discharged in 1919 Karl had been promoted to First Lieutenant. He married Mary Gwendolyn Burns an Ohio native, and the couple returned to Kansas City. Tragically in 1922 when their son James Burns Zahner was born, Mary died of childbirth complications. Karl remarried; he and Helen had a daughter Joan. Karl became proprietor of a restaurant equipment manufacturing plant.

* * *

When William Zahner and Frances Riebold were first married, William was employed at a tin shop in Kansas City, Missouri. Five years and two children later, in 1876, he opened his own tin shop at 937 Main Street in a partnership with another tinsmith.

William and Frances were another couple that couldn't turn away a relative in need of a home. At one point in time, both of their mothers were members of their household.

The 1880 census tells us that William's mother was afflicted with palsy, this description could have included anything from a mild tremor to paralysis. The census was taken June of 1880 and Louisa (Boehler-Zahner) Gatesman passed away August 12, 1880, in Kansas City, Jackson County, Missouri. She is buried at Calvary Cemetery in Kansas City. Her first husband's resting place was Clark County, Indiana, some years after his death a stone was erected by his children.

In addition to his mother, the William Zahner household was home to another Louisa, his mother-in-law Mrs. Francis Xavier Riebold. Like her housemate, this Louisa endured her share of tragedy during a challenge-filled life. William is described as a driven entrepreneur with a big heart, his generous traits are apparent when he created a small separate living area for Louisa, she enjoyed her privacy yet was just steps away from her daughter and grandchildren. To fill her idle hours, Louisa became a tireless volunteer for fund raising events of the Sisters of the Good Shepherd. She lived to her eighth decade, passing away November 14, 1903; her death certificate describes her cause of death as General Debility. Louisa (Kraft) Riebold is also buried at Calvary Cemetery, while her first husband John Meis was buried somewhere in Franklin County and her second husband Francis Xavier was buried at St. Francis Borgia Catholic Cemetery in Washington, Missouri.

When the new tin shop was just starting out William filled housewives requests for washtubs and coffee pots. Soon he began manufacturing stoves. As the business grew there was a need for additional space so he acquired an adjoining building. In 1894 there was a fire at his West Tenth Street building, but quick response kept the damage at a minimum.

As Kansas City grew, a new street cut through the Zahner property leaving a seven foot strip of land. This bit of land eventually became one of the most valuable plots of land in Kansas City. Around 1906 William sold it for eighty five thousand dollars which up to that point was the top price ever paid for real estate in Kansas City. This location became home to the Victor Building, a long narrow eight story building.

William's sheet metal company gradually expanded from building stoves and household products to manufacturing a wide array of restaurant wares. Their restaurant products were sold from coast to coast in the United States and internationally from Canada to Argentina.

William's sons joined the business and learned from the ground up. His second oldest son Edward Joseph thought there would be a good future in manufacturing metal doors and trim.

Industrial espionage was alive and well in Kansas City when Edward decided to go to work for a well known door manufacturer so he could see for himself how it was done. It didn't take very long before the manufacturer discovered who Edward was but he had already seen what he needed to see and turned in his resignation. This was the beginning of the next Zahner business.

The new endeavor took place in the early 1900s when industry was flourishing and competition was fierce. The Zahner's wanted their steel doors to stand out so they created doors that mimicked the appearance of mahogany or oak or whatever type of wood the customer requested. As with their other businesses, this one grew and prospered. In 1913 their door factory received an order to provide $100,000 worth of steel doors for the four million dollar Utah state capitol building. In addition to doors they also began looking at windows. On July 31, 1906 William filed for a patent for a Metallic Window,[34] his patent number was 865,286. The window was versatile and strong, it was made with sheet-metal, one of his specialties.

The business was outgrowing its space for the third time in its history and in 1919 the company moved to a three story building at 1213 Walnut

[34] U. S. Patent Office, September 3, 1907, page 241, patent number 865,286.

Street, their workforce at this point increased from 150 to 200 employees.

The stove business was changing, homes were being modernized and William was embracing innovations of the home heating industry. On April 7, 1924 he filed for a patent on an oil burner, the patent was issued March 3, 1925. The oil burning stove was complete with atomizer, overflow shut-off, high temperature shut off, pilot burner, an automatic fan when a certain degree was reached, it was even adaptable to a variety of fuels. The safety and automatic features of his stove were the key elements in his patent.

Even though much of William's time was spent growing and improving his businesses he did find time to become involved in other activities as well. He was a member of a fraternal benefit organization called the Catholic Knights of America. In 1896 at their national convention he was elected vice president, in 1898 he was elected treasurer. He was also involved in various manufacturing and sheet metal organizations.

Fannie died of bronchial pneumonia in 1928 and is buried at Calvary Catholic Cemetery. A year after Fannie's death, William remarried a woman who was thirty years younger. She was from Saint Louis and her name was Martha Elizabeth Smith, or "Mattie". William died in 1935 at the age of 88 from a cerebral hemorrhage; he is buried next to Fannie at Calvary Catholic Cemetery. Mattie died in 1942 and is buried in St. Louis.

(5). Louis Zahner was a twin born January 14, 1854, he survived for six months.

(6). John Zahner a twin to Louis was born January 14, 1854, died in 1918.

* * *

Of all the stories of hardship we've encountered and are yet to come, Louisa (Boehler) Zahner's has to be the most heartbreaking. She was a penniless woman with debt, five children, living in a strange land, no friends and no local relatives, a very bleak future indeed. There were a few glimmers of light. German neighbors and one American neighbor were willing to lend a hand, offering food and old clothing. The struggling family continued to rent the small farm over the next couple years and they lived in the run down shack that rested on its grounds.

Louisa's step-son Max spent most of his time working outside the farm to bring in funds to pay down their debts and the next oldest brother, Fred was only twelve years old but he was a lover of horses and handled most of the farming including plowing, harvesting and animal care. With poor living conditions and an absence of health care the family dealt with a never-ending string of sickness, but they were able to pay off their debts and it seemed the family's situation was improving.

With winter at their doorstep and thinking of the deteriorating shack they called home, Louisa was prepared to make a final attempt of providing a real home for her children. Like another Louisa we encountered earlier, she made a rash decision, and along with her entire family, she regretted the choice almost immediately. Louisa married their landlord, Charles Gatesman (or Goetzmann) in Jeffersonville, Clark County Indiana on November 5, 1857. On the positive side, he was a landowner, had a comfortable house and could provide a home for them.

Every family has a storyteller, but few put their words to paper. Thanks to a grandson and step-son of Louisa Zahner, we have a true and interesting history of the Zahner hardships. Edward Zahner, son of William, asked his uncle Maximillian Zahner for a family history, Max describes the situation from William's perspective as follows:

"Unluckily this man was of very eccentric habits, and being intoxicated most of the time, Mother did not better her situation as she expected and on account of the quarrelsome ways of this man, my brothers, Max and Fred and sister Mary had to leave home, when not a great while after this I myself was compelled to leave home at about the age of sixteen years."[35]

Louisa and Charles became the parents of two daughters, Johanna and Ozena. Johanna was born in 1858 (died in 1914) she married Marcus Zimmerman, they raised quite a large family in Indiana, the younger daughter, Ozena was born around 1860. The 1860 census listed a household of seven people; Louisa age 38, Charles 39, Johanna age two and Ozena Gatzman three months old along with the three youngest Zahners, John age 6, William age 13 and Mary age 14. After this census, no trace of Ozena has been located.

A short time into the Civil War, Charles was drafted; he enrolled with Company M of the 77th Regiment, 4th Indiana Cavalry on July 27, 1862. For the next three years there was peace at the Gatsmann-Zahner household. The first two years, an industrious William handled the farm, and then on May 2, 1864, he too was called into service. The question here, were Louisa and her young children able to plant a crop? There were Confederate sympathizers in their midst, making it possible that some of their neighbors may have been hostile. If neighbors couldn't or wouldn't assist, Louisa and the children could have planted enough to feed themselves and the animals and hoped for William or Charles to return before the next crop was ready for planting. *[more about William at Military Service]*

1856

---

[35] Zahner Family History written by Uncle Max Zahner for his Nephew Eddie Zahner (the last paragraph)

Ostwald Family
Dubuque County, Iowa

Herman Gerken was a lifesaver for the Ostwald family after they arrived in New Vienna, Iowa. Michael Ostwald and Anna Marie Gerken along with four of their children spent every penny they had to travel from Germany to New Orleans and finally to Dubuque. They thankfully accepted Anna Marie's younger brother's generosity, eventually moving to their own home in Western Dubuque County.

Michael was naturalized eight years later, in November of 1864 and died a year later. His wife Maria died a year after that. They are both buried at Saint Boniface Catholic Cemetery in New Vienna, Iowa.

(1). The ship manifest lists Caroline Ostwald as a passenger, this raises a question. She could have been Maria Agnes Caroline Ostwald, born December 12, 1830 but her age doesn't match the 22 years listed on the ship manifest. The next sibling, Elisabeth Catherine Ostwald born March 3, 1833, would have been twenty-two years old when the ship left the European port, in that case, her age matches but not her name.

(2). Anna Maria Elizabeth Ostwald was born May 6, 1834; she arrived in America with her family during April of 1856 and married Anton Mühlenkamp December 19, 1856. *[continued at Dreams Realized]*

(3). Maria Theresia Ostwald was born March 25, 1840, she was sixteen years old when she arrived in New Orleans. On September 30, 1861 she married John Henry Schroeder, a fellow German born around 1831. Their children were Mary, Margaret, Henry, Anna and Elizabeth. Theresa died in Dyersville, Iowa on December 30, 1905.

(4). Johannes Hermannus Ostwald was born June 29, 1844 in Hegensdorf, he was eleven years of age when he arrived in America. After immigration, records for Herman are quite sparse. If he moved north to Minnesota as some researchers believe, he is most likely the young man that enlisted for the Civil War at St. Peter, Minnesota, as a private in the 7th Minnesota Volunteer Infantry Regiment, Company K, on August 21, 1862, just after the Sioux Uprising began. This Minnesota Herman Ostwald died at a Memphis Tennessee hospital on February 11, 1865 of Chronic Diarrhea. His birth date was 1841 and some of his military documents do have his name spelled as Ostwald, an unusual spelling, burial at the Tennessee National Cemetery lists him as Herman Oswald. These are common errors for early military records, and with numerous records we're left with no certain conclusions as to the identity of this soldier.

1863

Elizabeth Greten Flammang

Came to America at the age of 62.

In current day America, Elizabeth Flammang would be eligible for Social Security and possibly in a quandary as to whether she should start collecting or wait. The Elizabeth we get to know on these pages would have definitely waited.

Elizabeth Greten was born November 1, 1800 to Francois Greten and Elisabetha Guttenkauff in Koerich, Luxembourg. It was there she grew up, was married and raised her family. Her husband and two of their daughters are buried in the local cemetery.

Eight years after the death of her husband, Elizabeth was preparing to leave her native land and travel to a missionary parish to join her son, the Reverend John Michael Flammang. It's not unusual for people to make changes during their sixth decade, but a change of this magnitude is quite uncommon, especially for a woman living with family. Whether it was her idea, or her son, asked her to come, we can be sure she didn't need a lot of time to contemplate her options, more than likely she was overjoyed at the chance to help her son in America. Elizabeth didn't come alone, she traveled with four of her daughters.

Elizabeth enjoyed her last years. She had an opportunity to spend time with her other grandchildren and she became a part of the parish her son was in charge of. During this time, Elizabeth didn't just sit back and let the world pass her by, she was a very generous, caring woman, she took in needy orphans with open arms and acted as mother to many young men away from home.

The following obituary of Elisabeth (Greten) Flammang is taken from the Luxembourg Gazette, the newspaper her son helped found, the obituary has been translated from German:

"We wish to inform our readers today of a mourning message. In Saint Donatus, Jackson County, Iowa this past Tuesday, 6 February blessed and strengthened with the Sacrament of the Holy Church, the mother of the local minister, Father J.M. Flammang, Elisabetha Flammang nee Greten, passed away. She was born on 1 November 1800 in Koerich of God fearing, pious parents, who had planted the seed of good deeply into the heart of the child, a seed which carried the most beautiful and richest fruit. In 1825 she gave her hand to J.P. Flammang, likewise from Koerich, to the eternal joining the stately list of 10 children resulted. Three sons and seven daughters were all carefully educated and knowledgeable with customs and religious training from her and her husband before going into the world. But they could not be saved from their cup of suffering, death snatched two daughters and on 23 January 1854 (Betrothal of Mary) her beloved husband passed away as well. She bore it and doubled the love for her children.

Their most ardent desire of fulfillment nevertheless, came through their oldest son, seeing J.M. Flammang in the office of priest. Over this she had still another cup of suffering to bear, separated he nevertheless for the distant mission country America, he headed there far from the Home Country.

"Mother planted the seeds of faith deep in the hearts of her daughters and brought the inclination that today resulted in 3 daughters joining the Sisters of Notre Dame (Milwaukee) as Sisters Irene, Chionia and Agape and a fourth joined the Order of Soeurs de la Doctrine Chretienne of Lintgen, Luxembourg. Also the fifth daughter, Margaretha, had stepped into a convent but left because she wanted to dedicate herself to care for her aging Mother. The second son Nikolas remained in his parents' house in Koerich, he is in agriculture as an economist and takes a position of Commons Member an honorable position the mayor's office already offered. The younger son Jean Nicholas moved later to America and established himself close to Saint Donatus, where he enjoys the highest degree of respect.

"Mother suffered to such a level in Europe that she decided in 1863 to spend her remaining days in St. Donatus with the Parish. There she concentrated the remaining years of her life with the works of Christian charitableness, prayers, and was respected by all. She acted as a second mother for some orphans, and some priest candidates without means.

"God knows it's final; God will recompense her. Blessed with prosperity, she made the best use of it. Bishop Smith never entered the parish house in St. Donatus, his blessed words were targeted at Mother Flammang. Her son remained with his loving Mother; he was her religious father. Since she entered the shore of the Continent, he did not treat anybody differently than her, nobody gave more to the Holy Sacrament than she. She was comforted in her short illness, he provided and he celebrated a High Mass. She was taken all too soon. But the Pater Noster with the words Fiats voluntas tua stochte was correct, with tears of overpowering sorrow.

"The Funeral was at 8 a.m., Priests Mr. St. Johannes of Dubuque, Jacoby of Lansing, Rottler of Sherrills Mount and Stritzelberger of St. Catherine hurried here. Participating in the ceremony were, as a Deacon Parish [Priest] Johannes, as Deacon Rev. Striszelberg, as Ceremony Master Father Rottler, Rev. Jacoby gave the final sermon.

"Spoken were abbreviated musical words, which went so deeply to the softly tuned hearts of the numerous good Parishioners and Friends that hurried to the funeral, they aired their many tears and made themselves also still go to the grave in quantity. Oh, Lucky a country, which has still such women, lucky the children, who have such a mother. Mother Flammang was an example of a friend, an example of a neighbor, an example of a wife, an example of a mother, and still she was the example of a Catholic mother.

God becomes your reward in the sunset, our words cannot describe. If the world had more women, if it had more mothers like the deceased, there would not be so much wretched, misery and wickedness as our earth goes around.

"Rest in peace good mother!

"We know what it is to have a good mother, also we had such, but too soon she was taken from us by death, may she rest in peace!"[36]

[36] Luxemburg Gazette, Dubuque, Iowa; February 13, 1877.

Zahner Siblings - William standing, Fred, Max and Mary seated

Left Photo - Louisa (Riebold) Zahner.
Right Photo - Alma Zahner, High School Graduation.

Alma, Karl, Edward, Frank, Margaret, Henry, Mary standing
Frances (Riebold) and William seated

Anton Muehlenkamp and Mary (Ostwald) Muehlenkamp

Back - William, Ted, Anna, Tony, Caroline, John, Joe Herrig
Front - Margaret, John, Helena, Christine, Lena Herrig

Left - John and J. P. Herrig Right - Nicholas and Christina (Herrig) Flammang

Mary Ann (Niemann) and Nicholas Flammang with daughter Elizabeth

Nicholas and Mary Ann with their grown family

Chapter 4

Dreams Realized

1855

Herrig Brothers

Jackson County, Iowa

Four Herrig brothers immigrated to America, and all four brothers became landowners in Jackson County or neighboring Dubuque County, Iowa. Eventually they would all four be clustered within a few miles of each other. The 1870 census shows William as a landowner and farmer, his next door neighbor, his brother Mathias was a Stonemason, he was not yet a landowner. Living with Mathias was their youngest brother John Peter who was also a Stonemason. Ten years later, William, John and J.P. were farming in northern Jackson county and Mathias purchased a farm just over the county border in southern Dubuque County.

Following is an interesting article translated from a March 1877 issue of The Luxemburger Gazette, this article shows how well connected families remained even when separated by an ocean, and cell phones a century away. The dates in the article are closely aligned with the dates obtained from census records.

"CORRESPONDENCE".

"A Double Celebration. A rare occurrence is to be reported today. On 22 February the long married couple from Wormeldingen, Michael Herrig and Catharina Herrig nee Thill, celebrate their golden anniversary. The bridegroom is at present 77 and the bride 74 years old; both are natives of Wormeldingen. Four of their educated sons were married in America, three in St. Donatus, Jackson County, and one in St. Catharine's Dubuque County near here. As soon as they heard the message, they also decided to celebrate here on the same day as over in Europe, on February 22nd. A ceremonial high Mass in the Parish Church of St. Donatus will be celebrated, with [priest] Father T. Nemmers from Gilbertsville and with [priest] J. M. Flammang as deacon and Father Strisselberger from St. Catharine as assistant.

"The lucky rejoicing pair educated six children, who are to them an honor in their aging days. The oldest son William moved to this country in the year 1854 and returned in 1864 to the old home of his parents which he in May 1865 again left. On March 4, 1857 the two sons Mathias and Johann landed on the shores of this continent. Mathias also went back in 1860 and quickly returned in 1861 to America. Mr. J. P. Herrig followed his brothers in 1868 into this country. Mr. Peter Herrig became an upper [class] teacher in the city of Luxemburg. Anna Ohms, nee Herrig, their daughter, still lives with her spouse with her aging parents in Wormeldingen. A brother of the Jubilates almost of the mentioned age lives in Seneca County, Ohio; also he will be celebrating his golden wedding in the near future. May the rejoicing pair live still for a long time and with peace and happiness with each other!"

(1). The children of Michael Herrig and Catherine (Thill) Herrig, were all driven to excel. Their first child was William Herrig, born March 19, 1828 in Wormeldange, Luxembourg. William immigrated in 1854 and was naturalized October 4, 1859 in Dubuque, Iowa. His marriage to Catharine Nemmers occurred July 10, 1861 in Dubuque County, Iowa. They had fifteen children, the following fourteen living to adulthood Matthew, Maria, Nicholas, Anna, Peter, Elizabeth, Michael, Catherina, John, Carolus, Elizabeth, John Michael, Mary Magdalena and George. William lived to the age of ninety one years.

(2). Michael and Catharine's second child was named Anna Maria Herrig, she died not long after her first birthday.

(3). Mathias Michael Herrig was born January 7, 1834, he immigrated to America in 1857 and was naturalized at the District Court in Dubuque in 1881.

On May 28, 1863, Mathias married Joanna Arens in Dubuque County, Iowa they had a daughter Anna born March 31, 1864, she was just a year old when her mother died. Anna married Theodore Nemmers, son of Michael Nemmers, Sr. and Anna Even, they had a family of eight children.

Mathias' second marriage was August 28, 1867 to Elizabeth Kaiser, their six children were John (b. 1865), Maria (b. 1868), Francis (b. 1869), Sebastian (b. 1869), Lena (b. 1871) and Annie (b. 1873, m. Andrew Wagner).

On a Sunday evening in April of 1890, Mathias discovered his brand new barn had been struck by lightning and was on fire. In an effort to save his horses he was overtaken by the fire and was severely burned. A doctor was called, but the severity of the burns offered little hope. Mathias was able to give his last will and testament and received the last rites of his Roman Catholic faith. He died the following morning leaving his wife and three daughters. Mathias is buried in St. Catherine's Cemetery, just north of La Motte, Iowa.

(4). Daughter Anna Herrig, was born December 6, 1836 in Wormeldange, Anna became a teacher and remained in Luxembourg. On February 8, 1867 she was married to Nicholas Ohms. They had at least one child, a son named Michael.

(5). John Herrig was born August 15, 1840; he arrived in America with his brother Mathias. John married Helena Haxmeier on October 24, 1868, she was the daughter of Johann Theodore Haxmeier and Caroline Nemmers, she was born August 6, 1850. Another family of fifteen! Caroline born August 30, 1869 married Anthony J. Till; Henry born in March 1, 1872, Anna born September 1, 1873 married Peter J. Till, William Joseph born September 28, 1875 married Caroline Poll, John Matthew born January 18, 1877 married Mary Ellen Horan, Mary, born February 28, 1879, Michael born November 19, 1880, Theodore, born April 23, 1882 married Christina Poll, George born December 26, 1883, Margaret born June 2, 1885 married Joseph John Till, Helena born June 29, 1887, married Charles M. Hilbert, Christina born October 29, 1888, married Nicholas Leo Flammang, Joseph born January 15, 1890 married Helena Ties, Mathias born January 15, 1890 and Anthony born April 15, 1893 married Regina Huilman.

John lived until April 16, 1911, the age of seventy years and his wife survived him by twelve years passing away at the age of seventy-three on October 31, 1923, they are buried in the Saint Donatus Cemetery.

(6). Peter Herrig is the only son of Michael and Catharine's that remained in Luxembourg. He married Margareta Reuther, and family stories say that he was a professor at a university in the area, perhaps the University of Heidelberg. Confirmed census information reveals that he was a head teacher at a high school in Luxembourg City, from there it is possible he moved on to the University.

(7). The youngest, John Peter or J. P. Herrig was born February 9, 1846, he emigrated on the Ship Belona from Le Havre to New York. He took the same route to America as his uncle John. This fact can be a strong clue when searching through ship records for the arrival of the other three brothers. Family members often traveled the same ports of embarkation and debarkation as those that first made the trip.

John Peter married Anna Haxmeier (a sister to Helena married to J. P.'s brother John) October 18, 1874 in St. Donatus, Iowa. Anna was a daughter of Johann Theodore Haxmeier and Caroline Nemmers. J. P. and Anna's children were Elizabeth, born September 6, 1876; William Peter born February 12, 1878 and married Mary Schons; Mary born February 2, 1880 married Peter Nemmers, son of George Nemmers; Henry born August 16, 1881 married to Mary Gehler; the first Michael born June 5, 1883, died as an infant; the second Michael born June 25, 1885, married Katherine Moran; Mathias was born February 10, 1887 and was joined in wedlock to Agnes Pollock; John Joseph, born May 30, 1889 was another child that died in infancy; Nicholas was born June 1890; Theresa on September 2, 1893, she married Leroy Lampe and the youngest Leo was born April 9, 1900.

Their oldest son, William Peter became a hardware store merchant. Perseverance and good management made his store popular and successful; he also became an inventor; his invention was a Well Rod Hook. William applied for the patent in 1912 and on April 22, 1913 the patent was granted.

All families have stories of their ancestors, most are forgotten after time, but there is one entertaining story that deserves to be shared. The story relates to J.P. and Anna's son Michael, their sixth child. He was born June 25, 1885. His brother William was his partner in the hardware business.

"John C. Haxmeier, Jr. of the firm of Herrig & Haxmeier, Lamotte, Iowa has sold his interest to Michael Herrig, brother of the senior member and the business will be continued under the name of Herrig brothers."[37] William had numerous business interests in progress and Michael took charge of the day to day operations of the hardware store. Under Michael's management, the store prospered but it lost some of its neat-as-a-pin appearance.

A former La Motte area resident recalled Michael's store and shared an amusing event pertaining to his business. Michael was a nice fellow and a popular businessman but his store was a bit disorganized or some would describe it as messy. The countertop was always cluttered and there was merchandise stacked everywhere, but Michael never had a problem finding what he was looking for.

One night there was a break-in to his establishment, the thieves were looking for cash and blew open the safe, not realizing the safe wasn't even locked. They had correctly assumed Michael hadn't gone to the bank but once the safe was open they discovered it was empty!

Michael had unwittingly outsmarted the thieves. The robbers walked right past the bank bag that Michael had tossed on the cluttered counter. In the end, the store was in need of a new safe, but the cash deposit was lying untouched in plain sight, ready for deposit at the bank next door.

Michael was a hard worker and he put in long hours. The 1940 census which was taken on April 2, 1940 asked how many hours the individual worked. Several people on the census page worked over 40 hours, Michael was tied for first at 72 hour worked. Interesting to note, the enumerator was George C. Nemmers.

---

[37] Farm Implements magazine of 1912.

1856

Anton Müllenkamp and Marie Ostwald

Delaware County, Iowa

Anton Müllenkamp's parentage and background remain mysterious. Census records show he emigrated around 1855 from Germany. Anton's great grandson William Millenkamp relayed a story that will become quite familiar. William said Anton immigrated with a brother; although the storyteller, was himself a veteran, he proudly classified his great grandfather as a "draft dodger," escaping the tyranny of his homeland like so many young Germans of the time.

Anton settled in Delaware County, Iowa where he began farming. Two years after immigrating, he married one of Michael Ostwald's daughters, Anna Marie (Marie) in neighboring Dubuque County.

Anton and Marie began farming near what is now Petersburg, Iowa, where he became a leading agriculturist of the county.

According to the book "Dyersville: Its History and Its People", in March, 1867 Anton was one of eight men appointed to a committee to study the need for a parish church in the area. A few businesses soon appeared in the area around the proposed church, this entirely Catholic community became Petersburg, Iowa. By November 1868 the first Saints Peter and Paul Church was built and ready for services. Anton and Mary are both buried in the Church Cemetery.

Nine children were born to Anton and Marie.

(1). Their firstborn was Margaretta Müllenkamp, arriving December 20, 1858, New Vienna, Dubuque County, Iowa. Her marriage to Frank J. Bohnenkamp occurred September 10, 1878 in Petersburg, Delaware County, Iowa. He was the son of Johann Herman Bohnenkamp and Antonia Floegel, a neighboring farmer. A few years after their marriage, the Bohnenkamps moved to rural Remsen, Iowa where they farmed. Their twelve children were Mary (m. James Peter Ludwig), Maria Rosa (m. John Ludwig), John Herman (Mary Elizabeth Kramer), Anna (b. 1887), Frank H. (b. 1889, m. Sophia Scharff), Henry Francis (b. 1891, m. Frances Tennessen), Joseph (b. 1893, m. Alma Cosgrove), Margaret (b. ~1895, m. Joseph Arens), Cecilia (b. 1897, m. Thomas F. McCarvel), Frances (b. 1897), Eleanor (b. 1900, m. John Henry Ortmann) and a baby that died in infancy.

(2). William Müllenkamp was born March 7, 1860 in Petersburg, Delaware County, Iowa, he married Mary Agnes Klostermann February 18, 1895, she was born August 21, 1876 to Frank J. Klostermann and Maria Catharina Kramer. They made their home in Remsen, Iowa and had seven children, Rose, William Frank, Frances, Marcella, Alfons, Louise and Clarinda. Not long after Clarinda's birth, her mother, Mary Agnes passed away.

(3). Herman Müllenkamp joined the family in 1863, he married Mary Overman in 1894. Their daughter was Anna, born in 1895. When she was a year old, her father died. Mary (Overman) Millenkamp remarried to August Detmer around 1907.

(4). Philomena Antonetta Mühlenkamp was born March 29, 1865 and died November 23, 1879.

(5). Mary Mullenkamp was born November of 1865; She married Franz Ferdinand Stuntebeck on April 5, 1888. They farmed in Remsen, Iowa and raised five hard working daughters, Anna Mary, Mary, Margaret, Katherine and Frances.

(6). Elizabeth Müllenkamp was born December 4, 1873; she relocated to Granville, Iowa where her sister Anna lived with her family. Elizabeth died in 1954 and is buried at St. Joseph's Cemetery in Granville, Iowa.

(7). Anna Müllenkamp was born November 26, 1875, she married Edward John Budden, son of Jan Hendrik Budden and Catherine D. Hargrafen. Their family grew to twelve, the first three were born in Petersburg and the next nine were born on their farm in Granville, Alfred, Edwin, Amelia, Melinda, Raynold, Coletta, Norbert, Amella, Albert Zeno, Emil D., Roman A., and Ima. Anna's sister Elizabeth was part of their household working as housekeeper.

(8). Anton Millenkamp was born September 13, 1880, Mary A. Kruse, daughter of Henry Kruse and Freda Buttenboehmer became his wife May 29, 1906 at St. Francis Catholic Church in Dyersville. Their son Cyril was born in 1907. Anton died in 1958, his wife in 1968.

(9). Katie Müllenkamp was born June 2, 1869, she died at the age of eight years.

Often the path leading from one spelling of a surname to another version seems random without a reason or explanation for the change. For William Mühlenkamp there is a story, and it was relayed by his grandson William. The name change was required to proceed with a legal case stemming from overpaid commissions for a 1914 land deal in South Dakota. William Mühlenkamp's attempts to take legal action were delayed until he had his name legally changed. The court did not have the ability to create a document with the umlaut needed to type his name on the document. After William legally changed his surname to Millenkamp he was able to file his lawsuit. From a newspaper article in the Remsen-Bell, William won the $600 overpayment through a jury trial.

1866

Peter Schartz and Angelina Philipps

Prairie Springs Township, Jackson County, Iowa

Peter Schartz returned from his service in the Civil War, reportedly weighing only seventy pounds. He was unable to walk and was carried on a stretcher. How did he end up in La Motte, Iowa? After immigrating to America around 1855, he settled in Cook County, Illinois where he farmed. Shortly after the war broke out Peter enlisted for Civil War duty. After the war, why didn't he return home to Cook County, Illinois? Was La Motte, Iowa his destination? Or was his intended destination Lamont, Illinois and he ended up in La Motte, Iowa? *[more at Military Service]*

In 1866 Angelina(Philipps) Welter arrived in the La Motte area with three children and a strong work ethic. She chose this destination because one of her brothers had bought a farm and was raising his family near Otter Creek. Angelina spent the next two years supporting her family by gardening and working odd jobs.

Angelina's three children, born in Luxembourg, grew up and spent their adult lives in Iowa. Peter, born November 1859, married Hannah Regan, they had one child Mayme Kelly. Mayme married Theodore Hingtgen, their five children, born near La Motte, Iowa were Cletus, Thelma, Raphael, Mildred and Merlin.

Katharina Welter was born September 20, 1859, she married Adam Seiler in 1877. He operated a shoe store on 723 Sycamore Street in Waterloo, Iowa. Their home was just up the street from the business. Their seven children were Margaret, Elizabeth, Anne, Catherine, Marie, John and Lena.

The youngest of the three children was Catherine, born September 12, 1861. She married Nicholas Ehlinger; like her brother, their family was also raised near La Motte, Iowa. Their thirteen children were Chris, Peter, Jacob, John, Margaret, Susan, Kathryn (Sister Mary Ephriam), Nicholas, Hannah, Joseph, Leo P., Lawrence and Aloysius.

On January 21, 1869 Angelina was married to Peter Schartz by the Reverend J. Michael Flammang. The newlyweds, along with Angelina's three children were now at home on Peter's Prairie Springs Township farm.

Peter and Angelina had two children, Catherine Anna was born October 22, 1869, and she was baptized October 26 at Saint Donatus by Reverend Flammang. Her godparents were Peter Schilz and Catherine Weber, the little girl died at the age of five years, one month and five days or November 27, 1874. Church records for her birth as well as death list her name as Catherine while census records have her listed her as Anna. Their second child was another daughter born March 12, 1871, she was given the name Margaret.

Because of his injuries during the Civil War, Peter became eligible for a pension. In the 1890's it was about $4 per month and increased to $8 by 1900. After Peter's death, Angeline collected a pension as his widow. Although his recovery was impressive, the effects of his injuries apparently remained. His condition was not discussed or passed down by family, however, after his death a short article in the Waterloo Dispatch described him as crippled. His death certificate listed his cause of death as consumption so the pensioner may have been a victim of Tuberculosis.

Peter had a sense of humor which he never lost through all he experienced in the war; his pension application included a question inquiring if he had been married previously and if so to provide the details. Most would simply write the word "no" Peter's written answer was "No Sir!"

Margaret married Peter Donatus Manders January 22, 1895; their married life began on the Schartz Farm where Margaret was raised. After their marriage, Margaret and Peter handled the farm, after the death of her parents they bought their own farm in Richland Township, where they were situated by the time of the 1910 census. On the 1915 Iowa Census we learn that Peter's income was $3,600 the prior year, his Richland Township farm was valued at $30,000 and he only owed $2,000.

(1). The firstborn of Peter and Margaret's children was Anna Angela Manders, born November 7, 1895, she married Peter Michael Koos on November 24, 1920. They were the parents of one daughter.

(2). Peter Manders was born November 5, 1896, he died April of the following year.

(3).George Manders was born January 3, 1898, he married Lena J. Till, daughter of Peter Till and Anna Herrig, granddaughter of John Herrig and Helena Haxmeier, Lena was born June 15, 1902. George and Lena raised a family of six children. George was a farmer near La Motte, he died June 20, 1969, Lena died November 30, 1986, both are buried at Holy Rosary Cemetery in La Motte.

(4). Leo Manders was born July 5, 1900, he married Lavina Lidwina Herrig on October 11, 1922, she was the daughter of Theodore Herrig and Christina Poll, granddaughter of John Herrig and Helena Haxmeier, Lavina was born June 6, 1905. Leo and Lavina's family consisted of two daughters.

(5). Mary Manders was born April 25, 1902 and married Leroy Manderscheid January 22, 1925. Leroy was born October 10, 1902, the son of Peter Manderscheid and Mary Gretchen. Mary and Leroy were farmers, they had one daughter. Mary lived to the age of 101, she died on June 2, 2003 at Mill Valley Care Center in Bellevue, Iowa.

(6). April 25, 1902 was the date of Catherine Manders birth, she married John Kaiser, they lived in a house near Holy Rosary Catholic Church in La Motte. John was a road worker for Jackson County.

(7). Mathew Manders was born August 8, 1906, and married Marie Arensdorf January 17, 1933 at Holy Rosary Catholic Church in La Motte. Mathew and Marie farmed near Bellevue, they had a family of eight children. He died May 10, 1996 at Mill Valley Care Center, in Bellevue,

Iowa.

(8). Christopher J. Manders was born December 29, 1907, he married Veronica Clasen June 26, 1934 at Holy Rosary Catholic Church in La Motte. They had eight children, Chris died December 19, 1954 when his youngest child was just six years old.

(9). Loretta Manders was born February 8, 1910, she married Louis J. Till a brother to Lena Till, the wife of Loretta's brother George. Louis was born April 17 1904. Loretta and Louis had two daughters. Loretta died August 10, 1969.

(10). Irivn Manders was born January 23, 1915 and was married to Vivian Junk on June 26, 1934, they had a family of three children.

* * *

In addition to farming, Peter Donatus took care of the local one room school building located near the farm; he and his family also provided a home for the teacher.

The Manders family was hard working but they were also a fun loving bunch, never passing up an opportunity to pull off a prank. Mary and Leo in particular enjoyed playing practical jokes. On occasion even their parents joined in the fun. One instance had Anna washing dishes, Mary and the country school teacher, Mamie Bordeau, who was living with them were also in the kitchen making plans for their next caper.

To keep their plans from becoming known they closed the door to the dining room. In the dining room Peter and Margaret figured the girls 'were up to no good' so Peter snuck out the back, came around and started rattling the outside door. The frightened girls tried to rush into the dining room but Anna was the first one to the door with slippery, soapy hands and the knob wouldn't turn. They were still struggling with the door when Peter entered the house, having a good laugh at their frightened reactions.

A sampling of their many tricks included Mary sewing Leo's coat sleeves shut, one of Anna's favorites was Leo placing a hairbrush under the covers of one of the girls' beds, sending a couple of her sisters shrieking out of the bedroom in a panic, thinking they just had an encounter with a small critter.

When they weren't working or pranking, the family enjoyed playing games, going to dances and having fun. Even when they were in their senior years these siblings enjoyed each other's company, at a family gathering you could tell by their smiling reaction when one of their siblings arrived at the event.

Peter died September 16, 1931, Margaret lived another 31 years. She spent her last years with her daughter Catherine or "Katie" in La Motte, Iowa, passing away at the age of 91 on June 18, 1962.

1868

Gerhard Herman Krogmann and Franz Henrich Olberding

Delaware County, Iowa

Petersburg is a small unincorporated village located in Bremen Township of Delaware County, Iowa. The village is situated on the western edge of the Township which shares a border with Oneida Township. Today, we might say that Gerhard Krogmann and Frank Olberding settled near Petersburg, Iowa, which is true, but at the time they arrived in Delaware County, the Village of Petersburg did not exist. The first store was built around 1873 and the community wasn't awarded its own post office until March 7, 1874, the post office was located in the store. The area was almost entirely German Catholic, and remained so for quite some time. Their own parish, Saints Peter and Paul Catholic Church, was established the same year as the post office, in 1874. There was also a school built about the same time.

Among the early settlers of Oneida Township were the Krogmann family, Gerhard, his wife Maria "Agnes" Froehle and their four children. Gerhard Heinrich and his family chose a growing German settlement near what is now Petersburg in Delaware County, Iowa. He was naturalized February 1879 in Manchester, Iowa.

On an 1894 plat map Gerhard is listed in Oneida Township, his land is located on a section neighboring section the Olberding property. According to this map he is farming 120 acres.

Their Children:

(1) Maria Anna, born March 5, 1850 in Steinfeld, Oldenburg, Germany, married Joseph Anton Lappe. Their children were Katherine M., Anton, Frank A., John, Anna, William, Joseph, Henry, Mary R., Clemens J., Clara Evelyn and Josephine, all born in Delaware County, Iowa

(2) Catharina Josephine was born January 15, 1852, she married William Woerdehoff and they had fourteen children, all born in the Petersburg, Iowa area. Their children were Mary Agnes, Margaret Mary, Katharine, Henry B., Aloysius Louis, Joseph, Anton, Rose, Andrew, Arthur, Josephine, William, Frances and Edmund E.

(3) Maria Elisabeth born August 19, 1854, died March 29, 1856 in Steinfeld.

(4) Francisca Carolina was born February 8, 1857 in Holthausen, she married Franz J. Bergman. They first settled in Carroll County, Iowa where Mary Magdalin, Elizabeth Mary and Bernard were born. Between 1883 and 1884 they relocated to Nemaha, Kansas, where there was another German settlement, and there the couple added eleven children, namely Josephine Caroline, Francis Henry, Anna Catherine, Frances Magdalin, Joseph Henry,

Edward John, Henry Leo, Wilhelmina Scholastica and Francis.

(5) Franz Joseph born August 12, 1859 and died December 22, 1867.

(6) Gerhard Henrich born June 29, 1864 and died January 22, 1865.

(7) Franz Henrich was born August 14, 1866 and was just a toddler at the time of emigration. He married Caroline C. Kramer, an Ohio native; this family was the smallest at just ten children. Those children were Alice, Mary and Joseph C. born in Petersburg, Iowa, then they moved to New Hampton, Iowa where Fred A., Edward Frank, Euphemia, Alve, Bernard, Olivia and Leo.

* * *

In search of land at the same time was Gerhard's friend, Franz Henrich Olberding, who emigrated with his wife Catharina Gertrud Froehle and five children. Their baby daughter died on the voyage so they were nearly heartbroken when they began their new life without their youngest child. Franz Henrich's parents were land owners in Germany and considered wealthy compared to a tenant farmer, but Franz wasn't the oldest, and not in line to inherit his parents' land or the rights that came with. (Franz was an uncle to Henry Krogmann, Sr. from Remsen, Iowa).

On December thirtieth of 1868, the Olberdings bought an eighty acre farm in Oneida Township of Delaware County. The price was thirty three hundred dollars or forty-one dollars and twenty-five cents an acre.

Franz only had six years to enjoy his dream of land ownership, on August 24, 1874, Franz passed away. At the time, the youngest child and only son Clemens, was four years old. Catharina didn't give up, she didn't sell the land, and twenty years later she was still listed on the plat map on the 80 acre farm her husband bought in 1868.

Their children:

(1) Marie Josephine Olberding was born September 17, 1853, she married Henry Harmeier, their seven children were Catherine, Josephine, John, Mary Clements, Louise and Henry. They initially remained in the Petersburg area, then relocated to Nebraska.

(2) Mary Elisabeth was born December 27, 1857, she lived at Petersburg until around 1910 when she moved in with her brother Clem.

(3) Catherine Bernardina was born December 18, 1859 and married John Richels a fellow German. Their twelve children were Anna, Henry, Elizabeth, George, Mary, John Henry, Katherine, Josephine, Frank, Rose, Margaret and Lawrence. The older children were born in Delaware County, by the time John Henry was born they were living in Hull, Iowa. The family then relocated to Le Mars Iowa where the youngest children were born. They eventually relocated to Wahpeton, North Dakota.

(4) Clemens August was born November 16, 1863 in Holthausen and

died January 20, 1865.

(5) Johanna Catharine, born May 20, 1867 died at sea on April 14, 1868.

(6) Clemens was born September 8, 1896 in Petersburg, Iowa, he married Mary Henkels on April 11, 1892. Their seven children were all born in Delaware County, namely Katie J., George H., Frank A., Rosie M., Andrew H., Annie F., and Cecilia.

1873

John J. Mulligan and Mary Ann Farrell
Vicksburg, Warren County, Mississippi

During the Civil War, Julia (Colliton) Farrell was a single mom with a young daughter. The "Fall of Vicksburg", their home town, is considered a pivotal event of the Civil War and was a traumatic event for residents. During the spring of 1863 the residents were warned but many still refused to leave. Once they realized their exits from the city were being cut off, it became too dangerous to leave. Homes and buildings became death traps, leading residents and refugees to use caves that had been dug into the hillside along the river the prior year. The civilians dug additional caves deep into the hillside to shelter as many as possible. As mentioned before, Mary Ann may have been sent to school in Saint Louis during the most dangerous days of the war, but her mother Julia was sure to have remained in Vicksburg.

The Siege of Vicksburg began May 18, 1863, as it continued, food and clean water became scarce, and as the days passed, the situation approached critical. The surrender of Vicksburg occurred on July 4th, 1863 a siege of 47 days. After the war was over, Vicksburg didn't celebrate the Fourth of July until after the turn of the century. At that time sporadic celebrations may have taken place but Independence Day didn't become an annual event again until after World War II.

John J. Mulligan and Mary Ann Farrell were married in Warren County, Mississippi July 29, 1873. John was born in Illinois, Mary Ann was born in Vicksburg, Mississippi, and they were both children of devout Roman Catholic parents. Over the next twenty-seven years they had fifteen children, eight preceded their parents in death, namely Mary Catharine, John Henry, William Victor, Wilfred, Mary Florence, Mary Josephine, Mary Finlay and Eleanor Mary. The seven children that outlived their parents were Edward Francis, Bernard Anistasius, Thomas Julian, Julia Blanche, Mary Genevive, Rosalie and Clifford Aloysius.

John Jacob Mulligan was the son of Irish immigrants; he was born between 1844, he 1854 and grew up in LaSalle, Illinois. Other than those few tidbits of information, there is little known of John's youth.

In the mid 1800's there were few Mulligan families in the La Salle area, only three of these families had a son named John and thus far no evidence has been discovered to definitively link our John to one of these Mulligan families. There is however 'circumstantial' evidence based upon an entry in an 1891 publication where John J. Mulligan is described "He came to Vicksburg in youth as a mechanic, having previously learned the trade of a tinsmith. He soon engaged in business for himself, and is now doing a very large, reputable and lucrative business"[38]. This biographical entry bolsters the likelihood that John was the son of Thomas Mulligan, a widower with a young son named John. Thomas Mulligan was a blacksmith and he was a local leader, one of fifteen men who voted to incorporate the City of LaSalle, Illinois. A son of Thomas' would likely have learned the trade of a smith at an early age and would have assigned high importance to the value of community involvement as his father did.

Among the long list of mysteries yet to be solved concerning John Mulligan is how he eventually ended up in Vicksburg. The move may have been linked to the Civil War, or possibly the lure of opportunity after the war. To grow their business and develop customers, many tinsmiths traveled around the area selling wares, and war torn Vicksburg was in dire need of a tinsmith's wares.

After the Civil War John was employed by the Vicksburg & Meridian Railroad as their repairman, and by the early 1870's John had established his first business on Mulberry Street in Vicksburg. He opened a wagon and carriage shop that grew and prospered for almost thirty years before it was destroyed by fire on October 9, 1901.

During their first years of marriage, John immersed himself in his business and worked hard developing his reputation as a respected Vicksburg entrepreneur. Initially, he sold small tin and iron wares such as pails, pots and pipes. From there John established a wagon business, soon adding harnesses and other accessories to his inventory.

The year 1878 brought John a couple of small misfortunes that were publicized. The first one, in February "about three o'clock yesterday afternoon, the horse attached to the spring wagon of Mr. J. J. Mulligan, was frightened by a number of little boys rolling hoops down the declivity of Walnut street, between Crawford and Clay streets, and ran away. The wagon capsized near Messrs. Wachenhelm & Horman's Beer Garden, and Mr. Mulligan was thrown out upon a dirt pile, in the vicinity of that establishment. No injury was sustained."[39]

The second was on May 18, 1878, when the most damaging tornado that hit the state of Mississippi in fifty years ripped through the City of Vicksburg. There was no loss of life but property damage was widespread.

---

[38] Biographical and Historical Memoirs of Mississippi Volume II, 1891.

[39] Daily Commercial, Vicksburg, Mississippi; Thursday, February 7, 1878.

"Mr. John J. Mulligan, who has been established in business for only a very short time, and whose energy and industry enabled him to erect an establishment of his own, is a very heavy loser; his damages amount to very near $2,500."[40] The tornado tore the roof off his business and the torrential rains that followed destroyed his inventory.

John was always open to innovation and new opportunities. From various city directory listings and news items we can follow changes in John's business interests and locations. In 1879, he was half of an innovative partnership contracted to install a street sprinkling system in Vicksburg that would eliminate the use of stagnant water for street cleaning. At that time he also had a copper, tin and sheet iron shop located on Crawford Street, in the late 1880's he saw a bright future in the emerging plumbing business hence, he expanded his services and had a second shop on South Mulberry Street. With his tinsmith background, he had an edge against competitors, helping his plumbing business to prosper. John J. Mulligan was known for having the first indoor plumbing in Vicksburg.

On January 3, 1893 he was one of three incorporators of Vicksburg Electric Transit and Light Company in Vicksburg, Mississippi where they had plans to erect an electric light plant. Whether their plans proceeded or he sold out are unclear, he was always thinking of ways to be innovative. In 1894 he returned to his experience with the railroad and was issued a patent for an improved Freight Car Door, two years later in 1896 after some refinements to his original patent he applied for and was issued a patent on a new Rail Car Door,

"My invention relates to an improvement in car-doors, and especially to and improvement in the doors of freight-cars; and the object of this invention is to provide a freight-car door or a door for similar purposes, which will be exceedingly tight when closed and which may be opened in an expeditious and convenient manner, being guided in its opening movement and held in proper relation to the body of the car.

"Another object of the invention is to provide a means whereby when the door is brought to the closing position it will substantially automatically lock itself, and furthermore, to provide a means whereby the door while being strong may also be made quite light and will be economic and durable in construction."[41]

Community involvement was an important part of his life. After settling in Vicksburg, John began volunteering for the local fire department. He eventually became president of his local Washington Street volunteer firefighters unit. John was known and respected throughout the city, and

---

[40] Daily Commercial, Vicksburg, Mississippi; Monday, May 20, 1878.

[41] *United States Patent Office. Specification forming part of Letters Patent No. 554,078, dated February 4, 1896. Application filed July 6, 1895.*

was later elected treasurer of Vicksburg's Washington Fire Company No. 3 and spent one term in 1880 as President and Marshall of the fire company. For a few years in the early 1880s, he was an alderman for the Fourth Ward of the City of Vicksburg. Also he was elected treasurer and eventually president of the Vicksburg Building Association.

John was instrumental in founding the Catholic Knights of St. John where he served as Captain. Over time the Knights of St. John faded in popularity, then in 1904 J.J. Mulligan and his son E.F. Mulligan were among the charter members of the Vicksburg Knights of Columbus.

As John and Mary Ann's children grew up they had the same entrepreneurial spirit as their father. Initially, they joined their father in the plumbing business, then as interesting opportunities arose, they abandoned plumbing and branched out on their own.

Business expansion continued until the 1901 fire, which destroyed his residential rental building, where the fire began, it spread to his warehouse storage facility for harnesses and buggies, and most devastatingly, the fire spread to John's tool and machine shop that housed his plumbing business. The machine shop contained the tools of his trade, many of which he had custom designed during his thirty years of experience and would not be replaced by the insurance company. After the 1901 fire, John substantially downsized his plumbing business. Working from his home he kept occupied with small plumbing repair jobs and the management of his properties. After a lifetime of work and community involvement, he and Mary Ann were semi-retired.

Around 1910 John moved his family to a newer Vicksburg development, their new residence was located at 1112 Harrison Street. Except for Edward, who was married and had children, the Mulligan siblings all lived with their parents.

Brothers Thomas and Bernard continued their father's pattern of investing in emerging fields. According to a 1911 city directory they had established a business called Mulligan Bros that included "Mulligan's Nusho" at 1408 Washington, a motion picture theater, and next door at 1412 Washington was "Mulligan's Lyric" also in the business of motion pictures. Their brother Clifford was an employee and their sister Genevive was bookkeeper. The brothers remained in the motion picture business for a few years before moving on to other endeavors. Bernard was elected vice president of the Motion Picture Exhibitors' League of Mississippi in 1913, he was also consulting for the motion picture business in Pensacola, Florida. Before WWI Thomas had left the business and by the time the war was over, the business had been sold or closed, the brothers going their separate ways.

In 1917 Mary Ann fell seriously ill; she died a few weeks later on September 9, 1917. An obituary described Mary Ann with the following words:

"She was ever thoughtful in behalf of her friends and never lost an opportunity to do a good turn or perform a kind service for her neighbors"[42].

John followed his wife eighteen months later in March of 1919, his obituary described John as a "prominent plumber and public-spirited citizen"[43].

1874

Herman Heinrich Krogmann

Clinton County, Iowa

Leaving Germany as a heuerling and stepping onto American soil with the prospect of becoming a landowner, filled Herman with anticipation. Once in Clinton County, settling onto to their new farm was exciting as well as challenging. The land included a small log cabin, an apple orchard and an old water pump. The cabin was crowded but served its purpose while a large house was built. The house was followed by a barn, outbuildings and a thriving operation. Herman was naturalized on January 5, 1883.

Although possibly incomplete, the following information includes the eleven children of Herman Heinrich Krogmann and Maria Agnes Nieberding.

(1) Maria Josephina, born December 21, 1858 in Steinfeld, she married John Horst and they farmed in Clinton County until 1897 when they moved to Poinsett, Arkansas with seven surviving children, Mary Anna, Mary Helena, Minnie, John, William Clemson, N. N. died as an infant, Louise Theresa died at the age of two, Emma Sophia, George Herman, and the youngest, Clara Frances was born in Arkansas. The relocation was a major event. The Horst family, was one of eight families that relocated to Arkansas.

(2) Maria Elisabeth was born September 20, 1860, she married Martin Bossen.

(3) Maria Johanna, born August 7, 1862 married Joseph Gasper, children include John, Joseph, Mayme, Agnes and Dora A. Their children were all born in Clinton, Iowa where Joseph operated a general merchandise store.

(4) Johann Henrich or "Henry" was born October 3, 1863 married Mary Theresa Holdgrafer, children include Herman Louis, John William, Henry Edward who died as a young child, and Mary Theresa. Henry and Mary

---

[42] Vicksburg Daily Herald, Vicksburg, Mississippi; September 10, 1917.

[43] Daily Herald, Vicksburg, Mississippi, 1919.

raised their family in the Clinton County area.

(5) Clemens was born January 3, 1866 in Steinfeld, he married Maria Carolina Christina Detterman. Their family included John Herman, Herman August, George Joseph, Rosa Sophia, Laura, Matt, Pauline, Mamie and Ruby. Clemens and family also remained in the Clinton County area.

(6) Franz Thomas "Frank" was born in Steinfeld, Oldenburg, Germany July 28, 1867 and married Sophia Caroline Detterman on January 26, 1886 in Lyons, Iowa. Here we have another large family that was raised in Clinton. Children were Joseph Herman, Benjamin, Anna Francisca, Frank, Martin John, Clara L., Mary C., Rosala, Herman H. and Agnes. Frank died January 1, 1941 and is buried at Saint Irenaeus Cemetery, in Clinton County, his wife was buried beside him in 1954.

(7) Joseph's date of birth was November 12, 1869, he married Frances Holdgrafer. After their marriage they bought the home farm which they operated a few years before selling to the youngest brother John and purchasing a different farm, also in the Clinton area.

(8) Bernard was born in Steinfeld on October 14, 1871, possibly died before emigrating, no additional information located.

(9)Magdalena "Lena" was born in Clinton County in 1874; she married John Caviezel around 1895. Lena and John with their baby, John Jr. were among the group that initially relocated to Arkansas. The Caviezel's however returned to Clinton County. Additional children include Frank Henry, Barnard, Rose and Frances.

(10) Herman was born around 1876 in Clinton County. Herman had an undisclosed disability that listed him as crippled or paralyzed on various census records.

(11) John B. was the youngest, born in 1878. His wife was Anna N. Hass. Their children were Alice A., Milo J. and Grace. John bought the home farm from his brother Joseph, but he too sold the farm. From there the family may have moved on to Minnesota, then back to Iowa.

After Josephine and family moved to Arkansas, Herman and Agnes, along with Agnes's sister Elizabeth also moved south. Who could blame them, no snow and warm winters! Herman bought a farm in partnership with another German. A couple years later, Herman became ill and died in Waldenburg, Arkansas. From conflicting records, the year was 1903 or 1905. Herman is the only Krogmann buried in the Waldenburg Cemetery. His wife Agnes returned to Clinton after his death, but her sister Elizabeth or "Lizzie" remained in Arkansas where she died in 1914. She is also buried in the Waldenburg Cemetery and she is the only Nieberding buried there.

1878

Franz Henrich Krogmann

Delaware County, Iowa

Every now and then there is a family connection you're almost positive exists, but can't find solid evidence to back it up. Franz Henrich "Frank" Krogmann was one of those cases for many years. This connection was not confirmed until recently.

Delaware County, Iowa immigrant, Franz Henrich "Frank" Krogmann born in Oldenburg, Germany, March 26, 1861 was the son of Franz Henrich Krogmann and Maria Catharina Berding, thus being a grandson of Franz Ferdinand Krogmann and Maria Engel Suennenberg, and second cousin to Henry, Sr. of Remsen, Iowa.

Henry, Sr. made occasional visits to South Dakota, these visits were continued by Henry's son when he visited Frank's son Louie at his horse ranch. Louie was described by family as "relation" not a very specific description.

Frank's father's first wife was named Josephina Meyer, his second wife was Maria Catharina Berding, she was a widow of Henry Kolbeck with two children Henry Joseph and John Clemens Kolbeck, both of whom had previously emigrated and eventually ended up in Remsen, Plymouth County, Iowa.

Frank arrived in America 1878 and located in Delaware County, Iowa. He married Agnes Macke, a native of Germany who was born on October 28, 1873. The couple began their family in Salem, South Dakota, relocated to Osceola County, Iowa for several years before returning to South Dakota.

Of their fifteen children, Clem and Kate were born in Salem, South Dakota, Mary, Frank Daniel (he became the Mellette County Sheriff for several years), Elizabeth, Annie, Louie (he was the owner of the Krogman Quarter Horse Ranch), William, John and Pauline were born in Sibley, Iowa and Clarence, Louise A. Clara F., Lawrence S. and Harold H. were born after the family returned to South Dakota.

1878

Carl Anton Krogmann

Iowa Counties of Delaware, Carroll, Sioux and finally Osceola

Starting out in Delaware County, Carl Anton joined his brother. However, greener pastures were calling and he soon joined other Germans and relocated to Carroll County, Iowa. There were other Krogman families in the area. Their youngest daughter, Margaret was born near Carroll before the family relocated again, this time to Hull, Iowa. There were numerous Krogman families in Sioux County.

His wife died in 1887 while they were still living in Hull. The next relocation took Carl Anton to Ashton, Osceola County, Iowa, where he remained until he passed away in 1910.

The children included Maria Josephina (b. 1858, m. Gerhard Heinrich Berning Jr., their home was in Lismore Minnesota); Herman Henrich (b. 1862, m. Josephine Anna Rosener, m. Anna Edelhide Wess, they also eventually settled in Lismore) and Frank (b. 1866), August (b. 1871, m. Katherine Gratz, their home was in Hennepin County, Minnesota), Anton (b. 1873, m. Katherine Tremmel, made their home in Ashton, Iowa), Maria Catharina (b. 1877, m. Henry Ebbers, their home was in Slayton, Minnesota) and Margaret (b. 1882, m. Anton Honkomp, their home was in Ashton, Iowa).

1882

Johann Heinrich Krogmann

From Clinton to Sioux to Plymouth County, Iowa

Working as a farm hand was a popular way to earn money for new immigrants in the 1850's and continued to be the case in the 1880's. Johann Heinrich Krogmann was living with neighbors of his uncle Herman in Clinton County, Iowa as of the 1885 Iowa census, he was living with the Bernard Manaman family. Thirty nine months after officially immigrating, Henry made his Declaration of Intention to become an American citizen. A week later, on January 11, 1886 Johann Heinrich Krogmann "Henry" and Christina Caroline Schmidt "Lena" were married in Jackson County, Iowa.

After their marriage the couple began farming 80 acres in Welcome Township, near Hull, in Sioux County. They had so little money that on November 4, 1886, Henry took out a two month chattel mortgage for twenty six dollars and thirty-five cents from H. J. Baumann. He used his fourteen year old dark brown unencumbered mule as collateral; the loan had an interest rate of ten percent per annum and was payable January 4, 1887.

The newlyweds were looking forward to a bright future working their farm and raising a family. With numerous German friends and relatives in the area, a farm with fertile land and a growing Roman Catholic parish in Hull, they didn't imagine that in a few arduous years they would be in search of a new home and ultimately relocating.

October 11th of 1888 welcomed the birth of their son John Henry Krogmann. The following year, October 2, 1889, Henry Sr. became a naturalized American citizen in Orange City, Sioux County, Iowa.

A search of the Hull Catholic Church's baptismal records found only one additional record of a child born to Henry and Lena, that child was a daughter named Mary Elizabeth, born in 1891.

By 1892 their situation was rapidly deteriorating, they were mourning the death of their baby girl Mary Elizabeth and many of their German friends and neighbors were relocating. They were weary of the never-ending difficulties of living with the Dutch and began to move to nearby counties. There was little cheer around the Krogmann home as they contemplated a move. The big question was where should they go? Many of the German families moved to the Ashton area in Osceola County, a few moved to Le Mars in Plymouth County.

In 1894 Henry and his family joined the exodus and relocated to rural Remsen, in Plymouth County, Iowa where Henry purchased 120 acres of land for $35.00 per acre.

The Sioux County, Iowa story of the Dutch Calvinists goes back to 1869 when they were scouting for an uninhabited area to build their dream of a Dutch-only settlement. They chose northern Sioux County, and reserved 60 blocks of land for their friends and relatives. In March of 1876 a Plymouth County paper announced "Twenty-three Holland families from Michigan to settle in Sioux county expected here to-day or to-morrow. A Holland colony of 200 families will move into Sioux county before the breaking season opens."[44]

As the Dutch relocated and consolidated their holdings, they took control of the county government, schools, banks, as well as the 'Main Street' businesses. Calvinist teachings forbade many leisure activities the German families enjoyed such as piano playing, singing, playing cards, dancing, smoking cigars and close to the top of the list was drinking alcohol. Not something a German was likely to abandon.

When one of the local Germans went into a Dutch general store to buy supplies, he might be told there was no sugar today, but a few minutes later, a Dutchman asked the same question and had their request filled. Not to mention the banks seldom lent money to the Germans, shopkeepers wouldn't offer credit, the feed store "didn't have" supplies they needed, the vet couldn't make it to the German farm for another day or two, and the list went on.

There was more going on here than the Dutch wanting their Dutch-Only settlement. The German settlers were almost all Roman Catholic and the Dutch feelings toward the Catholics dated back in history to the carnage and atrocities they suffered at the hands of the Catholics during their fight for independence from Spain in the 17th century. The Dutch had a long memory and in a nutshell, this predominantly Dutch settlement would have been a very hostile environment for a scattering of German Catholic settlers.

How many families relocated? That question would require some in-depth research into the land records; the number would most likely cover most of the Germans in the area. This list just includes the Krogman

[44] Le Mars Sentinel, Le Mars, Iowa; March 23, 1876.

families and relatives that have been identified:

- Franz Joseph Krogman and his wife Gertrud Mary Heisterkamp; they were in Hull when, son Franz Anton was born in 1885, daughter Mary Josephine in 1888 and son Joseph Franz in 1892, they eventually relocated to Le Mars, Iowa. (Franz Henrich was his father, Herman Heinrich (b. 1798) was his grandfather and Henry Krogman, Sr. of Remsen, was his second cousin).
- Carl Anton Krogman and his wife Maria Agnes Rosenbaum had moved to Carroll, Iowa, then relocated to Hull during the late 1880s and finally settled in Ashton, in Osceola County in the early 1890s.
- Gerhard H. Berning and Josephine Krogman lived in Hull in the late 1880's and relocated to Ashton, then to Lismore, Minnesota. (Herman Henrich (b. 1798) was his father and Henry, Sr. was a first cousin once removed).
- Herman Henrich Krogmann (b. 1862) and his first wife Josephine Rosener baptized a son Anthony in Hull in 1887 and with his second wife, Anna Wess had three children baptised at St. Joseph's Catholic Church in Hull, the oldest, unnamed, was baptized in 1888, Mary Elizabeth March 10, 1889 and Mary Caroline on April 3, 1891. Their relocation took them to Nobles County, Minnesota. (Carl Anton born in 1831 was his father, Herman Heinrich (b. 1798) was his grandfather and Henry Krogman, Sr. of Remsen, was his second cousin).
- Clem Kolbeck and his wife Elizabeth Krogmann baptized son Frank in 1886 and daughter Lizzie in 1888 and Anna in 1892 at St. Joseph's in Hull, Iowa. The family relocated to Ashton, Iowa where Elizabeth died. Clem and his second wife are buried at St. Mary's Cemetery in Remsen, Iowa. (Clem is a stepchild of Henry, Sr.'s uncle Franz Henrich Krogmann).
- John Richels and Katherine Olberding went from Delaware County to Sioux County where they resided when their son John Henry was born, from Sioux to Plymouth County, Iowa in the 1890s. (Katherine was a first cousin to Henry, Sr., daughter of Henry's mother's brother Franz Henrich, who was a witness at Henry Sr.'s parents' wedding, he immigrated in the 1870s, settling near Petersburg).
- Johann Henrich Krogmann and Anna Bockelman moved from Carroll to Sioux County. Their daughter Anna Mary was baptized August 20, 1887 and son Francis was baptized September 7, 1889. They relocated to Ashton by 1891. (Franz Henrich (b. 1821) was his father and Herman Heinrich (b. 1798) was his grandfather and Henry Krogman, Sr. was his second cousin).
- Other German families that relocated from Hull to Ashton during

the same time period included the William Bausch, Anton Berneman and Clem Krogman families.

* * *

The relocation was paying off. By the late 1890's Johann Heinrich and family were experiencing success in their farming operation. They hired a young German farm hand named Bernie Albers who lived with them for several years.

At the time of the 1900 census Lena reported having five children with only one, Henry Jr., still living. Not surprising, this took a mental and physical toll on Lena. Still wanting to add to their family, later in 1900 Henry and Lena took in a young Orphan Train child. Her name was Katherine Keller; she was born November 1, 1896 in New York, New York. At two weeks of age, Katherine was dropped off at the New York Foundling Hospital by her mother Elizabeth, the date was November 15, 1896. She was baptized the following day in the facility's Chapel by Reverend J. R. Kennedy.

At four years of age, Katherine boarded a train with a carload of fellow orphans bound for Iowa. The specific destination for each orphan from the New York Foundling Hospital was known before they left New York; Midwestern parish priests learned about interested parishioners, applications were made and the hospital tried to match the children with the request. Prospective parents were screened; an effort was made to be sure the request for a child wasn't to fill the need for a farm laborer or housekeeper. Other institutions weren't always as conscientious.

The list of traumatic events littering Katherine's childhood was still in progress. Six years after arriving in Iowa, in 1906, her new mother, Lena died of cardiac failure. Her death certificate also says an indirect cause of death was appendicitis, with a duration of 115 days and a contributory cause as hepatic abscess with a duration of 20 days. Family stories from multiple sources state Lena died on a flatbed railroad car on her way to the hospital in Sioux City. The version printed by a local newspaper states:

"Lena, the beloved wife of Henry Krogmann of Meadow Township was relieved from her sufferings through death at 8:30 a.m. Friday April 13 after having two operations at St. Joseph's hospital in Sioux City. Mrs. Krogmann was taken home as a convalescent on the 9th of April but her condition changed for the worse and the end came at the time stated. Mrs. Krogmann was born near Bellevue, Iowa as the daughter of Mr. and Mrs. Andrew Schmidt 41 years ago. With her husband, one daughter and one son, morn her untimely loss. The large attendance at the funeral last Monday demonstrated only partly in what degree the decedent was beloved in the community."[45]

Although newspaper accounts refer to Katherine Keller Krogmann as the adopted daughter of Henry Sr. and Lena, Katherine was never legally adopted, and when Henry's will was probated she learned she would not be an equal heir. It was after Henry's death that Katherine contacted the New York Foundling Hospital, and suffered a second disappointment. She learned her mother's name but little else; her file was sparse, there had been no visits or inquiries relating to Katherine, consequently there was only the information offered by her mother when she was dropped off.

The year of Lena's death, Henry Sr. was listed among the leading farmers in Meadow Township, but there was little thrill in the honor without his wife by his side to share the joy. Henry Sr. was only forty-five years old when Lena passed away. Henry did not remarry, and over the years he never parted with his wife's possessions. After he bought a house in town, he moved all her possessions to a spare room. The only people allowed to disturb her possessions were his dear grandchildren. His granddaughter Florence recalled how much fun it was playing dress-up when they were at Grandpa's. And the girls always returned their grandmother's clothing and jewelry to the same organized condition in which they found them.

A news bit in the Le Mars Globe-Post reflects his attitude about becoming a proud doting grandpa. "Grandpa Henry Krogmann came in to tell us of the arrival of a son at the home of Henry Krogmann Jr., of Meadow township."[46]

His son Henry Jr. was married to Anna Mary Stuntebeck October 8, 1907. It was at that point Henry Sr. began to step back allowing his capable son to take the reins.

Less than two weeks after the young couple was married, a Remsen News headline read "A Bride Very Ill." Anna had been taken to Sioux City for surgery after being diagnosed with appendicitis. This must have been extremely unsettling for Henry, Jr. since his mother's death followed appendicitis complications. Anna was young and healthy, her recovery was swift.

Henry Jr. was a savvy businessman, it took no time at all before Henry Sr. knew his farm was in capable hands. Henry Jr. purchased the farm from his father; the 1915 Iowa Census lists its value at $24,000 with an encumbrance of $15,000, Henry's prior year income listed as $400. Henry, Jr. had many interests; the Northwestern Iowa Polled Hereford Breeders' Association included Henry among the "nine herds of Polled Herefords, consisting of some of the best of the breed."[47] It was a profitable time for a

---

[45] The Le Mars Sentinel, Le Mars, Iowa, April 15, 1906.

[46] Le Mars Globe-Post, Le Mars, Iowa, November 29, 1910.

[47] The American Hereford Journal, September 15, 1920.

sensible farmer and Henry, Jr. took advantage of a variety of opportunities.

On the political front, the 19th Amendment was ratified in August of 1920. Although many women didn't feel it was necessary to vote, Anna was eager to take advantage of her new responsibility. At the age of 31, Anna's first opportunity to vote was the upcoming presidential election between Warren G. Harding and James M. Cox, undoubtedly, Anna was at the polls to cast her vote. Anna was a supporter of the Democrats and their policies, however German-Americans and Catholics felt betrayed by Wilson's broken promises after the Paris Peace Conference in 1919, which may have drawn her to Warren G. Harding and contributed to his overwhelming victory.

Farm prices continued their growth for a few more years and Henry continued managing his finances like a pro. His farm and money management skills turned out to be a godsend in the late 1920's when farm prices were plummeting. In spite of the economic hardships that falling prices posed for most farmers, Henry was considering building a new home for Anna. It may have actually been the dismal economic times with low prices on labor and materials that tipped the scales in favor of building.

The Krogman barn dances were popular for many years, an announcement for an upcoming dance read as follows: "Public Dance. The Meadow township farm bureau baseball team will give a public dance on Tuesday evening, July 2, at the Henry Krogman farm. Best place to dance, and the best music. Everybody cordially invited."[48] The Krogman barn dances attracted large crowds, reportedly at least 150 couples would attend. The dances were held in the hayloft of their barn and the floor was said to have been comparable to many area dance halls.

The house in which Henry and Anna had lived since their marriage was the same home Henry Jr. grew up in. This was a typical 19th century Iowa farm home, a compact two story, white clapboard surrounded by trees and a huge garden. For winter heating, the house had a corn cob and wood stove.

Adjacent to their house was a summer kitchen or a separate small building used during hot summer months to keep the cooking heat out of the main house, they also used their summer kitchen for separating cream from milk and churning cream into butter.

In 1928, shortly after their youngest was born, Henry and Anna selected their new home from the Sears and Roebuck catalog, it was delivered on a railcar with all the parts cut and pre-fitted. The house was built near the original farm house. It was a $2,500 five bedroom American Four Square style with a coal and wood furnace. (Plumbing and wiring extra). The original Krogman home was moved across the road and became the

---

[48] Remsen Bell-Enterprise, Remsen, Iowa, June 2, 1929, page 6.

residence of their hired hand for a time, later it was rented out with farmland, and after that became the home of their youngest son.

In 1963 the home was obliterated by a tornado. Their son and his family miraculously survived to tell their story.

The Krogman's were music lovers, Henry, Jr. played the accordion, his oldest son Clarence played the violin, Frank played the guitar, Marie the piano and they all sang.

Around 1910 Henry Sr. moved to Remsen, he purchased a house just up the street from Frank Stuntebeck's, between St. Mary's Catholic Church and the railroad tracks. It took no time at all for Henry to learn he was going to enjoy retirement. He was a happy-go-lucky German that enjoyed visiting with the townsfolk, playing cards, having a beer and maybe smoking a cigar.

According to his granddaughter Florence, he raised chickens, chewed tobacco and even though he was German, he enjoyed playing pinochle during the afternoons at the Luxemburger Bruderbund, a brotherhood normally limited to Luxembourgers. When he was a winner at the card table, Henry gave his winning chips to his grandchildren to trade in for a soda at the counter.

He also loved entertaining his grandchildren, telling them stories, and making them laugh, sometimes he sang German songs to them. He told stories of his father, a big man that enjoyed smoking cigars, and he never failed to bring a bag of chocolate candy bars when visiting his grandchildren.

Over the years Henry Sr. kept in contact with his sisters in Germany. In 1908, two years after Lena's death, he applied for a passport; the reason given on his application was to travel to Germany to visit relatives. In 1925, traveling on the S.S. Columbus, Henry took a second trip back to his birth country. Henry regularly corresponded with his sisters; after WWII he shipped food and supplies to them, resources were scarce and at times they were near starvation. Crates of food and clothing were sent for almost twenty years. After Henry, Sr.'s death the tradition was carried on by his son until the 1960's.

As age began to get the better of him, his foster daughter, the Orphan Train rider, Katherine (Keller) Pick, stepped in to care for him. Henry Sr. died in October of 1942 at the age of 80 years, 10 months and 22 days. His cause of death was cardio renal vascular disease caused by arterial sclerosis. He had been sick for five years. Both Henry and his wife Lena are buried at St. Mary's Cemetery in Remsen, Iowa. In the words of his granddaughter Florence Krogman Schumacher "he was a dear man, so kind and loved having us [his grandchildren] there, he sang German songs, and he made the best chicken soup – he raised chickens. In the summer he rode out to the farm in his horse & buggy, he always had a sack of candy bars for us kids. He had a barn next to his house in Remsen where he kept his horse and buggy, a coal bin and a room for the chickens he raised."

Henry's great grandson Jack said with a chuckle, "his horses could always find their way home even when Henry partied too much during the evening".

1884

Koos Brothers

Richland Township, Jackson County, Iowa

After nineteen years as a farm boy, Peter Koos was coaxed into giving big city life a try. Peter grew up in a rural community with a handful of residents, his father was a farmer, and the only occupation he was trained for was farming but his American destination was a growing city with a population well on its way to one million residents. Peter was planning to test the waters in Chicago, the home of his mother's younger brother.

Peter Reiland lived in Cook County, Illinois, arriving not long before Chicago's Great Fire of 1871. After the fire, hundreds of multi-story buildings were installing wooden barrel type water towers in case of fire. This was a dream come true for a cooper, he had more work than he could handle.

He was looking forward to having his nephew work for him, he needed a trustworthy hard worker.

Nephew, Peter gave it his best shot, but the city lifestyle and building of wooden water tanks did not impress Peter Koos and before long he was back on the road.

The young man continued his trek west, crossing the Mississippi and stopping in a small rural community with a concentration of Luxembourgers. That community was La Motte, Iowa in Jackson County's Richland Township. An interesting note about his destination, had he continued another 25 miles due east, he would have been in Richland Township, Jones County, Iowa where a great-uncle of his was farming. This great uncle Nicholas Koos, was a brother to Peter's paternal grandfather. This makes one wonder if he stopped in La Motte by mistake and his planned destination was his great-uncle's farm.

Life as a farmhand was much more suited to Peter, and before long he felt at home in La Motte. On December 29, 1885 he married Margaret Banks, the third daughter of Henry Banks and Mary Hoffmann. It was a double wedding ceremony along with Margaret's sister Katherine and Nicholas Kayser who happened to be a cousin of Peter's from Luxembourg. Fourteen months later on February 14, 1887 the young couple, Peter and Maggie Koos acquired the Banks-Marso farm in Richland Township, for three thousand dollars. Mary and Jacob Marso then headed for Sully County, South Dakota with their farm implements, livestock and horses. Many of their possessions were transported by rail.

Money was tight for the young couple and banks weren't always the most trustworthy places for a farmer to borrow money. Their interest rates were high and if they were willing to lend money they were known to be vague in their explanation of terms. Peter went to the bank to borrow money for three cows but it turns out he didn't have to worry about the bank's possible shady practices since they wouldn't lend him the money. This was just a slight stumbling block in Peter's path, he still wanted the cows, so he called upon neighbor after neighbor. He did this for three days and finally his quest came to an end. The result, he was able to borrow a hundred dollars, the lender kept ten for interest and Peter paid him a hundred dollars a year later. We can be confident the lender was a fellow Luxembourger.

There was a brief period when all four brothers lived in the LaMotte area. Joseph and Nicholas lived with Peter when they first arrived in Jackson County; Joseph then lived with Henry for a short while before he ventured out on his own. Joseph's future was that of a well-respected photographer in New Hampton, Iowa. He was naturalized June 26, 1902 at Maquoketa; and he died on December 2, 1924 of Erysipelas. His brothers Peter and Henry went to New Hampton to attend the local services. After the services they returned with the body. Joseph is buried at Holy Rosary Cemetery.

Little is known of the fate of Nicholas, except he died about two years after immigrating and is buried at St. Theresa's Cemetery near La Motte. Peter and Henry remained in the La Motte area where they married two of the Banks sisters and raised their families.

One of Peter Koos's daughters was proud of the fact that the first four families in the area to own an automobile were Pete Koos, Henry Koos, John Kilburg and a Beschen family.

(1). Peter and Maggie's children numbered ten, beginning with Nicholas, born August 31, 1887. He married Margaret Hingtgen September 21, 1909, she was born March 26, 1889, the daughter of Nicholas and Catherine Hingtgen. Nicholas and Margaret were farmers in La Motte, Iowa, they had nine children, and seven lived to adulthood. Margaret died in childbirth with their ninth child, the child also died, March 29, 1929.

Nicholas didn't continue his father's serious outlook on life, his granddaughter, Shirley McDermott recalled a story she and her brother Roger heard from their aunt Coletta while standing on a snow covered hill, the same hill this incident occurred.

Coletta recounted a memory involving her father Nicholas. The setting was a snowy winter in Iowa and Coletta along with some of her siblings were enjoying the season by sledding down a steep hill near their house.

The hill was a sledder's dream and the youngsters attempted to persuade their dad, Nicholas to join in the fun and take a turn. It took some convincing but he finally agreed, and climbed on the sled. The hill was covered with compacted snow and it didn't take long to build up speed. The hill was also part of a field that was home to the family's horses. As Nicholas began gaining momentum he could see imminent disaster ahead . . . maybe he closed his eyes, maybe he didn't . . . he was heading straight for a large horse, then suddenly the animal was gone. The horse had calmly stood still while Nick went flying between the horse's legs, instinctively ducking his head as he passed under the animal. After Coletta's story, her niece and nephew were allowed to sled down the same hill their grandpa came close to experiencing catastrophe.

(2). Henry was born January 17, 1889, he married Catherine Hingtgen, a sister to Margaret the wife of Henry's brother Nicholas. Catherine died during the birth of their only daughter on April 28, 1913, Henry named his daughter Catherine. Henry then married Gadzelle Stover, a teacher; in fact she was Henry's teacher when he was in school. Gadzelle raised Catherine as her own; she died at the age of 62 on June 25, 1937. Henry's third wife was Mary Lemke; they wintered in Tampa, Florida, and returned to La Motte every summer. Henry lived until February 15, 1980.

(3). Peter Michael was born August 21, 1890, he married Anna Angela Manders on November 24, 1920. The couple farmed just south of La Motte, Iowa and were the parents of one daughter. Anna died August 22, 1970 and Peter died the next year on October 7, 1971, they are buried at Holy Rosary Cemetery, in La Motte.

(4). Mary was born September 16, 1892, her husband was Andrew Wathier, the couple farmed near La Motte, Iowa, they had no children. From all accounts Mary was an incredibly talented cook.

(5). Louis was born December 27, 1893, he married Anna C. Hingtgen. The couple had two daughters, Vivian and Yvonne. Their farm bordered Louis' brother Peter's farm on one side and his father Peter's farm on another side. Louis Died September 19, 1966. He and his wife are both buried at Holy Rosary Cemetery in La Motte, Iowa.

(6). Josephine was born December 1, 1897; she married Joseph Kilburg on January 25, 1920. They had no children. Josephine died March 6, 1981; Josephine and Joseph are buried at Holy Rosary Cemetery.

(7). William was born August 30, 1900, he spent his entire life, except for his time in a nursing home, on the farm on which he was born. William died July 5, 1980.

(8). Florence was born November 24, 1902, she married Leo Sprank and spent their married life on a farm near Cottonville, Iowa. Florence died April 7, 1986 and Leo followed less than a year later on January 18, 1987.

(9). Around 1905, Frank joined the family and like his brother William he spent his entire life, except his nursing home time on the home farm. Frank died at the Mill Valley Care Center in Bellevue, Iowa on January 28, 1998 at the age of 93.

(10). Virginia was born March 14, 1907, she was the only child born in the new house Peter built for Maggie. Virgie died at the age of 84 on August 30, 1991.

The children were all born and raised on the farm that was purchased by Henry Banks. They worked hard, not only on their farm, also on other farms. During harvest season, initially Peter and his brother Henry offered their services with their threshing machine, and later it was Peter with his sons, making the tour around the county.

There was the possibility their routine was endangered in 1917. The evening papers of June 5th headlined "Nation's Young Men Respond to Call" the article continued "White or black, married or single, sick or well, alien or native born - even enemy subjects of the kaiser - all men between the ages of 21 and 31 were expected to present themselves today between 7 a.m. and 9 p.m. for registration."[49] World War I was raging in Europe and the Selective Service Act had been enacted two weeks previous.

On this day, four brothers, Nickolas, Henry, Peter M. and Louis Koos registered for the Draft. Peter was the only one called to service following the next harvest season.

Sometimes you hear a family tale that sounds a bit like fiction, maybe with a hint of truth buried deep within. There was such a story pertaining to Peter Koos, Sr. When I first heard the story, it was told by a great grandson who heard it from his father. The story was simple, Peter kept his money in the form of gold coins stored in a trunk in an upstairs bedroom and the trunk was mighty heavy, too heavy to move.

In prior generations, distrust of the banking system was widespread, if an individual hadn't lost money themselves, they surely knew of someone who had. During the financial crisis of 1893, between April and August alone, at least thirty one Iowa banks failed, most of their depositors losing almost everything. Borrowers also had troubles as banks began calling in loans to reduce their exposure.

The story of Peter's banking habits gained traction after sharing this story with other grandchildren and great grandchildren. The response was almost unanimous. They heard the story from people with first-hand knowledge, from their parents or grandparents and the story was firmly believed.

He may waited a few years before taking his cash to the bank, but after the Banking Act of 1933, people had much more confidence in their local banks that were FDIC insured.

[49] Evening Times Republican, Marshalltown, Iowa, Tuesday, June 5, 1917.

* * *

Henry, the second Koos brother to immigrate, married Anna Banks, a sister of Margaret, the couple had two children. Henry and Anna began their married life as farmers. Henry was a man of many talents, and many interests; in addition to farming, he was a skilled tinsmith with a knack for soldering. When he tired of farming Henry invested in a hardware store in La Motte, Iowa, the store was called Ehlinger & Koos. Business was going well so the partners added farm implements to their inventory.

Henry never lost his love for heights while working for his uncle in Chicago. He loved climbing local windmills to perform routine maintenance when he was at an age where most of us would hesitate before climbing stairs without a railing.

The two brothers were as different as night and day, the older one, Peter was serious and somber, while Henry was fun loving and always ready to party. Peter had no interest in music and his brother was a music lover. A story shared by his grandson Bob, illustrates Henry's attempt to combine his fondness for partying with his love for music. Henry and his friends were planning a party on one of the islands in the Mississippi River, they planned to do the party up right, including music, so they were taking a piano along. The party goers made it to the island in fine shape but the piano rests as the bottom of the Mississippi.

A 1928 ordinance the town of La Motte enacted wouldn't even have created a blip on Peter's radar, Henry on the other hand no doubt left town that Memorial Day holiday. During February of that year the town council "passed an ordinance prohibiting dancing and all forms of public sport including the playing of baseball, May 30, Memorial Day."[50] People who ignored the ordinance could be fined up to $50 or jailed for ten days, keep in mind $50 was a pretty steep fine in 1928.

There was a family activity they both enjoyed. During the 1930's and '40's the Koos family held annual picnics in the late summer before the harvesting season began. It was really more of a feast than a picnic. Maggie and her daughters made their famous homemade ice cream, Pete and Anna brought Trenkles hot dogs, which were always a hit.[51] The picnic was held on Peter and Maggie's farm in a pasture. They had table cloths spread out on the ground for the food and plates. The entire clan, their spouses and children all sat on the ground; Peter Sr. and Maggie were the only ones that sat at a table. The seating arrangement was often the same, the Koos sisters

[50] The Victoria Advocate, Victoria Texas, February 21, 1928.

[51] Trenkle Meats was established in Dubuque in the 1890's by a German immigrant, using their original family recipe; they closed in the 1970's

would sit together and the brothers and their families sat together.

Other Koos relatives that immigrated included the boys' uncle, Nicholas Steven Koos; born in Bilsdorf, Luxembourg, August 22, 1843. At the age of 23, in 1866 he immigrated to America, initially settling in Ohio where he married Susan Konz. His naturalization occurred January 27, 1873 in Cincinnati, Ohio. Nicholas Steven, commonly known as "N. S." later moved west to the Kenosha, Wisconsin area, and he married Elizabeth Schill. For years he made his living with hide tanning in conjunction with a rendering business. In addition, in 1898, with his son Edward, he began his own fertilizer company which grew into a large thriving business.

Nicholas Steven or N. S. enjoyed traveling and never hesitated to send a penny postcard announcing his most recent adventure. One of his 1913 postcards to Peter, in La Motte translates to "Haven't heard from you since you've been in Kenosha. I'd like to hear from you. Last May I was at the Pacific Ocean, and now at the Atlantic Ocean. N. S. Koos." It was sent from Fortress Monroe, Virginia. N. S. also made occasional visits to La Motte to visit his nephews.

After WWI when Peter M. Koos returned from his military service in France, his father Peter, Sr. was encouraged to visit his homeland. Peter Sr.'s uncle N. S. was also interested in returning to his native land. As noted earlier, communication and coordination was impressive, considering the technology available. The passport for N. S. was issued April 28, 1920 and Peter's was issued April 29, 1920. Uncle and nephew traveled together, N. S. paying for the tickets and Peter Sr. promising to pay him back. The pay-back never happened.

Unaccustomed to being hoodwinked, N. S. was determined to get what was owed to him. Alfred Koos, a great great grandson of N. S. shared the end of the story, N. S. then ordered a load of hay from Peter, once he had the hay in his possession he felt they were even and never paid the bill for the load of hay.

A grand uncle of the four La Motte brothers was Nicolas Koos, apparently the first of this Koos family to emigrate from Luxembourg. Born April 6, 1813 to Michel Koos and Therese Mathieu, he emigrated with his third wife, Susanna Kuntsch. He was living in Richland Township in a neighboring county when Peter arrived in Iowa.

Nicolas' first wife Marguerite Maillet, died in 1839, with his second wife Anne Catherine Schartz, he had three children: John, Josephine and John M. there may have also been a daughter named Anne, born 1848, died 1868. Nicolas married Susanna Kuntsch on May 30, 1860, daughters Mary (b. 1861, m. Patrick Rogers) and Catharina were born in Luxembourg. Nicolas immigrated with his family around 1864, they settled in Wisconsin where their youngest, Anna was born in 1865. By 1870, the family had relocated to Jones County, Iowa when the census included Nicolas,

Susanna, John, John M. Mary, Kate and Anna. After the 1870 census, son John located in St. Donatus, he died there on October 17, 1873.

Other relatives that immigrated included several Reiland cousins that made Wisconsin, their destination, not far from Peter Reiland in Chicago, John Reiland (b. 1840) settled in Wabasha County, Minnesota where he and his wife Mary Bartholome raised their family. There were also Kayser relatives that immigrated; the Kayser's chose farming communities in Iowa and South Dakota as their destinations.

1885

Stuntebeck Brothers

Iowa, Minnesota and Wisconsin

Three Stuntebeck brothers with three distinct personalities will eventually plant roots in three different states. Even with the miles separating them, these brothers saw each other just as often as many brothers living in the same county.

FRANZ FERDINAND STUNTEBECK

The wages from Frank's years of hard work as a farm hand were about to pay off, he used the savings to purchase a farm east of Remsen in Plymouth County, Iowa, near the Bohlke property where he had been working as a farm hand.

In 1888 Frank Stuntebeck and Mary Mullenkamp were married. Frank and Mary's family would grow to five, all five were daughters . . . not exactly the gender mix most farmers hoped for but Frank didn't allow gender to interfere with his farm operation.

Frank was an exceptionally hard worker. The Stuntebeck farm flourished with his corn crops and hog operation. As his assets increased he purchased additional farmland. When his daughters began approaching their teen years, they were expected to contribute. The girls spent as much time working on the farm as any of the neighboring boys.

(1). The firstborn Stuntebeck daughter was Anna Mary, born April 24, 1889. She developed a fancy for the boy next door, and the feeling was mutual. Henry Krogman would hop on his bike and ride over the mud road to visit the love of his life. Henry and Anna were married October 8, 1907. They made their home with Henry's father who bought a house in town a few years later. The couple raised nine children, Clarence, Frank, Marie, Henry, Helen, Irene, Florence, Joseph and Jeanette.

(2). Mary Stuntebeck was born February of 1892; she married William Beckmann in 1913. They also farmed in the Remsen area where they raised four children, Frank, William Jr., Lewine and Mary. William Beckman Sr. lived to the age of 77 and his wife Mary died in 1971 at the age of 79.

(3). Margaret or "Maggie," the third daughter was born July 6, 1894, she married Peter Lanners January 16, 1917. Maggie and Peter had one son Frank P. who died in North Africa July 12, 1943 during WWII. Margaret lived to the age of 85.

(4). Katherine or "Kate", was born August 1897, she married Theodore Hansen February 22, 1916, their daughter Mildred was born a year later.

On November 19, 1918, Theodore died during the flu pandemic which was referred to as the Spanish Flu or La Grippe. With a victim count of 20 to 40 million people, it was seen as a global disaster. The pandemic took more victims than WWI and more than the four years of bubonic plague. This illness was most deadly to the young healthy adult age group.

After Theodore's death, Kate and her daughter Mildred moved back with her parents Frank and Mary until October 10, 1925 when Kate married August Haack, a Remsen farmer.

(5). Frances, the youngest, was born 1898. She married Ferdinand Arens February 14, 1919, the couple farmed in the Remsen area. They raised two children, a son and a daughter. Frances died in 1982 at the age of 84.

* * *

The patriarch, Frank suffered a fractured collar bone in 1906 after a run-away team mishap. Frank was in Remsen on Main Street with his team, pulling a wagon of hogs. Another team was startled and in their panic ran into the back of Frank's wagon, startling his horses. As Frank's team bolted, Frank was thrown from his seat, landing on his side.

It was also in 1906 that the Plymouth County Atlas named Frank Stuntebeck as one of the leading farmers in Marion Township. In addition to farming, Frank helped organize the Remsen Farm Co-op and was director of the co-op for several years. He was also a township assessor for Marion Township, one of his grandsons, Joseph F Krogman, Sr. would eventually follow in his grandfather's footsteps, holding the position of assessor for Meadow Township for many years.

In the winter of 1916 Frank and Mary (Mullenkamp) Stuntebeck retired from farm life. Their retirement event did not follow the pattern of preceding generations. Frank and Mary held a public sale and moved a few miles west of their farm to the northern edge of Remsen, Iowa, purchasing the former Jess Rann house.

Frank had worked hard his entire life and his decision to retire came as a surprise to many. It was wondered how he would spend his time. They needn't have worried. Frank could always find something to occupy his idle hours. One of his favorite benefits of retirement was that it allowed him the freedom to go fishing at will and he rarely returned home empty-handed.

Retirement from farming didn't mean retirement from an active business life, Frank remained quite active as a businessman. Newspaper accounts provide an inkling of his "retirement" years. Among his business transactions, in 1924 he purchased or exchanged the 240 acre Carl Hanson farm, with property of a similar size that he owned in New Hampton, Iowa. In 1932 he purchased the Joseph Treinen farm located NE of Remsen, his plans at the time of purchase were to have his grandson Clarence Krogman operate the farm. His goal achieved, he was happy when he was able to provide each of his daughters a farm. Payback for their hard work when they lived on the farm.

Frank and Mary enjoyed each other's company and Mary loved spending time with her grandchildren. Around 1922 Mary's health began to give her problems, eventually she was diagnosed with diabetes. During her last six months she was confined to her bed, cared for by her husband and daughters. On the third of November 1928 at the age of 63, Mary (Mullenkamp) Stuntebeck died of diabetes mellitus.

In 1931 Frank went on a three months' sojourn to Europe. "While Mr. Stuntebeck was in Europe he visited with his brother, August Stuntebeck and family, who lives in Damme Oldenburgh, Germany, and he spent a few weeks with his cousin, Father Petrus Ernst, a Franciscan Father at the Kloster Korham, at Siegmarrigen, Germany. Mr. Stuntebeck reports that the crops in the vicinities he visited are in excellent condition."[52]

Frank enjoyed spending winters on the California coast where he spent time with old friends that had retired to the warmer climate, and he enjoyed taking daily walks on the beach. Frank never remarried; he played pinochle with friends, worked in his garden, and took long walks after lunch, and he always enjoyed dropping a line in the water and possibly bringing a bullhead home for dinner.

In the morning Frank made egg drop coffee. To prepare this morning drink, while the water is heating, break up an egg, shell and all; then mix in the coffee grounds, if it's too dry to stir, add a splash of liquid. When the water begins boiling, stir in the coffee-egg mixture until well blended, remove from the heat and allow the pot to sit quietly for a few minutes before gently pouring. With this method, even your last cup should be free of grounds! (This was well before coffee filters).

Where health was concerned, Frank was before his time. He considered diet and exercise top priorities in daily life. His afternoon walks were mentioned earlier but he also enjoyed a healthy diet, especially fruits and vegetables, many he grew in his own garden. As he reduced his gardening exercises, his daughters, especially Anna, showered him with fresh fruits and vegetables.

---

[52] Le Mars Semi-Weekly Sentinel (Le Mars, Iowa) September 18, 1931.

One thing about Frank that his grandchildren and his great grandchildren remember was his mustache. Of course the mustache was a curiosity to children and they would reach for it. Jack Krogman, great grandson wrote, "I used to try and grab his mustache and he would act like he was going to bite me." It didn't matter which child was reaching for the temptation, Frank's actions could always elicit a squeal from the youngster.

During his later years Frank sold his house and when he wasn't in California, he alternated his time between his five daughters, primarily the oldest, Anna. He remained active and was rarely idle. He still enjoyed solitary activities like gardening, fishing and walking around the property. He would sometimes grab a tool and walk out to the corn field to chop weeds paying no attention to the heat of the summer. Not watching the time, he worked until he was tired and would repeatedly arrive late to the dinner table, much to the aggravation of his daughter Anna.

In 1954 as his health began to deteriorate, he no longer moved from one daughter to the next, he remained at Anna's home, the last three months he spent in the hospital in LeMars, Iowa.

Frank Stuntebeck died September 24, 1956 at the age of ninety-one. According to his death certificate he died of uremia due to carcinoma of prostate and blood. The Stuntebecks were a family gifted with longevity. In 1934 Frank's aunt Mary Bohlke died at the age of 97. His brother Henry lived to eighty-two and his brother Leonard surpassed everyone by living to the age of 101!

HENRY AND LEONARD

In the early 1890's the two younger Stuntebeck brothers joined their older brother Frank in Remsen, Iowa. They weren't there long; Henry was restless and soon headed north. It wasn't long before Leonard joined him in the farming community of Wilmont in Nobles County, Minnesota. The brothers went into business for themselves and opened a saloon. This was about the same time Herman Heinrich Krogmann (b. 1864) moved to Nobles County with his family. Their paths surely crossed at some point.

According to family forlklore, the saloon venture took a wrong turn when one of the brothers, in an attempt to keep it safe, took the money bag along when he visited the outhouse. Once he was ready to leave, the sack was left behind. When the brothers discovered the bag was missing they rushed to retrieve the missing funds but it had disappeared. The story passed along to descendants says this misfortune marked the end of their saloon. Remarkably, this was not the case, although the incident may have put them on the brink of closing, the business did survive.

In 1901 Henry married Mary Fritz, a fellow German immigrant; their first child was born in Minnesota in 1901. Henry was a free spirit; even a growing family didn't deter him from re-settling. In 1902 they moved to

Rice Lake, Wisconsin where they had two more children. From there, around 1906 Henry and Mary moved to Kimball, South Dakota where the couple had seven more children, then in 1917 with their ten children, the family relocated yet again, this time to Marshall in Dane County, Wisconsin. There they had their eleventh child, and their adventurous lifestyle came to an end, they remained in Dane County. Henry died in 1952 at the age of 82.

When Henry left Minnesota in 1902, Leonard continued operating the saloon. During his travels visiting brothers and friends, Leonard met Charlotte Marie Drier (Lottie) from Doon in the northwest corner of Iowa. They were married in 1911 and relocated to Kimball, South Dakota, initially living with Henry and his family. Leonard and Lottie soon began farming on their own; they were happy with Kimball and decided to raise their four children there.

(1). Leonard "John" was born August 28, 1912; he married Alma Nicholas and raised one son and one daughter. John lived to the age of 96.

(2). Frances Marie was born October 22, 1913; her family was heartbroken when she choked on a cherry pit and died in her father's arms. Frances was 3 years, ten months and 28 days old.

(3). Edward William was born March 17, 1915; he married Alma Petula, who was born February 9, 1920. The couple had one daughter. Alma died April 20, 1984; Edward lived to the age of 75.

(4). The youngest, Josephine Charlotte was born February 20, 1917. Josephine was a teacher in Kimball for many years. She was a great help in supplying family history information relating to her father Leonard and family. It was surprising that even though the brothers were separated by distance, they remained close, and never allowed too much time to pass before visiting each other. Descendants of both Henry and Leonard recalled visiting Uncle Frank in Remsen, Iowa, and a few of the Krogman grandchildren remembered occasional visits from their Wisconsin and South Dakota relatives.

The Stuntebeck brothers had learned to read and write German in their native land. All three learned to read English after living and working here for several years. According to Leonard's granddaughter Jo, he learned to read English, enjoyed the newspapers and he could sign his name but like many immigrants of the time, he saw no practical need for writing English.

Among the memories of his native land, Leonard said they raised cattle on the family farm. He also recalled using wood dishes and one of his favorite homeland meals included sauerkraut.

REAL HEROS

If we had the opportunity to step back in time and speak to individuals that have long since passed away, most genealogists wouldn't select a historical or famous figure, it would be one of the most interesting or mysterious ancestors on their family tree. In my case it would definitely be one of the women who charged forward after a devastating loss; women who overcame hardship and were forced to make difficult and life changing decisions to provide for their children. It is hard to imagine the despair they must have been feeling when their situation was at its bleakest point, and trepidations they felt as they were about to make a decision that would change their future forever.

In recent years the liberal usage of the word hero has diluted the value of its meaning. Webster's definitions of the word include "one that shows great courage." This meaning can be applied to the majority of the individuals covered within these pages. And with no stretch of the imagination, our immigrant ancestors, and those that suffered the loss of a spouse, can certainly be classified as heroes or heroines.

UNTANGLING FAMILY TWIGS.

Family history researchers experience very high highs of excitement and accomplishment, often following the low lows of repeated failure. Rather than giving up, there are times when it's wise to set the research aside and return later with a fresh outlook. Hurdles aren't always the inability to locate records on an individual, sometimes there are too many records. Finding ten Johann Heinrich Krogmanns is exciting until the weeding out process becomes overwhelming. And what are the odds there would be two Johnann Heinrich Krogmanns that within a few years of each other married Catharine Olberdings, all living in Oldenburg Germany?

Naming traditions also confuse the situation. Many German families and a few Luxembourg families followed traditions that create chaos for curious descendants. If all the boys in a family named their oldest son after their father's father, and they all lived in close proximity, you can be looking at numerous individuals with the same name with birth dates spread in a relatively short time span. The research is further complicated when two brothers married two sisters and both followed the naming traditions.

Then we have the use of first and middle names. In the overall picture this is a relatively new practice that became especially prevalent among Germans and Luxembourgers. There was an area of Germany where the tradition was to give their children a first name in honor of a favorite religious figure, for instance, all boys in a family could have a first name of Johann followed by their middle name, it was the middle name by which the child was called. The American version of naming continued the first and middle names but discontinued naming in honor of a favorite historical or religious figure. There were families that followed the tradition for some children, but not all, and there were families that used the first name of a specific ancestor rather than a meaningful figure.

Families we've met like the Niemanns, Theodore and Henry, didn't strictly adhere to the tradition, but the two families each had several children given the same name as their neighboring cousins. Henry (son of Henry) was born in 1855, his neighboring cousin Henry (son of Theodore) was born in 1852. Both ended up settling in Marcus, Iowa after marriage and both opened retail stores. The first was Cousin Henry with a hardware store followed by Cousin Henry with a jewelry store. They were both considered leading business men in the Marcus area. The same was true for the Haxmeier family, Theodore and Henry lived next door to each other and each family had several children with names matching children in the other family.

* * *

Much has changed since our ancestors settled in the Midwest, and many of these changes have made it possible to live safer, healthier lives. A person with depression or suicidal thoughts is no longer carted off to the nearest insane asylum. Safety nets exist for those facing adversity, but the situation for many senior citizens is less stable than that of their great grandparents.

Attitudes are different today. Seniors have no desire to move in with their children, they don't want to be a burden, and they hope to maintain their independence as long as possible. Unfortunately, if we live long enough, most of us will need help. How to pay for care has become a serious hurdle. Some will move in with one of their children and many relocate to a nursing home in a community near their children, in doing so they lose contact with their friends and familiar surroundings.

More seniors are looking for a way around the current system, hence the *new concept* of Aging in Place. As the senior population grows, so does the list of laws in place to protect their well-being. We will never return to the system that worked so well for our ancestors, but affordable options for seniors to maintain a decent quality of life is a goal for which we should aim.

Angelina (Philipps-Welter) and Peter Schartz

The Peter Manders Children
Back - Mary, George, Katie, Leo, Anna
Front - Loretta, Matthew, Christopher, Irvin

John J. Mulligan

Mulligan children - Bernard, Ed, Clifford, Julia, Thomas and Rosalie.

Left - Maria Agnes and Herman Henrich Krogmann.
Right - Johann Henrich Krogmann (b. 1828)
(Herman Henrich and Johann Henrich are brothers).

Henry Sr. (b. 1861) and Lena (Schmidt) Krogmann
(Henry is a son of Johann Henrich above).

Lena, Henry and Henry Jr. (Circa 1890)

Clarence Krogman and Myra Pockes Witnesses for the marriage of Ollie and Catherine (Keller-Krogman) Pick.

**Anna (Stuntebeck) and Henry Krogman marriage.
Witnesses, John Bohnenkamp and Mary Stuntebeck.**

Henry and Anna After Sixty Years of Marriage!

Henry Krogman Sr. in front of his Remsen, Iowa home.

Jacob Marso & Mary Hoffmann-Banks

Joseph, Henry and Peter Koos

Brothers Peter and Henry Koos and their families.

Peter, Maggie and their ten children. Circa 1910

Peter and Margaret (Banks) Koos

The annual Koos picnic, this one was celebrated September 1937

Henry & Mary (Fritz) Stuntebeck wedding, and Leonard Stuntebeck birthday

Maria Elisabeth (Backhaus) and Johann Stuntebeck
(First cousin to the three Stuntebeck brothers that immigrated).
Note the resemblance.

Frank Stuntebeck and Mary Mullenkamp

The Stuntebecks - Anna, Frances, Kate, Margaret, Mary, Frank and Mary

Chapter 5

Lead By Faith

Religious rites and traditions played an important role in the spiritual lives of our ancestors long before coming to America. They had hopes of improving their economic status in their new homeland, but certainly not at the expense of their faith. Our ancestors were experts at finding solutions to seemingly insurmountable problems - no church building, no problem - a devout local would step up and offer their home as a meeting place until a church was built.

As their numbers multiplied so did the likelihood of securing regular visits from a pastor. The next step of finding a permanent priest or minister presented a bigger problem, but most were satisfied if they had a monthly visit from a traveling pastor, the person offering their home for services also offered their home for the pastor's lodging.

When it came time to build, land was often donated as well as labor, pews and other necessities. For many of our ancestors, supporting their church was as important as putting food on the table.

Church membership was also a way to make social connections and regular opportunities to visit with neighbors. Isolated farmers could spend weeks not seeing anyone other than their family and would excitedly look forward to the monthly visit of a distant pastor. The following glimpses of individual and family life will show how deeply devout and incredibly generous some of our ancestors were.

1853

John Michael Flammang

Roman Catholic Missionary Priest.

The twenty eight year old seminary student just arrived in Iowa and he was eager to complete his education and begin the fulfillment of his dream. Bishop Mathias Loras sent the young man to the Mount Saint Bernard Seminary at Key West, Iowa, just south of Dubuque.

John Michael Flammang was ordained by Bishop Loras on April 18,

1854 at the old St. Raphael's Cathedral in Dubuque, Iowa. His first parish responsibility was Saint Kunigunde in Davenport, later spending time at parishes in Muscatine and Old Mission in Festina, Iowa where a few years later the "smallest church in the world" was built.

In December of 1859 Reverend Flammang was assigned to St. Donatus a parish in a town of the same name. This was a stagnant parish that had recently lost its first buildings by fire, Reverend Flammang was residing in a poorly furnished rectory beside the shell of a church with construction at a standstill. Activity at the church may have been stagnant, but the Reverend soon learned there was a thriving business at the three local saloons.

Rev. John Michael Flammang's name will forever be linked with the small Iowa parish of Saint Donatus, Iowa where his list of achievements related to building up the struggling parish are long and varied. He arrived in December of 1859 after he was asked to take over the responsibility of the struggling parish and its mission churches of Saint Catherine's in La Motte and Saint Nicholas in Spruce Creek.

Rev. Michael wanted his parishioners to be dedicated to family and lead by faith; he had no problem visiting the local saloons and sending the patrons home to their loved ones. His obituary in the Luxemburg Gazette describes the problems he faced after his arrival in St. Donatus:

"There the conditions were mournful. It was a splintered and neglected parish, the four walls and the roof of a place of worship. But he said nothing and wavered not. He was impelled to buy furniture and build and with time it was one of the most beautiful churches in the west which appreciated in value and stood as a sedate chattel. But the most attention was the current increased and loving subordinate parishioners. He reached them through teaching, preaching, admonishing, warning and threatening the latent evil and was able to create a parish with the little money that was his to use, not a large proportion, small by present day standards. He was not limited to St. Donatus - St. Catharine, Springbrook, Spruce Creek, were his and eventually Bellevue was separated from his mission. Also there he cared for church and school and the sick people needing him whether by day, whether by night he didn't need to be called twice, whether it snowed, hailed or flash flood he was ready in a minute."[53]

At the point of his arrival in St. Donatus, there were only irregular classes taught by the local priest, Rev. Flammang immediately began holding classes for adults as well as children three times per week in local homes, he then developed an innovative circulating library to allow scriptures to reach a greater number of people. In 1860 the new church was finished, a year later classes were being held in the church basement.

---

[53] From his obituary in the Luxemburger Gazette, December 1883, translated from German by Mary Kay Krogman.

The most famous of his building additions was one of the earliest. In 1861 he built the outdoor Way-of-the-Cross, fourteen brick shrines that takes the visitor up a hill that some compare to Calvary. The Way of the Cross has become a popular site for visitors during the Easter season; it is also a tourist stop for people passing through.

The shrines or stations were completely paid for by the parishioners from their personal funds, there were no fundraisers, the individual stations cost $24.00. The contributors included many people from the pages of this book. Father J. Michael Flammang paid for Station I, the Haxmeier brothers paid for station VII, N. Nemmers was a contributor towards Station X, Mich. Nemmers contributed $7.00 and N. Hoffmann contributed $3.00 towards Station XIII and finally M. Manders contributed $3.00 toward Station XIV.

A new rectory and a grade school were added and during the Civil War, in 1864, building had begun on a four story convent high school and boarding school. The school's late 1860's ad in a Dubuque, Iowa paper read:

INSTITUTE OF ST. MARY
(St. Donatus) Jackson Co. Iowa.

This institution conducted by the Sisters of Notre Dame of Milwaukee, offers unusual advantages to young ladies to acquire a thorough and practical education. It is situate in a highly picturesque and healthful locality and within two hours ride of Dubuque.

TERMS-Board and tuition in English, German, Needle-work, and Vocal Music, per annum, $120.00.

The regular session will commence on the
First Monday of September.
For further information address:
REV. J. M. FLAMMANG
St. Donatus, Jackson Co., Iowa.
July 22.

J. Michael Flammang was a leader for his church, he was respected and included in many area events. One example is the 1870 dedication of the original St. Joseph's church in Cresco, Iowa which was presided over by "Rev. Father Flammang on the 18th day of December, 1870."[54]

Around 1871 Reverend Flammang was instrumental in establishing a weekly Catholic paper called "The Luxemburger Gazette" it was based out of Dubuque and even today it is a valuable source of information for family history researchers.

---

[54] Cresco Plain Dealer, Cresco, Iowa, February 23, 1917

The year 1872 showed the addition of a large sacristy and 1875 included a high school for boys along with a two story teacher's house.

In 1879 Reverend Flammang returned to Europe to visit family and schedule an audience with Pope Leo XIII. He returned to Europe again a couple years later in hopes that a break from the responsibilities of a busy parish would rebuild his failing health. While there, he convinced Margaret Flammang, his niece, (a daughter of his brother Nikolas) to return to America with him and join the Sisters of Notre Dame.

No information was available from the Vatican on Father Flammang's trip there. Unfortunately, according to their library, visitor records do not date back that far. For an ambitious researcher they suggested a possible article in the Vatican newspaper which is part of their historical library. At this time a researcher would be required to visit in person.

August 5, 1883, his niece Margaret was graduating at Sisters of Notre Dame in Milwaukee; she asked Father Flammang to witness the event. He was ill but made the trip, after all, she was there because of him. While in Milwaukee, his condition deteriorated to the point he became bed ridden. Over the next months as the outcome of his condition became inevitable, his brother and three of his sisters made the trip to Milwaukee to see him.

The Reverend died in Milwaukee on his birthday, December 6, 1883, four months after his niece's graduation. There were sixteen priests at his funeral, along with most of his parishioners as well as people from neighboring parishes. He is buried in St. Donatus, next to his mother, Elizabeth.

1854

Henry Niemann

Bellevue Township, Jackson County, Iowa

Friends, family, Ankum-Germany and St. Nickolaus Catholic Church were all dearly missed by the Niemann brothers Henry and Theodore. There was little they could do about seeing their old friends, family and home town. There was however one thing they could do. Three Ankumites set out to create a little bit of home in Iowa by creating a Catholic parish and Henry led the charge.

The Niemann brothers Henry and Theodore were among the first white settlers in Jackson County, Iowa. When Henry and his young bride Elizabeth began their life together, Bellevue Township was sparsely populated. Even though there were a number of Roman Catholics in the area, it was challenging scheduling religious services.

Henry is mentioned in J. W. Ellis' History of Jackson County, Iowa, in describing the establishment of Bellevue's St. Joseph's Catholic Church. "Father Parodin, then stationed at Garry Owen, attended to their spiritual wants at indefinite intervals, saying mass in a private house owned by Henry Nieman."[55] The Niemann home was always open for Father Parodin to spend the night and enjoy a hearty meal before he traveled on to his next stop. As the population grew and more people joined their meetings, they lobbied for a new church, eventually their request was approved.

Three neighbors, brothers Henry and Theodore Niemann along with Henry Rolling donated 12 acres of land in section three of Bellevue Township in July 1854 for the new parish. They chose the name of their hometown parish in Germany, St. Nikolaus. Building of a stone church began immediately and by wintertime the House of Worship was ready. The young parish thrived for years and in 1869 a larger church was built along with a rectory and the original stone church was used as a school; the area behind the buildings was the parish cemetery.

As the landscape changed and more families arrived, new parishes were established and parishioners broke off and joined more convenient parishes. In 1928 Spruce Creek's St. Nicholas Parish became part of Jackson County history. The newer church was eventually torn down, the old parish rectory is also gone. The original stone church still stands and the cemetery is still maintained. (As of 2015)

1864

Five Flammang Sisters

Three joined the Sisters of Notre Dame

Ever wonder how nuns came up with names you've never heard of? The ultimate decision of selecting a name was in the hands of the Mother Superior. Although the aspiring nun could make a proposition there was no guarantee the suggestion would be followed. In the case of the three Flammang sisters, whether the girls had any input is not known, but the choice was fitting for three sisters who were so close.

We met Annie in an earlier chapter when her mission in America was to act as housekeeper for her brother Rev. Flammang. Anna Maria was born November 11, 1830, she grew up in Koerich and spent a few unhappy years in America. Not long after returning home to Koerich, her mother, Elizabeth (Greten) Flammang, now a widow, made the decision to spend her remaining days in America helping her beloved son. It was not a plan of Annie's to leave Luxembourg a second time but in 1863 she was on a ship with her mother along with three of her sisters sailing to America.

Annie was thirty-three years old and was sure she was too old to join the Milwaukee convent where her twin sisters were preparing to attend. She had no desire to be burdened with another disappointment in her life, but

[55] History of Jackson County, Iowa by James Whitcomb Ellis, Volume I, 1910.

the persistence of her twin sisters eventually convinced Annie to have their brother make a request. Annie was beyond thrilled when she learned she had been approved. She joined the Sisters of Notre Dame August 30, 1864 and the following year was given the name Sister Maria Irena Flammang.

For many years Annie was a cook in Hokah, Minnesota and later she went to Krakow, Missouri. In 1901 Annie along with her sister Maria (one of the twins) were allowed to retire together at the Sancta Maria home in St. Louis, Missouri. Annie died of Arterial Sclerosis at 81 years of age on the 11th of May, 1912.

Barbara was a twin to Maria; she was born November 11, 1839. According to convent records in Milwaukee, once in America, her brother was concerned for the "welfare" of his sisters. He applied to Reverend Mother Caroline at Milwaukee's Sisters of Notre Dame for permission for his twin sisters to enter the candidature. Permission was granted and the rest is history.

Barbara was given the name Sister Chionia, she received her veil August 22, 1865 and made her first vows August 28, the following year. Sister Chionia taught needlework in Fort Madison, Iowa and at St. Francis and St. Ann's in Milwaukee. According to her companion Sisters she was pious, charitable and loved silence. After teaching for 45 years Sister Chionia began to lose her hearing and her strength until a "quiet peaceful death" closed the book on this phase of her story. Sister Chionia or Barbara died at the convent in Milwaukee, Wisconsin at the age of 71 on May 24, 1911.

Twin sister Maria, was given the name Sister Mary Agape Flammang and began teaching in 1867 at Saint Charles, Missouri. During her career she also taught in Cross Plains, Eagle Point and Eau Claire, Wisconsin, finishing in Washington and Krakow, Missouri. Her health began to fail in 1901. Sister Agape (Maria) died on May 3, 1909, two years before her twin sister.

The three Flammang sisters, Annie, Barbara and Maria, were given the names of three sisters born over 1600 years earlier. The Holy Martyrs of Agapia, Chionia and Irena (Love, Purity and Peace) were three sisters who were martyred for their faith at Thessalonica, Macedonia on April 3, of the year 304. The girls were in possession of Christian writings of which they didn't wish to part with, this was a crime punishable by death, they not only had sacred scriptures, they also refused to eat the meats offered to the gods, they were all three sentenced to death.

There was a Flammang sister that remained in Luxembourg. She joined the Soeurs de la Doctrine chretienne, 1864.

The youngest of the girls Anne Marie was born January 9, 1844, she joined the order Soeurs de la Doctrine chretienne in Lintgen Luxembourg and entered the convent in Luxembourg shortly before her mother and sisters left Luxembourg for America. After she took her vows, Anne Marie became Sister Marie Lybie Flammang. Sister Lybie was a teacher from 1869 through 1920 when she retired. At various times in her career she taught almost every grade level from first grade through high school. She died at the age of 77 years and 11 months on December 6, 1921.

There is a fifth sister that deserves mention in this chapter. Born in 1837, Marguerite or as her friends called her, "Maggie" was the seventh child, of John Peter and Elizabeth; she followed a slightly different path than her sisters. In Luxembourg she had joined a convent, but left to help her mother after her father passed away. Once in America, Margaret didn't follow her sisters to Milwaukee. She remained in Saint Donatus with her mother and once Annie was accepted by the convent and left St. Donatus, Margaret took on the responsibilities of cook and housekeeper for her brother.

Maggie worked as housekeeper until a few months after Rev. J. Michael Flammang's death, when she returned to her native home of Koerich, Luxembourg. There are few details available, but according to a letter she sent her brother Nicholas after her return to Luxembourg, has a translation of "No one has treated me like the two priests in St. Donatus. I forgive them, but I can't forget how badly I was treated." . . . a curious situation . . . did they kick her out after the death of her brother? Fire her?

We'll probably never know the details, but Suzanne L. Bunkers offers some insight on the situation. One of her books refers to the disarray that enveloped the St. Donatus parish after Father Flammang's death, parishioners complained and "Finally, the pressing request was granted, and unexpectedly, on April 30, Sister Sebastiana landed at St. Donatus. The good old priest was happy to have someone to acquaint him with the customs of these Luxemburgers. Peace and order were restored."[56] It sounds like a priest unfamiliar with Luxembourger customs was wreaking havoc in the parish by changing routines and habits.

After joyfully returning to Koerich, Maggie enjoyed another twenty-seven years in her beloved Luxembourg; she passed away on January 11, 1913.

1865

Anna Richels

Sisters of Saint Francis, Dubuque, Iowa

Anna Richels was born at Petersburg, Iowa on May 14, 1878 to John Richels and Katherine Olberding. Her family had moved to Sioux county for a few years, then relocated near Remsen in Plymouth County, Iowa. After completing her basic education at the Remsen schools, Anna continued her education at the Sisters of Saint Francis in 1895.

---

[56] Diaries of Women and Girls by Suzanne Bunkers.

The Sisters of St. Francis in Dubuque, Iowa was "Founded in 1875 by Sisters from Westphalia, Germany. The Sisters conduct an Orphanage, Industrial School and parochial schools in the archdiocese of Dubuque and diocese of Sioux City".[57]

" . . . Anna was received into the community of the Sisters of St. Francis on June 3, 1896 and from that time on was known as Sister Sophia. She made her first vows Aug. 2, 1898 and her final vows July 21, 1908."[58]

Shortly after her first vows, Sister Sophia became gravely ill, her father being called to Dubuque because of the seriousness of her condition. She soon recovered but various symptoms lingered. Sister Sophia contracted tuberculosis and died at thirty years of age, her burial is at Mount Calvary Cemetery in Dubuque, Iowa.

1869

Meysenburg Family

Butler County, Nebraska

Being an early settler of Butler County, Nebraska there was no Catholic Church for the family to attend in 1869. For the next seven years, sporadic services were held at the home of P. N. Meysenburg. Most of the Butler County Catholics were Luxembourgers and they were well acquainted with each other. In 1876 the visiting priest suggested they build a church and subscriptions or promises began pouring in. Numerous contributions of $25 were among the listing; P. N. Meysenburg's donation at $50 was the largest. Quite a sum for 1876.

John Meysenburg donated a two acre parcel of land to the church, under the proviso that if the church was ever closed or removed, land ownership would return to Mr. Meysenburg or his heirs. A year later Saint Mary's Mission Church was dedicated.

Ten years later they were outgrowing the small structure and again began collecting for a new church which was dedicated February 2, 1890. Later on the same day of the first Mass at the new church, fire destroyed the new building. Services returned to the original church. Again, the Luxembourg settlement came together and donated for yet another new church which was dedicated in 1891.

1871

Mary and Margaret Haxmeier

Sisters of Notre Dame

---

[57] The Official Catholic Directory for the Year of Our Lord 1905.

[58] St. Mary's Catholic Church Centennial, Remsen, Iowa, 100 Years.

Teenaged sisters Mary and Margaret Haxmeier knew their calling early in life. Their parents, Theodore Haxmeier and Caroline (Nemmers) Haxmeier were both devout Roman Catholics and raised their families as such. They lived near St. Donatus, Iowa and were members of the local church where Reverend John Michael Flammang was the resident priest. In addition to transforming his parishes into financially stable and growing organizations, Rev. Flammang was also well known for his successful recruitment of young parishioners into religious orders.

At the age of seventeen, the second oldest Haxmeier daughter Mary, entered the Sisters of Notre Dame convent in Milwaukee, she was followed on September 8, 1871 by her sixteen year old sister Margaret. We learned in an earlier chapter that Mary, the first to join, had a tragically short life, not even finishing her educational training and never having an opportunity to display her talents. During this woeful time of her life Margaret focused on her studies and her future.

Margaret was focused on making a difference; she reached a level of success that would have made her sister and parents very proud. When she became a novice, she was given the name Sister Mary Prosper. She had every intention of making a difference during her life and by 1910 Sister Mary Prosper was Mother Superior at St. Michael's in Rochester New York, a school with over 1,000 children. She had 16 Sisters under her direction as well as the lay teachers of the school. If she were alive today, Sister Prosper would be disappointed to learn the innovative "H" shaped school closed in 1975. It was allowed to deteriorate for years until it was finally sold. The building has since been refurbished and is a 28 unit senior facility called St. Michael's Apartments.

When Sister Prosper was in her sixth decade, she retired from the Mother Superior position but had no desire to stop working. She became one of over thirty teachers at a large Baltimore, Maryland Catholic School. Even her seventh decade didn't lure her into retirement; however, she allowed the work load to lighten. Sister Prosper brought her career to a close at the small parish of Saint Joseph in Taneytown, Maryland.

Sister Prosper lived to the age of 82; she passed away in 1937 and is buried at Glen Arm, Maryland.

1879

Margaret Flammang

Sisters of Notre Dame

Margaret was a daughter of Nikolas, the Flammang brother that remained in Luxembourg on the Home Farm. In 1879, her uncle, Reverend J. Michael Flammang, as mentioned earlier, was visiting Europe, his sister and housekeeper Maggie accompanied him. While visiting his brother Nikolas and family in Koerich, Reverend Michael convinced them to allow their daughter Margaret to travel to America where she would join the Sisters of Notre Dame in Milwaukee. Their return trip on the S. S. Halley took them from Germany to Rio de Janeiro, Brazil and finally to New York.

Once she arrived in America, Margaret joined the Sisters of Notre Dame and studied to become a teacher. In 1883, her goal achieved, she began her profession with the name Sister Mary Michael. Her name assuredly was in honor of her uncle Rev. Michael.

At the turn of the century Sister Mary Michael was teaching at St. Stanislaus in Chicago, Illinois, the school is still in operation today. She had a brother J. P. that became a priest in Luxembourg, he read the Mass in Koerich when his aunt Marguerite died. (The Flammang sister that returned to Luxembourg).

1874

Nemmers Family

Saint Donatus, Iowa

Nicholas and Catherine (Weber) Nemmers immigrated in 1847; they were another devout Roman Catholic family, their strong beliefs passing from generation to generation. Two of their grandchildren were led by their faith to lifelong professions, and others were key players in their local parishes. From a history of the St. Donatus Catholic Church "First religious services were held in the Tritz and Nemmers homes."[59]

A story included in a LaPorte City, Iowa newspaper, recounted one of Reverend John Nemmers' family stories. The family hadn't been in Iowa long when they received a visit from Bishop Loras. The Bishop arrived, forgetting to bring communion hosts. In English he asked Nicholas Nemmers, Jr. to mix flour and water and bake the hosts between two irons. Nicholas was still in the process of acquainting himself with the new language and understood flour, water and two eggs. The result didn't look right so Nicholas and his wife Catherine thought they should leave out the yolk, the color improved but the consistency was worse. They had no intention of disappointing the Bishop so they walked over to their neighbors, an Irish family, and explained the situation. She knew immediately the word wasn't eggs, it was irons, knowing a little German she said "buegeleisen" and the instructions became clear. They rushed home and had the communion hosts ready in time for Mass.

1874

---

[59] Centennial History of the Archdiocese of Dubuque by Rev. M. M. Hoffmann

Nicholas B. Nemmers
Organist and Choir Director

Nicholas B. was a first cousin of Reverend John Nemmers, born to Michael Nemmers and Anna Even in 1852, in Tete des Morts Township, Jackson County, Iowa. After his parochial school education in Saint Donatus he studied music at Pio Nono College in Wisconsin, where he graduated in 1874. Once he returned to La Motte, N. B. used his musical talents at St. Theresa's church where he organized a choir, he was also their organist.

N. B. was instrumental in obtaining permission from the bishop to build a second Roman Catholic Church in La Motte, Holy Rosary. Once the church was built, he became their organist and organized their choir.

1875
Michael Ludwig Nemmers
Writer of Religious Music

A brother to N. B. Nemmers was Michael L. Nemmers, Jr. and from an early age he had a passion for music. As a youth he attended the Catholic School at Saint Donatus, again, his parish priest was J. M. Flammang. At the age of sixteen, Michael was accepted to the newly founded Holy Family Normal School in Milwaukee, located near Pio Nono where his brother was studying. Four years later he graduated first in his class. Music was Michael's life; much of his career was spent in the Milwaukee area. A book covering Catholic Church music describes his dedication, "During his long career as organist, teacher and composer, Nemmers founded his own company to publish church compositions."[60] The M. L. Nemmers Publishing Company continued for years after his death, it was still in business in 1961 when they were sued by a foreign company for unfair competition and duplicating the plaintiff's works. The decision in a United States District Court in Wisconsin was found in favor of the M. L. Nemmers Publishing Company.

Erwin Plein Nemmers was one of two children of Michael Ludwig Nemmers he chose the profession of attorney after beginning his educational career with an undergraduate A. B. degree in music from Marquette College in 1898, followed by a Master's degree in music from Georgetown University in 1899, and a Ph. D., in 1900, an LL.B. in 1901

[60] Renewal and Resistance: Catholic Church Music from the 1850s to Vatican II, edited by Paul Collins, 2010, Peter Lang, Bern, Switzerland.

and LL. M. in 1902 all from Georgetown University. Michael's daughter Adalina Plein Nemmers graduated from the Wisconsin College of Music, then traveled to Vienna, Austria to study voice and piano under Maestro Theodor Leschetizky. He was a well-known virtuoso in Europe before reaching the age of twenty.

The next generation, Erwin Esser Nemmers and Frederick Esser Nemmers were the sons of Erwin Plein Nemmers and Methchild Esser. The brothers became the principal owners of the church music company the M. L. Nemmers Publishing Company, and on a small scale, Erwin also had musical compositions published. Combining some of their own wealth with profits from the publishing company, the brothers were able to bequeath fourteen million dollars to Northwestern University which now funds four biennial prizes of $100,000 to $200,000 each to recipients of the Erwin Plein Nemmers Prize in Economics, the Frederic Esser Nemmers Prize in Mathematics, the Michael Ludwig Nemmers Prize in Music Composition and the Methchild Esser Nemmers Prize in Medical Science. The recipients are selected for their contributions of "work of lasting significance"[61] in their respective fields.

Even more so than his father, Erwin Esser Nemmers accumulated degrees at an obsessive pace; his first was an A. B. in music in 1938, it was awarded from Marquette University. In 1939, A. M. from the University of Chicago, next he earned his LL. B. in 1941, from Harvard University; an aeronautical engineering degree from the University of Iowa and two doctorates from the University of Wisconsin, one in law and the other in economics.

Erwin Esser Nemmers list of accomplishments is long. During his early years he was a research fellow in law at Harvard, a member of the Wisconsin Bar Association, a certified public accountant and a professor of economics at Marquette University. He was also a professor at the University of Wisconsin in Madison and a professor of economics at Northwestern University's Kellogg Graduate School of Management for almost thirty years. He published articles on philosophy and law, wrote numerous books on economics and finance. His first book was published in 1949; it was related to the family business "20 Centuries Catholic Church Music." His knowledge was also respected outside the education community where he was on the board of US Controls Corp. in New Berlin, Wisconsin.

1875

John N. Nemmers

First Iowa-born Roman Catholic Priest, Ordained December 19, 1875

[61]Excerpt from http://www.nemmers.northwestern.edu/economics.html

As a young boy, then a young man, John N. Nemmers' future was formed under the tutelage of Reverend John Michael Flammang. In many respects Reverend Flammang developed John in his own image.

John N. Nemmers, a grandson to Nicholas and Catherine was born in Jackson County, born October 16, 1847, at St. Donatus, lowa, the fourth of 13 children. He was the child born to Nicholas and Maria Catherina (Freymann) Nemmers three months after the family's arrival in America.

Their arrival in Jackson County preceded the parish of Saint Donatus Catholic Church, they were among the first members of the parish and were staunch supporters of Reverend Flammang as their parish priest. One of John's instructors was J. Michael Flammang, well known for recruiting young people to religious vocations, Latin was among the lessons he learned from Rev. Flammang.

John's studies continued at a Milwaukee seminary, where he was a member of the first class to graduate from that seminary in a class of three, he was ordained a Catholic Priest, December 19, 1875 becoming the first Iowa-born Catholic Priest. On the day of his ordination, Rev. Nemmers was assigned to Gilbertville, Iowa's Immaculate Conception Church and was commanded by Bishop Hennesy to leave for his new charge first thing in the morning. John knew his family was looking forward to attending his first Mass, followed by a family celebration. The Bishop allowed Rev. John to say an early Mass, which was publicized by word of mouth and widely attended, but he was not allowed to remain for the celebration. Rev. John left for Gilbertsville, Iowa by a hired driver with a horse and carriage and there he spent the next fifty three years and is buried in the church cemetery.

Reverend John Nemmers' handling of his new parish mirrored many of the procedures that Reverend Flammang followed. He brought order to the parish, set up a school, taught at the school, added to the church building and purchased furniture. After first arriving, Rev. Nemmers spent six months living with a nearby farmer until a small rectory was erected, he lived there for 25 years when in 1901 a modern rectory was built.

John was a very active person. During the early years he helped clear land and build his own rectory. When a new church was built in 1888 there were eight hundred thousand bricks among the construction material. Not standing by to watch or direct activities, he joined in to help unload the bricks. No matter what the project, he was there to help, no job was to dirty or labor intensive. And when it came to his salary, he rarely used it, just added the money to the church funds for day to day needs.

For the first fifteen years the school was taught by lay members of the parish, including John Peter and Henry Nemmers, after 1892 the Sisters of Notre Dame were installed as teachers, at this point the school had expanded to over 200 students. It is very unusual for a Roman Catholic priest to be assigned to a single parish for decades, and even more rare for a priest to spend his entire career at a single parish.

Officials at his funeral included Monsignor George Haxmeier of Lansing, Iowa, a first cousin of Reverend Nemmers and the Archbishop of Dubuque, who preached the sermon.

His obituary in the Waterloo Evening Courier spoke of his tactics with the liquor industry of the town. "Father Nemmers fought liquor as he fought the Iowa early day wilderness. On one occasion he entered a saloon at 1 a. m. Sunday, personally ejecting the patrons at the bar. From then on he fought, with the parish on his side, he enforced the Sunday closing law. . . Once Got A Saloon License. According to the mulet law, Gilbertville's population entitled it to license two saloons. There was one there. Another was projected. To thwart the plan, Rev. Fr. Nemmers made a fast trip to the county seat and himself applied for license to run a saloon, a license which was granted but never used. In retaliation the saloon crowd staged a beer party in a vacant lot opposite the church. The priest, undaunted, dispersed them with a club." [62]

Mary Gedeona Nemmers

Sisters of Notre Dame

A sister of Father John N. Nemmers, Mary Gedeona Nemmers was born February 13, 1852. Following the parade of young women from Saint Donatus, Sister Mary Gideona joined the Sisters of Notre Dame. First she was a teacher at Saint Boniface Catholic School in Quincy, Illinois from 1876 to 1892, from there she went to Saint Michael's in Chicago and taught for another ten years before rheumatism prevented her from leading an active life. Sister Gideona died at the age of sixty-six, in 1919.

1879

George L. Haxmeier

Priest in Lansing, Iowa

A first cousin and neighbor of the Haxmeier sisters mentioned earlier was George L. Haxmeier. George was born September 20, 1856 to Henry Haxmeier and Susanne (Nemmers) Haxmeier. After his education at St. Donatus he attended Mount Calvary College in Fond du Lac, Wisconsin, St. Francis Seminary in Milwaukee and Grand Seminary in Montreal Canada, where he was ordained on December 20, 1879. He began his priestly duties in St. Donatus for several months before being assigned to Immaculate Conception Catholic Church at Lansing, Iowa. It was there he spent 62 years.

---

[62] Waterloo Evening Courier, Waterloo, Iowa, September 7, 1928.

According to the February 14, 1921, Washington D. C. Evening Star, On February 13 during a Knights of Columbus Ceremony, the Very Rev. G. L. Haxmeier was appointed by Pope Benedict to be one of his domestic prelates.

1893
Elizabeth Flammang
Sisters of Notre Dame

A more recent generation of Flammangs also had a pair of siblings dedicate their life to religious orders. In this case it was the oldest daughter and youngest son of Nicholas Flammang and Mary Ann Niemann's thirteen children.

When reflecting on her childhood, Elizabeth's obituary lists one of her favorite childhood memories, "When I was but three and a half years old, my father took me to church. I can well remember how after a few minutes, I looked right and left. Suddenly my father's big hat was over my face and I knew that looking around was not allowed. I was happy in church and did not want to forfeit the pleasure of going again."

Elizabeth was born November 1, 1868, attending Saint Donatus Catholic School until she was thirteen years of age, when she remained at home to assist her mother in caring for her seven siblings, with more to come. She then followed the same footsteps as three of her aunts. When Elizabeth reached her twenty-first year she went to Sisters of Notre Dame in Krakow, Missouri where her aunt was working.

Elizabeth was soon sent to Milwaukee to further her education; in June 1891 she was given the name Sister Mary Clarella. She began her teaching at Eau Claire, Wisconsin where she spent sixteen years, then a year at St. Michael's of Milwaukee followed by a couple years at St. Michael's in Chicago. From a big city in Illinois she moved on to the small community of New Trier, Minnesota. Three years later she was sent to St. Michael, Minnesota where she spent sixteen years. She had an undisclosed illness but returned to teaching at Wabasha when age and declining health interfered with her duties she became a substitute teacher at various missions. Finally at the age of seventy-nine she retired and moved to the Mankato, Minnesota Motherhouse.

Sister Clarella was a beloved teacher; she didn't fall into the mold of the nun recalled by many parochial school students. Her biography said "she had a special gift for handling handicapped and neglected children. More than one wayward child stopped at a convent door years afterwards to inquire - Is my Sister Clarella still living?"[63]

---

[63] Northwestern Province, 1954, page 143.

On July 29, 1953, Sister Clarella had the pleasure of celebrating her diamond jubilee. Elizabeth died at the Motherhouse on February 4, 1954; she is buried at the School Sisters of Notre Dame Cemetery in Mankato.

Theodore Joseph Flammang
Carmelite Brothers

Not all ancestors who dedicated their lives to their faith, spent their time teaching. Theodore Joseph Flammang was born in Tete des Morts Township January 9, 1890 to John Nicholas Flammang and Mary Ann Niemann, we learned about his family in a previous chapter.

By 1928 Theodore was living in Chicago near St. Clara's Church. It was here Theodore became interested in a life dedicated to his faith. He discussed his thoughts with the parish priest who shared general information, including a Vocation Book. His interest grew and Theodore wrote a letter to Mount Carmel College. This letter was included in this obituary:

November 25, 1928
Mount Carmel College
Niagara Falls, Canada

Dear and Reverend Sirs:

For several years it has been in my mind to enter into a religious order, and with this thought before me, I am writing to ask you for a little information.

Have you any booklet describing the lay brotherhood in the Carmelite Order, or can you give me the daily duties of a brother? There is only one doubt in my mind and that is that I may not be strong enough. I am now 38 years old, have never been seriously sick during my life, but at one time I did have nervous trouble which forced me to give up office work. Since doing work requiring physical exertion, my difficulties have almost left me entirely. A recent examination by an expert physician showed that I am in good health. The doctor gave me a thoro examination and asked me to take up some constructive work.

I went to the Very Rev. Lawrence O. Diether, O.Carm. for advice; he gave me your catalogue of Mount Carmel College. He told me to come back in a week, but did not tell me to write to you. It has been my desire to join the brothers of the Society of the Divine Word at Techny, Illinois, but I have prayed much to St. Therese at her Shrine here in Chicago during the last three weeks and I now feel as tho I could become one of her Brothers.

A few words from you as to the daily duties of a Carmelite Brother will be greatly appreciated.

Sincerely,
T. J. Flammang

Things moved quickly after that letter and on August 15, 1930 he recited his vows and Theodore became Brother Angeles. He was immediately assigned to Mount Carmel High School in Chicago. This assignment lasted for two years, and in 1932 he relocated to Englewood, New Jersey, where he eventually retired.

After arriving in Englewood, even though doctors orders were to involve himself in physical work to reduce the tremors he endured since the Army incident, he spent his time working in the office of the parish as well as the high school and eventually the bookkeeper for St. Cecilia's. He watched every penny, turning off lights when leaving a room, and always looking for ways to cut costs. He also managed the cemetery funds, keeping his finger on the pulse of the stock market, making and selling investments when he felt the timing was right.

The V. Rev. William J. Harry, O. Carm. Shared a great story about Brother Angeles and his financial prowess:

"One story that I heard early in my years with the Carmelites is that the provincial treasurer was in Englewood lamenting that we needed some money for some project. Br. Angelus had been in charge of the cemetery for many years by then and, because he ran it efficiently, everyone left him alone. But as he heard the province needed some money, Br. Angelus said he could give out some of the funds he had collected from the cemetery. So the treasurer asked how much he could afford to give and Br. Angelus said "Oh, a million dollars." If you have ever been to the Carmelite circle in the cemetery that Br. Angelus is buried in the center. Many of us believe he got such a prominent spot because of the million dollar gift at a critical moment."

Even after retirement, Brother Angeles wanted to review bank statements to confirm the funds were being properly managed.

1920

Peter Koos

Holy Rosary Parish, La Motte, Iowa

The Roman Catholic religion has numerous holy days and feasts throughout the year. One of these, not limited to the Roman Catholic faith, is The Feast of Corpus Christi which is celebrated 60 days after Easter, or traditionally the Sunday after Trinity Sunday. The Roman Catholic event begins with a Holy Mass followed by a procession where the Eucharist is carried and displayed in a decorative vessel (a monstrance) which the priest holds out in front of him and above eye level. The procession can include a canopy which is held over the priest protecting the Eucharist. The tradition has faded away in many American parishes, but has remained very active in a few European as well as South and Central American countries.

One parish that carried out this tradition for many decades was Holy Rosary Catholic Church, located in the rural community of La Motte, Iowa. This church, although closed by the archdiocese in 2007 had a rich history of generosity and volunteer spirit. Father Friedman was a long time priest for the parish. Shortly after WWI he convinced a Luxembourgian immigrant, Peter Koos, Sr. to buy a canopy for the annual Corpus Christi procession, in return he told Peter that his boys could be the bearers of the canopy as long as they were willing. Peter accepted the offer and went all out, he purchased a top-of-the-line beautiful canopy or baldachin supported by four processional poles, the canopy itself was made of a white sturdy brocade material with gold threads and shimmering gold fringes hanging around the perimeter.

The baldachin was not light in weight, it required strong individuals to balance, carry and stand with the structure, especially if the day was breezy. Donned with suits and white gloves, the initial carriers were four of Peter's sons; Peter M., Nicky, Louis and William. The procession was led by first, second and third grade girls, students at Holy Rosary. They wore white dresses, tossing fragrant peony flower petals from their baskets as they walked. Throughout the years, Peter's young granddaughters all had opportunities to be among the young flower girls in the procession.

As the years passed, Nicky's health began to fail and carrying the baldachin had become too strenuous, his son Irvin took his father's place. This Koos tradition lasted over twenty years; it came to an end a few years after the departure of Father Loosbrook. The new resident priest had a vision for his own traditions and the parish purchased an inexpensive canopy that only required two bearers selected by the priest. This marked the end of the Koos brothers' prominence in the Corpus Christi procession. At this parish, the Corpus Christi procession continued until the 1960's when the tradition was abandoned after the arrival of yet another new priest.

1917

Gerken Brothers

Dyersville, Iowa

The brothers Leo and Rudolph Gerken, were sons of William Gerken and Mary Elizabeth Sudmeyer. They were second cousins to Mary (Mullenkamp) Stuntebeck.

Rev. Leo Michael Gerken was born in Dyersville, Iowa on April 5, 1885. He was ordained in Baltimore in 1919 and served at parishes clustered near his home including Dyersville where his first Mass was said, and other northeastern Iowa communities of Cascade, Independence and Oelwein.

Leo's brother Archbishop Rudolph A Gerken was two years younger, born March 7, 1887, and was ordained in Texas in 1917. A mere ten years later he was named bishop of a newly created Amarillo Diocese; at forty years of age. He was the youngest bishop in the United States.

In 1933 Bishop Gerken was named Archbishop of Santa Fe, New Mexico. One of his accomplishments during this time was the establishment of Cristo Rey Catholic Church in Santa Fe, New Mexico around 1937. This church is the largest adobe church in the United States, and one of the largest in the world. It is considered an architectural masterpiece.

TODAY'S VOLUNTEERS

The Midwest is long past the need for missionaries to help establish community parishes. Parishes have been long active and now are struggling to find enough priests to staff the numerous small parishes. Many churches our ancestors worked hard to build have now closed due to financial or staffing shortages. Locals with a closed church within walking distance are now required to drive or find transportation to more distant churches.

Volunteers now focus on education and hunger outside the boundaries of their religious communities. Volunteerism has become an integral part of many religious organizations, and their generosity is isn't limited to parish members. Even the volunteers at major parish events may be from outside the parish or outside the particular religion of the parish. While our ancestors were concerned about building churches for the local worshipers, their descendants are now handling food drives and fund raising activities from these churches to help others in need.

Rev. Flammang, his mother Elizabeth and sister Maggie

Rev. John Michael Flammang

Holy Rosary Cemetery - Land Donated by Koos Family

Holy Rosary Catholic Church - La Motte, Iowa

Chapter 6
Military Service

It's a sad fact of human history; all generations of our civilization have in some way been affected by war. Family history researchers with Luxembourg ancestry undoubtedly have distant cousins that fought as part of Napoleon's army. In this case, numbered among Napoleon's army are Nicholas, an older brother of Mathias Manders Sr. as well as a distant ancestor of Peter Koos. Germany and Russia's armies included many Luxembourgers as well. If we step back far enough, even the Romans were marching through what is now Luxembourg and Germany.

The first American conflict experienced by many of the ancestors on these pages was the Civil War. As the war began, people on both sides felt it would be over quickly and of course each side saw themselves as the victor. Then the conflict began to drag on; quotas, draft ages and enlistment periods changed. Initially, each state was issued a quota and the states in turn distributed the quota among their counties. If volunteers didn't fill the quota, the shortfall was filled by conscription, the draft method wasn't consistent across the country, different states, and even different counties used different guidelines. Some communities would actually target the poor, drafting them into service, while other communities utilized a random selection. Random selection had its drawbacks too. Once drafted, the wealthier men had an option of paying a substitute to take their place. Initially the draft age ranged from 18 to 35. As the war continued, in 1863, the upper limit jumped to age 45. The Union soldiers earned a whopping $13 per month, which came to $156 for a year's worth of service.

Artillery units were smaller and in general didn't work as a fighting unit. These units broke off in smaller groups to provide support to infantry and cavalry units. Peter Manders of Iowa and William Zahner of Indiana were members of artillery units; they were better armed, carried more dependable equipment and customarily had top of the line horses. Because of this, they could break off and move quickly to provide support for fellow soldiers.

Infantrymen or "foot-soldiers" made up the bulk of Civil War soldiers;

these soldiers included Peter Schartz, Michael Manders and John Peter Manders. Infantry soldiers carried all their personal equipment, supplies and extra clothing with them, all together their burden could exceed fifty pounds. They were issued a belt that carried everything from a lined cartridge box with 40 cartridges to a cleaning kit along with a bayonet to attach to the end of their rifle or musket. In addition, they carried a canteen for water, a knapsack that presumably included a tin cup for coffee, a plate, utensils, blanket and in a perfect world, extra clothing. Their pockets were weighed down with an additional 20 to 40 cartridges.

A sampling of familiar names included in U. S. Civil War Draft Registration records for Union Soldiers in Jackson County, Iowa included Michael Hoffmann, Henry Banks, John Peter Manders, John Herrig, William Herrig, Peter Manders, and Mathias Herrig.

1812

Nicholas Manders

Napoleon's Army.

Napoleon's soldiers weren't limited to the French, many Luxembourgers were enumerated on Napoleon's rolls. His foot soldiers were mostly young working class men. Farmers were Napoleon's favorites since they were strong, resilient and could march forever.

Nicholas Manders was born March 27, 1793 to Nicholas Manders and Magdalena Capesius, he was three years older than his brother Mathias, Sr.

His service lists his birth date as March 27, 1793 and his place of birth Sandweiler, he served in the 24th Regiment of an infantry unit from 1812 to 1814, dates matching Napoleon's Russian Campaign, a brutal conflict which began June 24, 1812 with over a half million soldiers made up of Austrians, Prussians, Polish and French.

As the campaign began, Napoleon was surprised by the Russian tactic of burning their own lands as they retreated. The Russian goal was to starve the French Army, it didn't matter that their own people were starving in the process. After the bloodiest day of the campaign, Napoleon's Army arrived in Moscow which to his dismay had been evacuated. Between the bitter cold and lack of supplies the Grand Army returned to France after less than six months in Russia and having suffered casualties of 380,000.[64]

One would wonder if Nicholas survived. The odds aren't good, but his service date continued from 1812 to 1814, making it appear that he did survive the French Invasion of Russia and continued to serve in Napoleon's Army.

[64] The Wordsworth Pocket Encyclopedia, p. 17, Hertfordshire 1993.

Johannes Heinrich Gerken
Napoleon's Army

Johannes Heinrich Gerken, born October 4, 1773 was born in Hegensdorf, Germany and is another ancestor with a link to Napoleon's army and the Russian campaign. His name wasn't found on a brittle faded historical roster, instead, it was a family story passed down through the generations, and possibly expanded upon with time.

The Coat-of-Arms of Johannes Heinrich's great grandson Rudolph A. Gerken, the Archbishop of Santa Fe, New Mexico relays the family story passed along about his service with Napoleon. The story says Johannes was a member of Napoleon's personal bodyguard during the Russian expedition, that he was one of the lucky survivors returning from Russia. "Years after his death when his home was torn down workers found a box of personal effects and records that had been cached among the brick and stone of the chimney. In this box were found a document declaring Mr. Gerken's honorable discharge from Napoleon's army, and a soldier's chevron or decoration bearing the emblem of a bee."[65]

A Gerken family researcher, Tom Larson, doubts the validity of the story for several reasons. The soldier would have been almost forty years old, in addition, he was married with children, and it would be unlikely Napoleon had a Prussian in his personal service. That doesn't mean the discharge papers weren't valid from an earlier conflict.

1849
Mathias Manders
Luxembourg Militia

When Mathias Manders, Sr. obtained the passport to bring his family to America, one of his children was excluded from the names on the document. That individual was Mathias, Jr., a young man that was enrolled in the local required military service. Luxembourg Military history in the early 1840's specifies a five year military service length consisting of one full year followed by three months during each of the next four years. Then in 1846 there was a 20% increase in the size of Luxembourg's militia.

To a nineteen year old, four or five years is a long time to be separated from your loved ones. When the time came for the Manders family to board the ship, Mathias, Jr. was among the passengers. The details become a more apparent when reading an 1851 Luxembourg government publication of legislation and administrative announcements. From the

[65] Dyersville: Its History and Its People, by Rev. Arthur A. Halbach, 1939, page 289.

translation it appears Mathias had served his first year of service, having been called up in 1849. As the militia is determining the number of additional people required for the 1851 militia we have this notice translated from German "As replacement for Mathias Manders, liable for militia service in the 1849 call-up, stricken from the roll as a deserter."

Mathias' choice of leaving was a logical decision, he no longer had a home in Sandweiler, nowhere to live for the nine months each of the next three or four years when he would not be serving in the military. By joining his family on the voyage to America he could carry on with his life rather than put it on hold for the next three or four years.

1861

Peter Schartz

Civil War, Union Army

On November 29, 1861 Peter Schartz volunteered for the Union Army, he joined the 58th Illinois Infantry. Peter's residence was recorded as Cook County, Illinois and initially they enrolled him with the name of Schultz. It was finally corrected to Schartz when his pension application was processed.

Peter, a slightly built, mild mannered farmer had become a private in a regiment that was ill equipped to fight a war. The regiment left Illinois without training and was armed with defective weaponry cast off by other regiments. Additionally, security procedures didn't allow evening campfires and on more than one occasion it was documented where the regiment went without food rations for up to 48 hours. In spite of their limitations, the 58th Regiment had remarkable success during their first months of service. This luck however was short lived. A few hazardous months after volunteering, April 6, 1862; Peter was captured with most of his regiment at the Battle of Shiloh in Tennessee.

For the first ten days the prisoners were held in Corinth, Tennessee. On April 16, 1862 they were moved to a cotton warehouse in Montgomery Alabama where conditions were unquestionably deplorable. Many prisoners died from malnutrition and inadequate medical care. Water was so scarce the prisoners dug their own well in a darkened corner of the facility and sanitary conditions were non-existent.

On May 15, 1862, the 130 surviving prisoners were 'paroled' or released with restrictions and sent north. From Montgomery they traveled to Chattanooga where they took a train to St. Louis, arriving at their destination, Benton Barracks a week later. According to the Missouri Civil War Museum in St. Louis, "Benton Barracks included an encampment for paroled Federal prisoners released from the Confederacy. These paroled prisoners were released by Confederate authorities on the condition they would not bear arms against Southern forces until the expiration of parole." Peter spent three months at the Benton location and re-joined his regiment on August 18, 1862.

It is believed that the parole system prolonged the war since it enabled a continuous influx of soldiers for both sides; the rules were complex and seldom followed. When the parole system was abandoned, camps such as Andersonville prison became more common, with a scarcity of food for their own soldiers, feeding prisoners was certainly not a priority.

Peter was a dedicated soldier, he didn't have a wife waiting for him at home and he believed in the cause. On January 1, 1864 he re-enlisted for two more years.

On Saturday, April 8, 1865, along with thousands of other soldiers, they were directed to take control of Alabama's Spanish Fort. "For several hours the roar of artillery was one of the most awful I have ever heard, with the additional vociferations of 20,000 men."[66] This continued into the night until about two in the morning, when Spanish Fort had surrendered to the Union. There was little time for the soldiers to rest, for just hours after the capture of Spanish Fort the orders were given to attack neighboring Fort Blakely. Peter and his fellow soldiers were again preparing for battle.

One of the last major battles of the Civil War was The Battle of Fort Blakely, near Mobile, Alabama. On April 9, 1865 Major General Canby was preparing the Union troops for a general assault. As scheduled, at 6:00 A.M. 16,000 Union soldiers emerged from their trenches and stormed the Confederate soldiers. Soldiers at the front of the line included the 58th Illinois, whose job was to make way for the soldiers behind them, many were killed and injured as they charged toward the enemy over a third of a mile, unshielded, with over 1500 rifles attempting to shoot them down as they moved forward. "Each man must climb and clamber for himself, and that over a distance of nearly seven hundred yards through maize's of matted timber, which really seemed insurmountable."[67] An hour later Fort Blakely was in the hands of the Union soldiers. Though Peter had been seriously wounded during the attack, he was thankful to be alive.

After a month long hospitalization, Peter rejoined his regiment in May 16, 1865 but three months later August 13, 1865 he was sent to the post hospital "sick and wounded . . . nature of sickness and location of wound not stated". Poor initial care and lack of supplies to keep a wound clean presumably lead to infection and the second hospitalization. Peter

[66] From the Albany Evening Journal, Albany, New York, Tuesday, April 18, 1865 via Cincinnati, Monday, April 17.

[67] Excerpt from an in-depth newspaper article from the Milwaukee Sentinel, Milwaukee, Wisconsin on Thursday April 27, 1865, signed by Y. S. Special Correspondent of the Cincinnati Gazette.

remained hospitalized at least through October possibly December of 1865. After that point he was on detached service and remained in the Montgomery area until February 28, 1866 when he was described as separated from his regiment. Peter traveled home on a stretcher weighing less than 70 pounds.

Although his recovery was amazing, the effects of his injuries remained. His condition was not discussed by family, however, after his death a short article in the Waterloo Dispatch described him as crippled.

Peter applied for and received an Invalid Pension on January 31, 1882, after his death his wife applied for and received a Widow's Pension on August 26, 1901.

1861
Peter Manders
Civil War, Union Army

Three sons of Mathias Manders, Sr. and Elizabeth Hengen were soldiers in the Civil War creating four long years of stress and worry for a close and caring family. Of the 2.75 million soldiers in this war, over 22.5% became casualties, and experts feel the casualty number has been vastly understated. The Manders soldiers beat the odds, all three returned home to their families.

The first of the brothers to join was Peter, the oldest son, born December 29, 1825; he was a former stone mason, now a farmer by occupation. Peter enlisted September 16, 1861 at the age of thirty-five, leaving behind his wife Rosalie (Capesius) and three children, one being an infant. Peter served for one enlistment period; he was a member of the Third Independent Battery, Iowa Light Artillery, nicknamed "Dubuque Battery". Peter was mustered out December 13, 1863 at Jackson County.

Peter's unit was responsible for providing support for infantry and cavalry units, equipment included howitzers as well as various cannons and large caliber weapons. On March 7th and 8th of 1862 they were in Arkansas in a memorable battle referred to as Pea Ridge. This was an unusual battle in that the Confederate troops far outnumbered the Union troops. Heavy losses were taken on both sides but the Union soldiers were able to drive back the Confederates and take control of the battlefield. Captain Hayden describes the losses at Pea Ridge, "Our loss is two men killed and 17 wounded. We lost 23 horses killed and three disabled. Three of our guns and one limber were captured by the enemy."[68] There were a total of 290 men enrolled in the Third Iowa Battery. Incredibly only three

---

[68] The Report of Captain Mortimor M. Hayden, 3rd Independent Battery Iowa Light artillery, Sugar Creek, Ark. March 9, 1862.

died of wounds, disease however took an additional thirty-four men.

1862
Michael Manders
Minnesota Indian War and Civil War, Union Army

On Sunday August 17, 1862, Chief Little Crow and the Sioux War Council were gathered to discuss broken treaties, starving families and attacking the whites to rid the Sioux hunting grounds of the settlers. About the same time that day, five young Dakota Indians were on a hunting trip in Meeker County, Minnesota. Their trip began with a quantity of "fire water" which lead to boasts, dares and skepticism. The day ended in the killing of five white settlers.

It was also on August 17, 1862 that Michael Manders, age 28, enlisted in Company K, 6th Regiment of the Minnesota Infantry, he was mustered in at Fort Snelling. The day after his enlistment, August 18th, the Indian uprising began. Stories of horror spread like wildfire, stories included the discovery of mangled bodies of women and children brutally murdered with guns and hatchets. Colonel Henry Sibley was ordered to proceed to Fort Ridgely with four companies of raw and undisciplined recruits. Many of the men were on foot and travel was slow. The forces did not arrive at Fort Ridgely until August 28th, 1862.

Immediately, 6th Regiment Infantry volunteers along with mounted men " . . . aggregating in all, a force of over one hundred and fifty men, were sent in advance of the main army to protect the settlements from further devastation, and at the same time collect and bury the dead yet lying on the field of the recent slaughter."[69] Michael was among the men sent to carry out this gruesome task.

The burial party split into two groups, one scouting the north side of the Minnesota River and the other group the south side, they buried between 50 and 60 settlers.

On September 1st they all camped on the north side of the river at Birch Coulee, having seen few Indians during their trek, " . . . no immediate fears of Indians were apprehended; yet at half-past four o'clock on the morning of the second of September, one of the guards shouted "Indians!" Instantly thereafter a shower of bullets was poured into the encampment. A most fearful and terrible battle ensued, and for the numbers engaged, the most bloody of any in which our forces had been engaged during the war. The loss of men in proportion to those engaged was extremely large; twenty-three were killed outright, or mortally wounded, and forty-five so severely wounded as to require surgical aid, while scarce a man remained whose

[69] History of the Minnesota Valley by Charles S. Bryant, 1882.

dress had not been pierced by the enemies' bullets."[70] The welcome arrival of Colonel Sibley with the main battery of troops scattered the attackers and prevented the death toll from climbing much higher.

Michael, along with his fellow survivors, were glad to be alive. Although exhausted after a thirty-one hour siege with no rest, no food and no water. Days later, the recruits were back to their duty of protecting the fleeing settlers while Colonel Sibley tried working with Little Crow for the return of hostages. His efforts were futile.

Three weeks later on September 23 the third, sixth and seventh Minnesota Regiments marched against the Sioux and the battle of Wood Lake ensued. The soldiers were prepared for this engagement and the results favored Colonel Sibley's men, and the Sioux had suffered heavy losses. Because of the campaign's success Henry Sibley was promoted to Brigadier General.

Michael spent almost two years fighting the uprisings of the Dakota. Finally in June 1864, with the Minnesota problems under control, the regiment joined the Union efforts in the Civil War and moved south to Helena, Arkansas. Here, the malarial infested swamps proved more disabling than battle. The men had built up no resistance to fight the disease, and over 80% of them contracted malaria.

Private Manders, being a good soldier and a dependable leader, was promoted to Corporal while they were in Helena. Their assignments were varied; the soldiers transported prisoners and carried out traitor executions. One of these executions was Morgan Utz, a 23 year old Missourian who was caught transporting a wagon load of medical supplies to the Confederate army. He was charged with being a spy, recruiting men for the rebel army and carrying correspondence to the rebels. He was found guilty on December 24, 1864 and on December 26th, Michael and several other soldiers were assigned to carry out the hanging which took place at the Gratiot Street Prison in Saint Louis.

Soon after the hanging the Regiment began making their way south. In April of 1865 they were part of the capture of Spanish Fort and Fort Blakely. Michael was mustered out August 19, 1865 at Fort Snelling, Minnesota.

"While in the South, he became a good friend of Antonius A. Davis, a negro. Antonius came to Freeburg to visit several times. Mr. Manders said, "A negro is just as good as a white man . . ."[71]

Michael applied for an Invalid pension July 21, 1890, and on November 19, 1915 his wife Anna applied for and received a widow's pension.

---

[70] Ibid.

[71] Minnesota Lake Tribune, Our Civil War Veterans, Stories retrieved from the archives.

1862

Judge Anton Yerger

Civil War, Missouri, Union Army

Although today this is contrary to policy, during the Civil War family members often wanted to serve together, resulting in several family members serving in the same regiment. Such is the case with two of Francis Xavier Riebold's brothers-in-law and a nephew.

Judge Anton Yerger was Captain of Company F, 88th E. M. M. commonly known as Yerger's Jefferson County E. M. M. (Enrolled Missouri Militia) He was commissioned September 11, 1862, and promoted to lieutenant-colonel September 29, 1864. Other members of Company F included brother-in-law Ambrose Friedmann, and Captain Yerger's step son Leo Kohler.

Yerger's Jefferson County E. M. M. was not a combat regiment. Their terms of service were short, and they remained within the boundaries of Jefferson County. Commonly, men in these positions were older and duties consisted mostly of guarding buildings, bridges and supplies. Their exposure to danger, as well as their weaponry, was limited.

1862?

William Zahner

Civil War, Union Army

Considering the fact that William Zahner's time in America to this point had been anything but a smooth ride, going off to war for his new country enabled him to spend time away from his stepfather. According to William's obituary, "Although living in a southern state, young Zahner drove an ammunition wagon for the union forces in the Civil War."[72] He was living in Southern Indiana at the time, was a hard worker and had basically been on his own since a young age.

According to his granddaughter, Frances (Mulligan) Krogman, William was responsible for transporting a small canon. Combine this with transporting ammunition as noted in his obituary, would have placed him in charge of an artillery wagon. This position was not only difficult and time consuming, it also carried heavy responsibilities.

An artillery wagon that was fully equipped required 4 to 6 horses due to the weight it carried. In addition to carrying the weapon which traveled on two wheels, there was a limber attached, also two wheels. When fully loaded it carried three chests of ammunition and the driver's seat was the

[72] From family memorabilia, a Kansas City Times newspaper clipping.

front ammo chest. The driver, William was responsible for the artillery, the ammunition, keeping the wagon in working condition as well as caring for the horses. During battle, horses were moved to the back of the lines and the artillery section of the wagon was separated from the ammunition chests. The gun was positioned at the front of the line while the ammunition was kept several yards behind, ideally behind the protection of a berm, boulders or trees.

Finally, and a very important part of his job, he was responsible for keeping the wagon out of the hands of the enemy. Battles were scored not only by deaths and injuries to each side, but also by weapons and equipment that were gained or lost. His job included a very limited amount of down time.

1864

John Peter Manders

Civil War, Union Army

The year after Peter's return, his brother John Peter (J.P.) Manders, also a former stone mason, now a farmer, enlisted as a private in Company I of the 8th Iowa Infantry. He was mustered in at Clinton, Iowa on November 29, 1864. J. P. was thirty-six years of age when he went off to war, leaving his 160 acre farm, a pregnant wife and three small children.

Early in March of 1865 the regiment traveled to Orleans, from there they moved on to set up camp in Mobile Bay, then proceeding with the assault on Spanish Fort. A few days into the engagement, on March 28, 1865 J. P. was on picket duty and was shot in his hand. The injury was serious and J. P. was hospitalized until the end of the war.

Picket duty was a dangerous assignment where the soldiers were protecting the encampment from a sneak attack. Soldiers on picket duty were the first line of defense, consequently the first to be captured, wounded or killed.

The Eighth Iowa Infantry found itself in the midst of heavy fire on multiple occasions; in the end, they were instrumental in the taking of Spanish Fort.

During the war, the 8th Iowa Infantry Regiment had an enrollment of 1,589 men. 276 died of wounds or disease and 228 soldiers were wounded. Combined deaths and injuries for this regiments covered almost one third of the enlistment.

J. P. was mustered out August 15, 1865. The first years after the war held disappointment for many of the injured soldiers. They had been given to understand, if they didn't return to 100% of their original self, a pension was in their future. J. P. applied for an Invalid Pension March 17, 1866, the outcome was disappointing when the application was rejected, as were many of the early applications for less serious disabilities. He was, however, approved after a later application for he is included with the 1883 pensioners, his pension amounted to $3.00 per month due to his wounded right thumb.[73]

There is an interesting fact concerning the Battle of Spanish Fort in Alabama. The regiments of Peter Schartz, John Peter Manders and Michael Manders were all three involved in the battle and subsequent victory at Spanish Fort. There were over 15,000 soldiers from the Union Army so the three men weren't fighting shoulder to shoulder, but they each had a role in the final result.

1918

Peter M. Koos

World War I, France

Peter was drafted into the American Expeditionary Force during World War I. It was winter-time, February of 1918. The day before departure, the young men were given a special farewell "send-off" for which Maquoketa was well known. The festivities included a dance, movie and refreshments all free for the new soldiers. The next morning the local citizens and families of the recruits gathered to say goodbye.

A fire at the National Personnel Records Center on July 12, 1973 destroyed over fifteen million Military Personnel Files, among them were Peter's. This keeps us from learning the specifics of his service record such as illness, injury and assignments during specific battles. However, his battalion records along with information he shared, allow us to learn the generalities.

Peter was assigned to the 54th Engineer Battalion, training was completed at Camp Dodge, near Des Moines. Peter's transport to Europe was the S. S. Rhode Island, a twelve year old battleship that performed anti-submarine duties during the war.

Many of the A.E.F. units in Europe, especially the early ones, had little training and were poorly equipped. Weaponry wasn't top of the line, there was rarely extra clothing to change into when their uniform or socks became wet, even their food rations didn't arrive in a timely manner. Most soldiers carried an ammo belt, a canteen and a knapsack with a mess kit, shaving and medical supplies, a short-handled trenching shovel, wire cutters and extra clothing, also a rifle and maybe a .45 caliber pistol. They carried all this gear wherever they went.

The 54th Engineer Battalion was a combat support unit; they were sent to France where they were stationed east of Paris near the German border.

[73] Pension certificate number 90,559, post office location Saint Donatus, Iowa.

After arriving at their destination, Peter was partnered with a French soldier to perform what can best be described as scavenger missions. Peter spoke English and German while the Frenchman spoke French and German, they could communicate with each other as well as the French and Germans. This proved to be an advantage when they were sent on clandestine missions to appropriate food, medical supplies, machine parts or equipment. In the end, these soldiers with little training and equipment may actually have had an advantage. It was the well trained well equipped soldiers that were sent to the front lines. As scanty as the food rations were for the A. E. F. their European counterparts, and the enemy, operated with even smaller and less appetizing allowances. The A. E. F. rations included canned beef, canned peas and beans and sometimes pork & beans. The biggest problem for the A. E. F. was effective distribution. The war interfered with supply routes and it wasn't always easy to predict where the soldiers would be. When the supply delivery was delayed, Peter and his French counterpart were the salvation for their unit.

The A. E. F. soldiers survived in wretched conditions. Trenches were muddy, changes of clothing were rare and disease was rampant. Lack of sanitation allowed body lice to multiply unrestrained. In addition to the term "cooties" the soldiers had a variety of apt nicknames for the condition, "galloping freckles" being one of the more picturesque.

Not helping the situation, in France, where Peter's unit was stationed, the soldiers' non-combat time was often spent in rural and farming areas with the local farmers. They spent their time in local barns where unsanitary conditions exposed the unsuspecting soldiers to even more diarrhea, body lice and a variety of fevers. The soldiers with a farming background were surprised at the lack of sanitation on the local farms. The animals either lived in their own filth, or if an effort had been made to clean the area, waste was often piled outside the home rather than spread in a pasture or moved away from the living area. The French didn't have the advantage of wide open spaces the American farm boys grew up with.

There were few drugs and medicines to combat the many diseases that spread freely among the soldiers. Few precautions were taken; the soldiers lived in close quarters and food was often cooked in unsanitary conditions sometimes by soldiers who were ill themselves. Disease and illness far exceeded combat injuries when it came to incapacitating or causing the death of a soldier. In addition to measles, mumps, diphtheria and epidemic diarrhea we learn from the Surgeon General's report:

"The other epidemic and one which was much more serious as a cause of non-effectiveness, and as the case of the greatest mortality in the American Expeditionary Forces was that of influenza, which was and continued to be part of a pandemic of the disease which has within the past year affected all parts of the world. The disease in a mild form prevailed from the middle of April until the middle of July without interfering materially with the activities of the American Expeditionary Forces. There was much increase in non-effectiveness for a week or so while the disease swept through a command, but the recoveries were prompt, complications rarely occurred, and there were very few deaths from the primary infection or from complications."[74]

By October of 1918 the 54th Engineer Battalion was reorganized and became the 20th Engineer Regiment, Peter was a member of the 44th Company. The A. E. F. were among the first to arrive in Europe and many of the soldiers left long after the war was over. Peter's service was complete on July 7, 1919 when he left Newport News, Virginia. From there he sent his sister Florence a quick postcard and another postcard from Cincinnati, Ohio two days later while waiting for the train that would transport him home.

After leaving the A.E.F. Peter was offered an engineering job but his father convinced him there would be more opportunity by staying at home and working on the farm. Finally after three weeks of contemplation, Peter made the decision to turn down the engineering job and remain in Iowa.

1918

Frederick A. Krogman

Frederick Albert Krogman was born March 5, 1895 in Petersburg, Iowa. He was the son of Franz Heinrich Krogmann and Caroline Catharine Kramer. Fred entered the service May 27, 1918 and went to Camp Dodge, Iowa, for training. This was the same training camp Peter Koos was sent to and perhaps they crossed paths during their training. Fred was a Corporal in the 88th Division, Company G, 352nd Infantry. He died of disease in Héricourt, Haute-Saône, Franche-Comté, France on October 8, 1918 and is buried at St. Mary's Catholic Cemetery in New Hampton, Iowa.

* * *

NO END IN SIGHT.

Wars have been around a long time with no end in sight. Of our known ancestors, none were here for the War of 1812 or prior. Although WWII isn't covered in this work there were losses and service that should be mentioned.

Alvin Haiar of Jackson County, Iowa, was killed April 6, 1845 in Okinawa, Japan, leaving behind his wife Viola and two children.

---

[74] Report of the Surgeon General, U.S. Army To The Secretary of War 1919, Vol. 1, Washing Government Printing Office.

Donald Leroy Conarty of Nebraska was a widower; he was killed March 24, 1944 leaving behind two daughters.

Frank P. Lanners was the first overseas war fatality to befall Remsen, Iowa. Frank was an only child, leaving behind grieving parents.

World War II soldiers that lived to see their families again include Alve Flammang of Saint Donatus, Iowa; Joseph F. Krogman of Remsen, Iowa; James Flammang of Saint Donatus, Iowa; Nicholas Koos, La Motte, Iowa; Karl William Mulligan of Kansas City, Missouri; and Kenneth Adrian, Cassville, Wisconsin, who also served in Korea.

Following is a touching Civil War Poem written by Kate Putnam Osgood (1841-1910), first published in Harper's New Monthly Magazine in 1865. This is a poem about a farmer whose three sons joined the Union Army and went off to war.

DRIVING HOME THE COWS.

OUT of the clover and Blue-eyed grass,
He turned them into the river-lane;
One after another he let them pass,
Then fastened the meadow bars again.

Under the willows and over the hill,
He patiently followed their sober pace;
The merry whistle for once was still,
And something shadowed the sunny face.

Only a boy! And his father had said
He never could let his youngest go!
Two already were lying dead,
Under the feet of the trampling foe.

But after the evening work was done,
And the frogs were loud in the meadow-swamp,
Over his shoulder he slung his gun
And stealthily followed the foot-path damp.

Across the clover and through the wheat,
With resolute heart and purpose grim,
Though cold was the dew on his hurrying feet,
And the blind bats flitting startled him.

Thrice since then had the lanes been white,
    And the orchards sweet with apple-bloom;
And now, when the cows came back at night,
    The feeble father drove them home.

For news had come to the lonely farm
    That three were lying where two had lain;
And the old man's tremulous, palsied arm
    Could never lean on a son's again.

The summer day grew cool and late;
    He went for the cows when the work was done;
But down the lane, as he opened the gate,
    He saw them coming, one by one.

Brindle, Ebony, Speckle and Bess,
    Shaking their horns in the evening wind;
Cropping the buttercups out of the grass -
    But who was it following close behind?

Loosely swang in the idle air
    The empty sleeve of army blue;
And worn and pale, from the crisping hair,
    Looked out a face that the father knew;

For Southern prisons will sometimes yawn,
    And yield their dead unto life again;
And the day that comes with a cloudy dawn
    In golden glory at last may wane.

The great tears sprang to their meeting eyes;
    For the heart must speak when the lips are dumb,
And under the silent evening skies
    Together they followed the cattle home.

Printed in Harpers' Magazine[75]

---

[75] Poetry, Lyrical, Narrative and Satirical, of the Civil War, edited by Richard Grant White, The American News Company, New York, 1866.

Left - John Peter Manders. **Right - Michael Manders**

Peter Michael Koos (WWI)

WWI - New arrivals at Camp Dodge, Iowa.

The U.S.S. Rhode Island. Peter Koos's WWI ocean transporation.

Chapter 7

Daily Life

The Homestead

Immigrants arrived in America with varied traditions and customs. One old country practice that was for the most part abandoned by the newcomers was the use of a single building for living, crop storage and livestock or a combination house and barn. For them, it made sense to build a house-barn combo. First, building costs were reduced. Another reason, during the winter livestock shared their heat, and maybe most importantly, with limited land available they couldn't afford to squander any acreage that could be used to grow crops. The proximity to the animals also allowed the farmer to hear sounds of trouble, especially during birthing season. The practice of a single building began to fade away in the 19th century and the new immigrants to America were taking the opposite approach.

Jackson County, Iowa, with an abundance of trees and streams, was a dream-come-true for immigrants with plans of building a homestead.

The early settlers started small, first came the log cabin, then a small barn, and to protect the animals from the elements a lean-to was added. After their five year homesteading requirement was fulfilled, a new house was often the next construction project. Later in the nineteenth century large barns were constructed. They generally included a lower level for livestock and upper level for crop storage. Building the barn into a hill provided easy access to the upper level for hay and grains, equipped with a chute to conveniently drop feed to the animals below. The lower level had easy access for cows and other livestock to enter.

Barn raisings became common Midwestern social events later in the nineteenth century. The men erected the barn while the women prepared a feast, much like threshing. This is a tradition is still in use today by the Amish.

During this time-period, a chicken coop soon followed the house and barn. It was built closer to the home, it was a small structure, customarily with a slant roof, a roost and a couple rows of wooden nest boxes lined with straw or dried grass. Many chickens selected a favorite "nest" in which to lay their eggs. The eggs were collected twice each day, during the morning and evening chores. Chickens were easy to care for, they needed plenty of water but were not picky eaters. They happily ate grass, roots, berries and grains along with a few things we wouldn't even consider a food option. During the winter they enjoyed table scraps, including egg shells. Beginning in the later 19th century farmers bought oyster shell to feed their chickens for stronger egg shells and to assist in replacing calcium in the aging hens.

By the early twentieth century, once the barn became too crowded to store all the animals, crops and equipment, there was little hesitation before construction continued. Popular additions included a shed to protect farm equipment from the elements, an enclosure for pigs or sheep, and of course, a corn crib.

* * *

Some communities were not so quick to give in to progress. A 1929 news article headlined "Village Untouched by the Age of Jazz" says "St. Donatus still is "Old World" Territory; Has Not One Filling Station.

ST. DONATUS, Iowa, July 27.-In eastern Iowa, some 14 miles from Dubuque, there remains today a bit of "Old Europe."

In this village, where prohibition isn't a question because they don't have much of it and where the wheels of progress have not ground away natures's beauty, live 50 or 60 Luxemburgers whose forebears came to this country 50 years ago.

There are no railroads, no paved roads, no jumble of gasoline stations and road houses in St. Donatus.

"Old Dobbin" methods still hold sway in the town, but one will search far before he finds a group of persons living together in the contented atomosphere which surrounds the historic ground.

Few modern architects could match the craftsmanship which was employed in erecting the buildings. They are of heavy stone, covered with smooth cinder stucco composition. The proportions of their facades and the designs formed by perfectly arranged doors and windows give the buildings a remarkable degree of unity.

Only one change has come over the village since it was founded in 1849. That is the name by which the town is known.

Tete des Morts was the name of this Catholic settlement in the early days. The name, it is said, had its origin following a battle of two Indian tribes."

Shelter

Eastern Iowa's first settlers arrived to find land covered with trees, wildlife and brush. Preparing the land for planting the first crop was an extremely labor intensive process, but the first step of cutting down trees also provided raw materials for building their first shelter.

Finding the perfect spot for the cabin was dependent upon several factors. Among them were how level the plot was, exposure to water runoff and access to water. Log cabins were customarily built facing south to take advantage of the warmth of the sun shining through the open front door. If a compass wasn't handy, a pocket watch would assist the settler in aligning his new home.

To provide a solid base, large rocks or small boulders were embedded in the ground at the cabins four corners and the front door. The dimensions of log cabins were not random lengths of logs, they were a variation of two foot lengths, common sizes included 10 x 12 and 12 x 12. The size of the cabin was no larger than many living rooms are today. A separate measuring tool wasn't needed since the axe not only provided a means for chopping down trees, the handles of most axes also served as a two foot measuring tool.

If there were three or four men available, a cabin could be erected in a few days. If winter wasn't imminent, more time was invested. Logs were hewed with a broad axe, straight logs of roughly the same circumference were required for the cabin overall. Logs with the largest girth were used for the first layers, smaller ones as the layers multiplied. Seven to ten layers of logs completed the main floor area.

Nails were not required to hold the structure together, besides they were a luxury item with a hefty price tag. The ends of each log were notched and fitted much like Lincoln Logs. With an investment of sweat and a good measuring tool the settler could build a windproof shelter that provided a comfortable haven from winter. After the logs were in place the open cracks were filled with clay, sometimes a mud-straw mixture, wood chips, whatever was readily available, even corn cobs. A variety of materials were easily accessible in Jackson County for chinking the cabin; a mixture of clay, lime and water made a durable water resistant filler.

If a window was included, most log homes were initially outfitted with greased paper windows (or greased cloth when available). Animal grease was rubbed on the paper or cloth making it water repellant and a very economical substitute for glass, especially if the cabin was a temporary home until a more spacious permanent home was erected. Purlin roofs constructed of additional logs were used when a saw mill wasn't nearby, the pitch shallow except when a loft was to be part of the structure. Some roofs included hand split shingles.

Fireplace construction in Jackson County, Iowa was not as challenging as it was in many parts of the country, even other parts of Iowa. Stones were freely available for the firebox portion of the fireplace and using a thick clay-lime mixture for chinking made for an enduring fireproof material.

The front door was the most likely part of the cabin requiring an outside purchase. Nails to hold it together, hinges and a latch to complete the front door. Families like the Nemmers' with an in-house carpenter may have fashioned wooden nails and other hardware for their front door.

Keeping the Fires Burning

As farmlands became more crowded, if your fire went out you could take a cast iron container over to the neighbor and "borrow" fire or coals. But if you were alone out in the wilderness, miles from the nearest neighbor, a tinder box was a necessity. These little tin boxes had a lid or cover, they contained a steel striker shaped to grip with your fingers, some versions were shaped like a U, others like a flat C. The box also included a chunk of flint and of course some tinder. In addition to keeping the tinder dry, the tinder box served as the container to light the tinder. Once lit the fire was moved to the fire pit.

The Kitchen

CHURNING BUTTER. Homemade butter was always a treat, it didn't require special talents or experience and fresh milk is the only ingredient required. After the cow was milked, the milk was set aside allowing the cream to rise and skimmed off the top the following morning.

My grandmother had a Dazey churn she used to make butter, although it began to collect dust after she acquired an electric butter churn. I thought the Dazey churn was more fun, but my arm often fatigued before the cream became butter and Grandma had to take over the manual task to finish the project while her electric churn sat nearby. The Dazey contraption included a glass jar with a lid that screwed on, a wooden paddle rested inside the jar and a crank on top turned the paddle, churning the cream into butter, a strong arm with good stamina was the only other requirement. Before refrigeration was an option, butter was stored in small crocks in the coolest area of the cellar, a generous amount of salt was sprinkled on the butter for preservation purposes and a cheesecloth stretched over the top.

The byproduct of churning butter was buttermilk, a sour watery liquid that was then used in making hot cakes or biscuits, during the summertime some settlers had a custom of using the liquid as a preservative. Pouring buttermilk over a crock of fresh beef or pork stored in their root cellar or cellar would help keep the meat from spoiling but this wasn't a preferred method of preserving meat for it left a unique unpleasant aftertaste. It did however work well as a meat tenderizer for tough cuts of beef.

RENDERING LARD. As with many things in life, rendering lard is a simple undertaking, IF you know how it's done. The keys to success are timing and temperature, again, easy for an expert but trial and error are required for the inexperienced.

The best lard comes from the fat of a pig; it is simply melted, strained and stored in a cool location. When melting the fat, the temperature needs to be hot enough to melt the fat but not so hot as to burn, that's where the tricky part comes in, patience is required and experience helpful.

As the fat melts, there will be little non-fat crumbs or cracklings floating in the kettle. Once all the fat is melted, the hot mixture can be strained through a cloth and the lard stored in a crock or a jar. The cracklings are set aside, stored in a cool location and used as a savory addition or flavor enhancer to a future dish. Luxembourgers used cracklings in their blood sausage, a dish that sounds nauseating but when properly prepared is a very flavorful pork sausage.

MAPLE SYRUP. Jackson County Iowa had a wonderful assortment of trees, the most valued by the pioneer woman were trees that added delight to their meals. There were black walnut trees, hickory nut trees and maple trees. The maple tree was treasured for the sweet delicacy of maple syrup it provided. Every spring the farmer or his wife trudged out to a maple or two and inserted a metal spout into a chiseled hole, a homemade wooden spout worked just as well. A wooden pail collected the sap which was then used as sap directly from the tree or more often was boiled down to syrup. (40 quarts of sap boiled down to 1 quart of syrup). The maple had long been a favorite of the Native Americans and they had the method of collection and preparation of the syrup perfected.

HERBS & FLAVORINGS. Herbs were an essential part of pioneer gardens, they were used for adding flavor to bland dishes and even to help disguise the smell of food, especially meat, that was beyond its prime. Some herb seeds and plants were brought from the home country and many common herbs such as chives, lavender and parsley were discovered growing wild on their new farmland. The local Native Americans knew the herbs well, they were aware of the properties of almost every plant that grew in their home area. Gardeners grew sage, chives, thyme, basil or savory for use in the kitchen.

Settlers also grew herbs for medicinal remedies, chamomile and mint leaves made excellent teas for an upset stomach, and the soft leaves of lambs-ear were used to cover cuts and other wounds.

PRESERVING MEAT. Salt pork was salt-cured meat that could be stored in a crock or barrel for a few weeks or months, depending on the temperature. Preparing salt pork was simply meat cut into small pieces, usually the leftover parts of the animal, layered alternately with a salt mixture or stored in a very salty brine, the prime cuts having been used while at their freshest. The brine was a mixture of salt, water, saltpeter and sometimes brown sugar, salt being the main ingredient. When it was time to include the meat in a meal, it was thoroughly washed and re-rinsed to remove as much salt as possible.

A family recipe for Meat Brine began with the words "salt to carry an egg" which would mean to add enough salt to each of two pails of water to make an egg rise to the top. Then add two tablespoons of Salt Petre, one and one half pounds of brown sugar and pepper to taste. Mix well and your brine is ready for freshly cut meat.

For those with plenty of wood available, as in Jackson County, slow smoking meat was a tastier more time consuming option with less spoilage. Smoking or drying large cuts of meat or numerous fish worked best in a smokehouse but for small pieces of meat or fish it was possible to smoke over the home's fireplace. An actual fire wasn't a requirement, just smoldering embers providing continuous heat to remove the moisture from the meat.

MEALS. Three meals per day were standard fare, especially for pioneer farmers using a lot of physical energy to perform their daily chores. Typically, meal options were based on seasonal availability. If stored properly, potatoes could be eaten anytime during the year, but peaches could only be stored a limited amount of time. 19th century Midwest farmers often had a root cellar to keep their meats and produce from spoiling.

The breakfast meal was the most standard throughout the year. A farmer's breakfast may have included a hard boiled or fried egg, bread or fried potatoes, possibly salt pork and hot cakes which had flexibility since they could be made with corn meal or flour.

For Midwesterners, the noon-time meal is still called dinner by many with an agricultural background. It is the main meal of the day and was a hearty meal where meat and potatoes were the mainstay, maybe a vegetable, with bread and possibly a fruity dessert. Hunting was a good source of meat, rabbit and wild pig were early Jackson County settler favorites, but tastiest options were the farmer's livestock. Early winter made an optimal time for slaughtering a larger animal for family use, there was little waste as long as the meat could be kept cold. The better cuts such as roasts and steaks were used before warm weather arrived and salt pork and other cured and dried meats were saved for later. The price and availability of sugar often limited sweet desserts to Sunday Dinner when the best meat, vegetables and fruits were brought out along with the "Sunday" table cloth.

Supper was eaten after the daily work and chores were completed and was a no-fuss meal. It was a quicker lighter mean than dinner, and included items like bread, garden produce or soups, possibly made from dinner leftovers.

Secluded, financially strapped early pioneers, especially during their first years in America had more corn bread than flour bread due to the fact corn was more readily available. The dried field corn was first parched with a small amount of lard over the fire, once cooled it was ground up to a course powder with a mortar and pestle. In addition to a flour substitute, the corn meal was used for corn meal mush, a convenient staple for those without a nearby store.

CORN MEAL MUSH. This was a dish anyone could prepare by using 4 parts water and one part corn meal. Water is adjusted to determine whether the consistency is like a pudding or more like a pancake. The process began by boiling the water, next, slowly stir in the corn meal, a pinch of salt and a spoon of butter or lard. Cook for three or four minutes. It can then be eaten like oatmeal or cooked until very thick, cooled and sliced. Either way, honey or syrup were welcome additions along with butter when available.

After the farmer was on a profitable path he had the option of having the local mill grind the corn for him but by that point he was also able to buy wheat flour from the mill and corn bread became an option rather than a staple.

NO MEAT AVAILABLE? Beef wasn't plentiful but squirrels were very bounteous in Iowa. Not only did their meat provide a flavorful stew for a hungry family, a trained tanner could turn the hides into hats, mittens, boot liners and other clothing as well as using leftover strips of hide as short cords for tying and binding.

SUMMER KITCHEN. Summer kitchens became popular in the late 19th century and their popularity continued into the 20th century. The structure was a small one room building with a door, a window or two, a stove and shelves. It was usually located just outside the side door of the main house.

Without air conditioning, cooking, baking and extensive summertime canning made living conditions miserable but a summer kitchen allowed them to perform the heated tasks just out the door from the main house. An added benefit of the summer kitchen, during warmer months it provided privacy for family members to take a bath, hence they were more likely to bathe. A tub of water would serve to bathe most or all of the family, beginning with the youngest and women, ending with the adult men. During the winter the bathing occurred near the stove in the main house and for many it was limited to a weekly task or for special occasions.

After electricity and modern appliances arrived in rural areas their summer kitchens turned into tool sheds and storage buildings.

WATER PAIL & DIPPER. No kitchen was complete without a water pail and dipper, early ones were made by a tinsmith and the more "modern" versions were enameled. Sometimes the dipper rested in the water, other dippers had a hook, allowing the dipper to be hung outside the pail. Every family had different habits, some drank directly from the dipper, others poured the water into their cup, the latter becoming more common as the twentieth century began. The habit sounds very unhealthy by today's standards but the practice was widespread. Not only homes, but schools and public areas also had communal drinking vessels. As evidenced by a new ordinance in 1911 Chicago, there were also public drinking cups, used much like today's drinking fountains.

Drinking Cup Outlawed.

Chicago, May 9.-Chicago physicians united today in praising the action of the council in outlawing the common drinking cup. Under the terms of the ordinance, public drinking cups must disappear by August 8.[76]

Oil Cloth

Today's version of oilcloth is just another environmental nuisance, while the real deal used by our ancestors was totally biodegradable. An oilcloth used by our great grandparents was made with a heavy linen or cotton duck cloth purchased at the local general store. If the oilcloth was made at home, the cloth was stretched over a wooden frame or laid out on the table to limit wrinkles, linseed oil was spread or brushed over the cloth which was then allowed to rest and dry for a few days and the process repeated several times.

The result was a water resistant cloth with a variety of uses. Table cloths were at the top of the list and when used for that purpose they often had a decorative design, old table cloths were re-purposed as a protective cover for a mattress, and it was always handy to have an oilcloth jacket to stay dry when working or traveling in cold rainy conditions.

Root Cellar

A root cellar was a popular method for farmers to store their vegetables such as potatoes, carrots and beets through the winter. Apples would also enjoy an extended life in a root cellar. If the home had a dry cellar, a root cellar was a convenient addition. Otherwise it was located outside near the house. Digging the root cellar into the side of a south facing sandy-soil hill provided the cellar with good drainage and protection from winter winds,

[76] Springfield Daily News, Springfield, Massachusetts, Tuesday, May 9, 1911.

giving the cellar angled walls helped prevent cave-ins and digging to a depth of 9 to 10 feet kept the produce from freezing during the winter months. A wooden frame built into the hill around the entrance with a sturdy door provided security from wildlife and protection from the elements. Before storing the vegetables, they were carefully checked for any signs of rot that would quickly spread to the entire basket.

Wash Day

Today it is easy to multi-task while doing laundry. Toss a load in the washer while making dinner, transfer to the dryer before serving dinner, and fold or hang the load after the dishes are in the dishwasher.

For our ancestors it wasn't quite that simple. Wash day was planned around the weather. Each household had their own way of handling the dreaded task, but the basics were similar from home to home. A batch or two of laundry could easily fill a day, possibly two.

PATCHING. Our forefathers and mothers were very frugal people, a frayed hem or ripped cloth were not reasons to dispose and purchase new clothing. A day or two prior to wash day, the patching and mending was handled, if the item was beyond repair there was still plenty of life remaining in the cloth. If there were similar clothes in the household the item would be saved to repair these items. Lightweight or flowery materials were set aside for quilt or rug making and as a last resort, cloth was re-purposed as an everyday handkerchief or wash cloth or rag.

A needle and thread or yarn were used for the repairs, sewing machines were a luxury most often limited to tailors and dressmakers.

Washing - - - When the actual wash day arrived, requirements included a wash tub, preferably two, lye soap and a wash board, all of which made the task much easier. Wash tubs, made by local tinsmiths, were used to heat water, as well as washing and rinsing. Half of a wooden barrel was a suitable substitute for rinsing. My grandmother had an old oval copper tub with wooden handles on each side, which was ideal for heating water on a cook stove. In an earlier day an open fire was the only option.

Water was not always plentiful or easily accessible so it was not unusual for more than one load to be washed or rinsed in the same tub of water.

Wash day begins by building a fire, then carrying water to fill the tub about half full, after the water begins to boil, laundry is added to begin the soaking process. The "clean" load is handled first and water re-used for the next load. A wooden paddle makes a good tool for agitating the laundry in the hot water. Once the water is cool enough to immerse your hands you're ready for the next tools in the process, a wash board and lye soap.

With the wash board resting in the tub in front of you, the soiled areas of the clothing are pulled up over the board and rubbed with soap, the soapy cloth then rubbed over the ridges of the wash board, re-soaped and rubbed again until clean. This was a back-breaking and time-consuming process, and anyone new to the task is sure to finish the day with painful blisters.

As each item of clothing is finished the soap is rinsed off, excess water wrung from the material and the item is dropped into the cold rinse water. After the entire batch is finished, the clothing in the rinse tub has the excess water wrung from the cloth and it's ready for drying. This makes today's method of doing a load of laundry look like child's play.

On wash day, there was always hope for a bright sunny day to take advantage of the bleaching qualities of the sun. Creativity was the name of the game, each laundress had her favorite spots for drying clothes, using anything clean, ranging from a pile of rocks or a grassy area to bushes or boards supported by barrels. A well-equipped laundress strung a rope between a two trees, but hanging the clothing under the trees reduced the bleaching effects of the sun.

Drying inside by the fire was a wintertime or rainy day alternative, however care needed to be taken not to place the drying items too near the flames or the results can be disastrous, as we see from John Mulligan's experience described below.

1901

John J. Mulligan

Vicksburg, Mississippi

As the flames spread, John's concerns were no longer focused on his burning buildings, his fears rested with the safety of his tenants, praying none of them were trapped inside.

His feelings of helplessness intensified as his thoughts drifted back to his days as a volunteer firefighter, the days when he had the prerogative to take control. John wasn't accustomed to being a mere spectator and he certainly couldn't understand why the fire wasn't being brought under control. The local paper described:

"Quite an exciting, destructive and sensational fire broke out at 2 o'clock yesterday afternoon at the corner of Crawford and Mulberry Streets, which had the effect of bring a large proportion of the male population and not a few of its feminine members to that vicinity. The fire was the outgrowth of a washerwoman's work and originated at the back part of the Mulligan's tenement building, just back of the Bonelli office and store building and J. J. Mulligan's carriage and harness shop. A woman tenant in the premises, it seems, had been engaged in washing clothes on Tuesday, and it appears owing to the rain of that evening they could be dried quickly on the outside. Accordingly, she hung some of the articles indoors, near a rather hot fire, the fabric drying rapidly, and before the woman was aware of it several garments on the line had caught fire and shortly the whole room was in a blaze. She completely lost her head and ran into the yard screaming and beating her hands like mad. Under the circumstances the fire quickly gained headway, and got beyond local control."

This particular fire is covered in detail by Lt. John Lynn Yeager in his book "Wrapped in Flames" which imparts an interesting history of the Vicksburg Fire Department including the Mulligan fire and the complaints from citizens, property owners and insurance companies relating to the apparent mishandling of this and two other destructive Vicksburg fires.

* * *

The early 1900's welcomed a variety of wire clothes lines and an easier method of drying.

IRONING. Table cloths and Sunday dress clothing were ironed, there were some industrious home-makers that insisted on ironing sheets and every day clothing as well. An easy trick that homemakers used to make ironing easier, was to roll the cloth tightly while it was still damp, wrap a cloth around the bundle of clothing and set aside. Ironing damp material was much quicker, with smoother results than ironing dry cloth sprinkled with water. The actual ironing was done after the next meal, while the cook-stove was still heated, or sometime within the next 24 hours.

In the 19th century Flat Irons were forged by blacksmiths. They were simply a flat iron-shaped piece of iron attached to a wooden or spring handle. Regular cleaning and polishing was required to prevent rust and other contaminants from damaging their good clothing and table cloths. Two flat irons made the task move along much quicker while one was in use, the other was heating. An optional trivet provided a clean resting spot for the heated iron which was first tested on an old cloth for temperature and possible dirt. The actual ironing was often performed on the kitchen table. A variety of ironing boards were invented in the 1860's and came into common usage in the following decades as families could afford the new-fangled extravagance.

LYE SOAP. Early pioneers made their own soap using lye and the fat of a slaughtered animal. For settlers that made their own lye, the entire process could be done without expense since the ingredients are all waste materials from other processes.

The lye itself could be made using wood ashes from a fireplace or stove, they were placed in a leaky bucket or a container with a small hole at the bottom. Water was added to the container and as the water leached through the ashes, the caustic liquid dripped into a container below, this process took anywhere from a few hours to a day or two. It's important to note the process was done outdoors, during the summer time. Pioneers understood the health hazard posed by the caustic fumes released while making the lye.

Beef tallow or fat from any animal, was boiled in water to melt the fat which was then mixed with the lye. The lye and fat mixture was poured into a shallow or flat container and left to harden. The following day the Lye Soap was cut into chunks and the homemaker had her laundry and cleaning soap for the upcoming year.

My grandmother's recipe included several purchased items. Ingredients included ten pounds of melted and strained lard, cooled, two cans of Lewis lye and two quarts of water. The first step is pouring the lye over the cooled lard, next pour the water on the lye and finally add six tablespoons each of borax, kerosene and ammonia. Stir until it thickens. Note that coal oil, extracted from soft coal, was sometimes referred to as kerosene. It was mostly used as lamp oil. Petroleum based kerosene was an entirely different product.

Harvest

THRESHING BY HAND. The most difficult method of threshing was of course, handling the task without equipment. New immigrants brought few tools and their equipment was sparse. Initially many had only the wheat or oat seeds they brought from the old country. During the first year or two threshing by hand was the normal procedure for a pioneer settling on raw land with very little cleared land.

Once the crop is ripe the grain is separated from the stems and chaff, not an easy task. Separating several bushels of grain by hand could no doubt take an entire day of hard work. The crop selections for most Iowans were oats and wheat. Oats for the horses, wheat for personal use and to sell at the nearest mill.

With the manual process, the grain was cut with a scythe, the grain falling onto a cradle where it was bundled and stacked. A few days later the bundles were transported to their makeshift "processing" floor where the grain would be walked on, beaten with a flail or the family method they had learned from their fathers or grandfathers. Straw stems were lifted off and shaken to drop any remaining grain, the straw was later used for animal bedding, it also made an acceptable stuffing for a mattress. Finally, the chaff was fanned off the grain and seeds set aside for the following year. Any grain not needed to feed horses and livestock through the winter was taken to the nearest mill where part was milled for baking and food and the balance sold.

Promotional materials for threshing machines around 1920 claimed a modern machine could do the work of thirty men, with better results and less waste.

THRESHING WITH A CREW. Even as farming became modernized,

it wasn't practical for everyone to own a thresher and a steam engine. Learning how to safely operate the equipment was a completely separate issue. Every community included a few entrepreneurial types willing to invest in newfangled equipment, and hopefully learn its safe operation. By the late 1800's threshing machines were no longer operated by horse power. A steam engine, generally owned by a local farmer, traveled with the threshing machine from farm to farm.

In Jackson County, Iowa one of the local entrepreneurial teams was Peter Koos, Sr., along with his brother Henry. The young men invested in a thresher and steam engine and traveled around Jackson County from farm to farm with their threshing equipment.

This brings us to another story shared by Bob Koos several years ago. As the story goes, the two brothers were on one of their threshing trips with their steam engine and a threshing machine. Roads weren't quite what they are today and the brothers decided on a short-cut. Their path took them up a rocky hill, Henry was on the thresher operating the brake and Peter was driving the steam engine which decided to stall on the rocks. Henry couldn't stop both the steam engine and the threshing machine with the brakes so the entire ensemble began rolling down the hill backwards. Slowly at first, but soon picking up speed, Henry was a daring fellow but knew it was time to abandon ship and he jumped off. The thresher rolled down the hill and tipped over. Henry went over and inspected the damage, looked at his brother and said "Now you can grease it underneath!" They spent the rest of the day at the fair (Henry's idea I'm sure) and the following day they began the task of getting the thresher back into working order. And, before it was set upright, Peter presumably did grease anything he thought was necessary before the machine was set upright again.

When a threshing team arrived, the neighbors gathered from nearby farms and worked as a team to get the job done as quickly as possible. When one farm was finished they all moved on to the next farm until all harvests were finished. This was all coordinated without a computer, cell phones or a professional scheduler.

It wasn't just the men that gathered for the event, the women spent the day in a hot steamy kitchen preparing a lavish meal, each trying to prepare a favorite to feed fifteen to twenty men at dinnertime, the noon meal. After the work was done the locals went home and the traveling crew remained and enjoyed supper before retiring for the night. The meals were happy events, neighbors shared stories, laughed and when sitting down for a meal the workers knew they were in for a treat.

SETTING UP FOR THE CREW. The first step in threshing is knowing when the crop is ready; when a grain such as oats or wheat turns golden, and the grain itself is firm, not squishy, it is ready for harvest. First the grain is cut with a binder which used a sickle to cut the grain, the cut grain fell onto the binders' heavy canvas where it was bundled and bound with a lightweight twine, finally pushed off the back of the binder falling to the ground. The bundles were manually set upright, leaning a half dozen to a dozen bundles against each other with the grain side up, forming a shock. The shocks are given a few days for additional drying, when the threshing crew arrives with the threshing equipment the final steps would be completed.

On threshing day, the engineer in charge of the steam engine was the first to start work in the morning getting the engine fired up for the upcoming day. A good engineer was always vigilant in his job, a miscalculation could result in the explosion of the steam engine with horrific results. The steam engine was parked in line with the thresher close enough to allow the long drive belt to be connected from the steam engine shaft to the thresher. The belt always had a twist, after time, friction would fray the edges of the belt. It wasn't until recently, when I read a book by Cyril Jones did I learn why the twist was there, "A twist is made in the belt, so that it won't slide off too easily,"[77] an answer to a question I've wondered about since childhood. Once the belt was in place the steam engine was backed up until the belt displayed the perfect amount of tension. A process that generally required several adjustments.

The shocks were brought from the field by wagon, and bundle by bundle the grain tossed into the hopper, the twine was sliced as it was dropped in. The thresher now performing its job had paddles to beat the grain from the straw, the grain falling through a screen (a metal sheet with round holes) onto the next level where a similar screen with smaller openings did its job shaking the grain until it passed through to the next level, a fan circulating air through the separating area blowing away the dust and chaff. There were two grain collection sacks, allowing the process to switch to the empty sack as a full one was removed.

The 1920's offered new options for farmers willing to invest in more modern machinery. The introduction of the combine, or a combined reaper and thresher was slowly making its way onto farms. During World War II, the shortage of farm workers helped the combine become the norm and marked the end of an era. The sad result was that harvest season was no longer a social event.

PICKING CORN BY HAND. This was another job that was hard work. It was abrasive on skin, it damaged gloves and in Iowa, the weather was almost always cold when corn was ready for picking, making it hard on feet too. When the season brought an early snowfall, everything from picking the corn to transporting it became more challenging.

---

[77] Musings of a Middleton Boy, Growing Up on the Gower Coast by Cyril Jones, 2007, ISBN 978-0-59590-953-7.

At sunrise, a horse drawn wagon carried the pickers to the field, the entire family was involved. The wagon had a short side and a tall side, the tall side was simply a removable extension that was lifted on when needed and removed when corn picking was finished. The ear was broken from the stalk, husked and thrown into the wagon, the tall side of the wagon serving as a bang board when the ear was thrown over the short side. Bent and fallen stalks make the process tiring and wearing on the back, but every ear meant food or profit.

Smaller children ran around looking for fallen and trampled ears while other family members systematically went down the rows picking the corn; snow made the entire process much more difficult, deep snow would end the process until springtime. Around noon they climbed aboard and went back to the homestead for dinner, warmed their feet, possibly switched gloves and returned to the field, continuing the process until dark, only to rise the following day for more of the same.

Simple Pleasures

Penny postcards have a surprisingly interesting history. They were first issued in 1872 as a quick and inexpensive way to communicate and the price for Government printed cards remained at one cent for decades. Privately printed souvenir cards cost two cents, and the backside could only contain an address, no message allowed. In 1898 the price to mail a souvenir card dropped to a penny and in 1907 the post office allowed the back side to be split into an address section and a message section. The popularity of picture postcards exploded and greetings were sent for birthdays, holidays, vacations or just a quick hello that included a picture of interest such as the new parish church. This was a welcome and affordable option during a time when photos were an extravagance.

The cards became collectables and a new industry was born. People like Florence (Koos) Sprank bought an album to store her collection which included postcards from her brother Peter M. when he was in the A. E. F. in World War One. Collecting old penny postcards continues today.

Peter Koos Threshing Outfit, Steam Engine above, Threshing Machine below

Stack of Straw (Engineering marvel, built to shed water)

Between Threshing Jobs
During the later years, Peter M. became the steam engine operator

Supporting crew standing on the Steam Engine Water Tank

Biographies

BANCK, Henry. AKA, Henry Banks was born to Nicholas Banck and Elisabeth Kuhn in Kehlen, Luxembourg in April of 1836. He immigrated to America and settled in Jackson County, Iowa, it is reasonable to assume the locations was intentionally selected since a fellow Kehlenite had located there with her parents. Henry was married to Mary Hoffmann November 26, 1863 in Saint Donatus, Iowa. He died January 15, 1870 at the age of 33.

BANCK, Nicholas. The son of Peter Banck and Elisabeth Scholtes, born in Luxembourg on October 20, 1793. He married Maria Thommes February 18, 1817 in Kehlen, Luxembourg, the couple's children were Elisabeth, Peter, Peter and Maria Elisabeth, all born in Kehlen. His second wife Elisabeth Kuhn was born December 20, 1803, their marriage occurred January 13, 1830. Seven children blessed this marriage, all born in Kehlen, John Peter, Helen, John, Henry (b. April 8, 1836), Henri, Barbara and Michael. Elisabeth Kuhn died in 1846 and Nicholas lived another 24 years, passing away January 10, 1870 in Kehlen.

BANKS, Margaret. Margaret was the third of four daughters born to Henry Banks and Mary Hoffmann. She was born on their farm just south of La Motte, Iowa on March 23, 1867. "Maggie" married Peter Koos when she was nineteen years of age and raised a family of ten children, Nicholas (b. 1887, m. Margaret Hingtgen 1909), Henry (b. 1889, m. Catherine Hingtgen 1912), Peter M. (b. 1890, m. Anna Angela Manders, 1920), Mary (b. 1892, m. Andrew Wathier), Louis (b. 1893, m. Anna C. Hingtgen) , Josephine (b. 1897, m. Joseph Kilburg), William (b. 1900), Florence (b. 1902, m. Leo Sprank), Frank (b. 1905) and Virginia (b. 1907). Maggie died on September 30, 1949 at the age of 82; she is buried at Holy Rosary Catholic Cemetery in La Motte, Iowa.

BLOCK, Catherine. Catherine was born May 7, 1803 to Nicolas Block and Eve Rennet in Arsdorf, Luxembourg. On February 6, 1828 she was married to Jacques Reiland. Their children included Catherine (b. 1842, m. Nicholas Koos 1863), Eve (b. 1829, m. Henri Erpelding), Marie (b. 1833), Peter Reiland (b. 1834f, m. Mary Heinen 1885). Peter immigrated to America and settled in Chicago, Illinois.

BOEHLER, Louisa. Louisa was born October 7, 1818 in Liel Germany to Donat Boehler son of Ignaz and Magdalena (Zimmermann) Boehler and Elizabetha Hagenbach daughter of Joannes Georg and Magdelena (Diess) Hagenbach). She married Ludwig Louis Zahner June 30, 1842, the children born in Germany were Mary Eve (b. 1846) and William Ignasse (b. 1847, m. Frances Antonia Riebold ~1871) and twins born in America were Louis and John (b. 1854). Louis died at the age of six months. Louisa lived to the age of 87, she passed away August 12, 1880 in Kansas City, Missouri.

BONNEKESEL, Anna Maria Elisabeth. Elisabeth was born July 3, 1833 to Johannes Heinrich Bonnekesel and Maria Aleio Kuter. Her marriage to Andres Schmidt occurred around 1849. The couple had nine children, all born in Jackson County, Iowa. Andrew J. (b. 1850, m. Mary Schiltz 1872), Anna Mae Elizabeth (b. 1853, m. John Louis Ernst 1872), Catherine (b. 1854, m. Frank Stein 1874), Lucetta Elizabeth (b. 1856, m. John P. Franzen), William Frederick (b. 1858, m. Mary Kettman 1884), Edward C. (b. 1859, m. Justina Augusta Linneberg 1883), Christina Caroline (b. 1866, m. Johann Henrich Krogmann 1886), Mary Elizabeth (b. 1868, m. August Brinker) and Henry (b. 1869, m. Anna Bregenzer).

COLLITON, Julia. This Irish immigrant was born August 27, 1829 in County Kildare, Ireland to Frank and Catherine Colliton. She married William Farrell May 31, 1855 in Vicksburg, Mississippi, and they had one daughter, Mary Ann. Julia became a widow in 1858, remarried Edward O'Neil, a native of County Kilkenny, Ireland. They had one child, a son named Frank before Edward passed away. Julia died June 12, 1908 and is buried at Cedar Hill Cemetery, Vicksburg, Mississippi.

FARRELL, Mary Ann. She was the only child of William Farrell and Julia Colliton, born in Vicksburg, Mississippi between 1855 and 1858. Mary Ann married John J. Mulligan July 29, 1873 in Vicksburg. Their family grew to fifteen children, Mary Catharine (b. 1874), John Henry (b. 1876), Edward

Francis (b. 1879, m. Alma Zahner 1905), William Victor (b. 1881), Bernard Anistasius (b. 1886, m. Francisca H. Ward), Thomas Julian (b. 1883), Wilfred (b. 1887), Julia Blanche (b. 1888), Mary Genevive (b. 1890), Mary Florence (b. 1892), Rosalie (b. 1893, m. Robert Lee Grandberry), Clifford Aloysius (b. 1895, m. Nellie E. Maples, 1918), Mary Josephine (b. 1897), Mary Finlay (b. 1899) and Eleanor Mary (b. 1901).

FLAMMANG, John Nicholas. The fifth of ten children born May 3, 1833 (tombstone displays May 9) in Koerich, Capellen, Luxembourg to John Peter Flammang and Elizabeth Greten. He immigrated to America in 1855, spending a few years working as a farm hand. On November 21, 1866 he was joined in marriage with Mary Ann Niemann. Thirteen children were born to this union, all born in rural Saint Donatus, Iowa. He lived to the age of 85, passing away in Dubuque, Iowa on January 13, 1919 and is buried at Mount Calvary Cemetery in Dubuque.

FLAMMANG, Nicholas, Leo. The tenth of thirteen children, Nick was born November 22, 1882 in St. Donatus, Jackson County, Iowa to John Nicholas Flammang and Mary Ann Niemann. He married Christina Herrig January 18, 1910 at St. Donatus Catholic Church in St. Donatus, Iowa. Nick and Christina had eleven children, all born in Nebraska. He died February 18, 1950 in Dubuque, Iowa at the age of 67.

FLAMMANG, John Peter. J. P. was born on April 24, 1787 in Bour Luxembourg to Peter Flammang (b. 1755) and Maria Zimmer (b. ~1759). On February 2, 1825 he was married to Elizabeth Greten in Koerich, Luxembourg. The couple had ten children. J. P. died at the age of 66 on January 23, 1854 (unconfirmed date). His oldest child had recently left for America as a missionary, and his youngest daughter Anne Marie was ten years of age.

GERKEN, Johannes Heinrich. Was the fourth of seven known children born to Adam Gerken and Gertrude Cramer. He was born October 4, 1773 at Hegensdorf, Germany. On November 1, 1801 he married Maria Catherina Stratmann (b. 1779). Their seven children were Anna Marie (b. 1802, m. Michael Ostwald 1826), Johannes Adamus (b. 1804), Anna Maria Gertrude (b. 1807), Jodocus Wilhelmus (b. 1810, m. Maria Catherine Quante 1834), Maria Agnes Gertrudis (b. 1813), Joanne Herman (b. 1815) and Johann Heinrich Hermann (b. 1819, m. Maria Catherina Schulte 1849). Johannes Heinrich died October 24, 1823 in Hegensdorf.

GLAESENER, Catherine. Catherine was born September 24, 1807, to Carolus Gloesener son of Georges Gloesener and Anne Christine Bonnerts and Marie Catherine Mersch daughter of Pierre Mersch and Marie Catherine Roob. She married Michael Hoffmann on January 21, 1834 in Kehlen, Luxembourg. They had seven children, Michael (b. 1835, m. Marie Heiter 1867), Mary (b. 1836, m. Henry Banks 1863), Michael John (b. 1839, m. Anna Wagoner 1870), Franz (b. 1841, Susanna Heiter 1865), Angeline (b. 1846, m. Peter Entringer 1867), Nicholas A. (b. 1849, m. Elizabeth Mueller 1875). Catherine died October 31, 1899.

GRETEN, Elizabeth. Elizabeth Greten was born November 1, 1800 to Francois Greten and Elisabetha Guttenkauff in Koerich Luxembourg, Elizabeth married J. P. Flammang February 2, 1825 in Koerich. Their children numbered ten, John Michael (b. 1825), Nicholas (b. 1828, m. Frances Manz), Anna Maria (b. 1830), Marie (b. 1831), John Nicholas (b. 1833, m. Mary Ann Niemann 1866), Elisabeth (b. 1835), Margaret (b. 1837), Barbara (twin b. 1839), Maria (twin b. 1839) and Anne Marie (b. 1844). Elizabeth emigrated to America in 1863, she died February 5, 1877 in Saint Donatus, Iowa and is buried in the local Catholic Cemetery.

HAXMEIER, Helena. The second of seven children, Helena was born to Johann Theodore Haxmeier and Caroline Nemmers August 6, 1850 in Jackson County, Iowa. October 24, 1868 marked her marriage to John Herrig. They had fifteen children, Caroline (b. 1869, m. Anthony J. Till), Henry (b. 1872), Anna (b. 1873, m. Peter J. Till), William Joseph (b. 1875, m. Caroline Poll), John Matthew (b. 1877, m. Mary Ellen Horan), Mary (b. 1879), Michael (b. 1880), Theodore (b. 1883, m. Christina Poll 1904), George (b. 1883), Margaret (b. 1885, m. Joseph John Till), Helena b. 1887, m. Charles Hilbert 1916), Christina (b. 1888, m. Nicholas L. Flammang 1910), Joseph (b. 1890, m. Helena Ties), Mathias (b. 1890) and Anthony (b. 1893, m. Regina Huilman). Helena died in Saint Donatus on October 31, 1923.

HAXMEIER, Johann Theodore. Theodore was born January 7, 1814 in Leschede, Germany to Hermann Heinrich Lohenrich and Anna Greite Engel Rotgers Alf.[78] He immigrated around 1845 and began acquiring land early in 1848, and on September 25, 1848 married neighbor Caroline Nemmers. Theodore died in Jackson County, Iowa November 30, 1871.

HENGEN, Elizabeth. The fifth of ten children, Elizabeth was born in Sandweiler, Luxembourg, December 27, 1799 to Pierre Hengen (b. 1768) and Marie Verholgen (b. 1775). She married Mathias Manders January 9, 1823 in Sandweiler. They had nine children, Marie (b. 1823, m. George Hottua, m. Gerhardt Van Dillon), Peter (b. 1825, m. Rosalie Capesius), John Peter (b. 1828, m. Catherine Hentges), Mathias (b. 1830, m. Suzanne Meysenburg, m. Elizabeth Gluden), Marie (b. 1830, m. Carl Thimmesch 1851), Michael (b. 1834, m. Anna Katherine Schmitz 1869), Elizabeth (b. 1837, m. Peter Kass 1860), Eva (b. 1839, m. Theodore Fisch 1859), Sebastian (b. 1841, m. Elizabeth Capesius). Elizabeth survived her husband by six years, passing away on April 10, 1875.

HERRIG, Christina. The twelfth of fifteen children, Christina was born October 29, 1888 in St. Donatus, Iowa to John Herrig and Helena Haxmeier. She married Nicholas Leo Flammang on January 18, 1910 at St. Donatus Catholic Church in St. Donatus, Iowa. They had eleven children, all born in Orleans, Nebraska. Christina died at her rural St. Donatus home at the age of 79 years on February 5, 1968.

HERRIG, John. The fifth of seven children born to Michael Herrig and Catherine Thill, born August 15, 1840 in Wormeldange, Luxembourg. His immigration occurred around 1857. On October 24, 1868 he married Helena Haxmeier. John lived until the age of 70; he is buried in Saint Donatus, Iowa.

HERRIG, Mathias. The son of Dominic Herrig and Margaret Kelsen, Mathias was born March 19, 1765 in Wormeldange, Luxembourg. He was the oldest of at least nine children and grew up in Wormeldange. On December 26, 1792 he was married to Johanetta Punnel, daughter of Michel Pinnel and Maria Adam. Their children included Mathias (b. 1794, m. Anna Maria Hemmen), Magdalena (b. 1796, m. Mathies Theisen), Michael (b. 1800, m. Catherine Thill), Margaretha (b. 1805) and Johann (b. 1809, m. Susanna Bauer 1830). Mathias died on July 12, 1835.

---

[78] Rebecca Stewart's research on Haxmeier ancestors.

HERRIG, Michael. Born in Wormeldange, Luxembourg on December 19, 1800, son of Mathias Herrig and Johanetta Punnel. He married Catherine Thill February 21, 1827 and they had seven children, four of their sons emigrated.

HOFFMANN, Maria. The third of seven children, Mary was born November 25, 1836 to Michael Hoffmann and Catherine Glaesener in Kehlen, Luxembourg. She married Henry Banks, also from Kehlen, on November 26, 1836. They had four daughters, all born in Richland Township near La Motte, Iowa. Katherine (b. 1864 m. Nicholas Kayser 1885), Mary (b. 1865), Margaret (b. 1867, m. Peter Koos 1885) and Anna (b. 1869, m. Henry Koos 1897). Henry died in 1870, Margaret married Jacob Marso on February 15, 1871. They continued farming at Richland Township and added six children to the family. Elizabeth (b. 1872, Michael J. (b. 1873), John J. (b. 1875, m. Nina M. Jones 1903), Frank Joseph (b. 1877, m. Nellie Eliza Wilcox 1909), Suzie (b. 1879, m. Leo Schroeder 1908) and Mary M. (b. 1882, m. James I. O'Donnell 1903). In the late 1880's Mary and Jacob and their children relocated to South Dakota where they homesteaded land. Jacob died on May 20, 1927 at the age of 88 and Mary lived to the age of 92, passing away August 29, 1929 at Highmore, South Dakota.

HOFFMANN, Michael. The first of (at least) three children, Michael was born March 15, 1805 to Michael Hoffmann and Anna Marie Michels in Kehlen, Luxembourg. He married Catherine Glaesener on January 21, 1834 also at Kehlen. Their family grew to seven children, all born in Kehlen. Michael was a wagon maker in his native land, immigrating to America June of 1861. After arriving in Iowa he purchased a farm in Prairie Springs Township of Jackson County, Iowa. Michael was 92 years old when he died on February 2, 1898.

KOOS, Franz. Franz was born March 25, 1797 in Tarchamps, Luxembourg, his parents were Michel Koos and Therese Mathieu. On July 12, 1826 in Bigonville, Luxembourg he married Marguerite Muller. They had eight children, all born in Bilsdorf. Franz died April 17, 1862 in Bilsdorf.

KOOS, Charles Henry. The second of nine children, C. H. was born January 17, 1889 in Richland Township, Jackson County Iowa to Peter

Koos and Margaret Banks. He married Catherine Hingtgen on April 16, 1912. Catherine died in childbirth on April 28, 1913. The baby, named Catherine, grew up to be a teacher like her step mother Gadzelle Stover, Henry's second wife. Gadzelle died on June 25, 1937 and Mary Lemke became his third wife. Henry and Mary spent their senior years in Tampa, Florida, returning to Iowa a few months every summer. Henry died February 15, 1980.

KOOS, Henry. The fifth of nine children, he was born May 22, 1872 in Bilsdorf, Luxembourg to Nicholas Koos and Catherine Reiland. He immigrated in 1887 and like his brother spent time in Chicago before making his way to Jackson County, Iowa. Henry married one of the Banks sisters, Anna. They had two boys, John Joseph and Leroy F. Henry died July 10, 1956; his wife lived to ninety-four years, passing away September 16, 1963.

KOOS, Nicholas. The seventh of eight children born April 28, 1839 in Tintange, Luxembourg to Franz Koos and Marguerite Muller. He was married to Catherine Reiland daughter of Jacques and Catherine Block in Arsdorf Luxembourg on April 13, 1863. The couple became the parents of nine children. Nicolas left his wife a widow on March 31, 1878 in Bilsdorf, Luxembourg, he was 38 years of age, their youngest child, a son, was less than a month old.

KOOS, Nicholas. Nicholas was the oldest of Peter Koos and Margaret Banks ten children born in Jackson County, Iowa August 31, 1887. On September 21, 1909 he was married to Margaret Hingtgen, daughter of Nicholas and Catherine Hingtgen. Margaret died during the birth of their ninth child on March 29, 1929. Nicholas did not re-marry, he continued farming and passed away February 27, 1956; Nicholas and Margaret are buried at Holy Rosary Cemetery in La Motte, Iowa.

KOOS, Peter. The second of nine children born to Nicholas Koos and Catherine Reiland in Bilsdorf, Luxembourg on January 1, 1866. He arrived in New York on March 22, 1884, made his way to Illinois for a short time, quickly learning he wasn't a city boy he continued his westward trek to Richland Township, Jackson County, Iowa. After working as a farm hand for a year, Peter married Margaret Banks December 29, 1885. The couple remained on the Banks-Marso farm, eventually buying the property and there raised their ten children. Peter was eighty-nine years old when he died on February 13, 1955. He is buried next to his wife at Holy Rosary Catholic Cemetery.

KOOS, Peter Michael. The third of ten children of Peter Koos and Margaret Banks, he was born August 21, 1890 in Richland Township, Jackson County, Iowa. He was a soldier in the A. E. F. during World War I. Peter married Anna Angela Manders November 24, 1920 in La Motte, Iowa. They became the parents of one daughter. Peter died October 7, 1971 at the age of 81 and is buried beside his wife at Holy Rosary Catholic Cemetery.

KRAFT, Maria Louisa. Louisa's German background remains mostly hidden within undiscovered documents. Her birthplace was likely a location referred to as Rietbach in Bavaria, this has not been confirmed. The only family mentioned in any article was her obituary mentions a brother Fred Kraft of Saint Louis, who survived her. Louisa's life in Missouri took her on a wild ride. She was married to John Meis and had a daughter, Mary, in Franklin County, Missouri around 1842, her husband John Meis died, and Louisa married neighbor Francis Xavier Riebold June 20, 1849. The couple had five children, Anselimis (b. 1850, d. 1852), Frances Antonia (b. 1853, m. William Zahner ~1871), Francis Joseph (b. 1854), Josephina (b. 1856, m. Henry Ziegelmeyer) and Margaret Catharine (b. 1858, m. Edmund Gustave Pueschel 1874). Later during the year of Margaret's birth, her husband died. She married again to John Henry Holls, this marriage ended, probably by her choice and she relocated to Kansas City, Missouri where she supported her family by operating a boarding house. Louisa died November 14, 1903 after an extended illness that had her bedridden for two months; she is buried in the Zahner Family plot in Kansas City, Missouri.

KROGMANN, Franz Ferdinand. With records discovered to date, Franz was the fifth of five children born to Herman Henrich Krogmann and Anna Maria Osterhus. He was born October 8, 1801 in Steinfeld. On July 13, 1824 he married Maria Engel Suennenberg. Six of their children include Franz Henrich (b. 1830, m. Josephina Meyer, m. Maria C. Berding 1860), Johann Heinrich (b. 1828, m. Maria Catharina Olberding 1851), Herman Heinrich (b. 1834, m. Maria Agnes Nieberding), Franz Ferdinand

(b. 1837), Anton (b. 1845) and Maria Elisabeth (b. 1848). After he became a widower, Franz emigrated with his son Herman, settling near Clinton, Iowa. He likely died between 1880 and 1885.

KROGMAN, John Henry. The only one of five children to survive past infancy, Henry was born October 11, 1888 in Hull, Sioux County, Iowa to Johann Heinrich Krogmann and Christina Caroline Schmidt. When he was about six years old his parents left Hull, and re-settled near Remsen, which had a growing settlement of Germans and Luxembourgers. Neighbor, Anna Mary Stuntebeck became his wife October 8, 1907. They had nine children, all born at their home near Remsen, Iowa. Henry lived to the age of 92 and is buried next to his wife at St. Mary's Catholic Cemetery in Remsen, Iowa.

KROGMANN, Johann Heinrich. The fifth of five known children born to Johnann Heinrich and Maria Catharina Olberding. He was born November 29, 1861 in Steinfeld, Oldenburg, Germany. Officially emigrated in 1882, traveling from Bremen to Baltimore where he worked in a brewery before continuing on to Iowa. He married Christina Caroline Schmidt on January 11, 1886. They had five children, just one survived to adulthood. Henry died October 21, 1942 in Remsen, Iowa.

KROGMANN, Johann Heinrich. The second of six known children born to Franz Ferdinand Krogmann and Maria Engel Suennenberg, Henry was born September 27, 1828 in Steinfeld, Germany. He married Maria Catharina Olberding in Holthausen, Germany on February 17, 1851. Their children numbered at least five. Although his father and his youngest son emigrated, Henry spent his years in Germany, he died around 1901.

MANDERS, Anna Angela. The oldest of ten children of Peter Donatus Manders and Margaret Schartz, Anna was born November 7, 1895 in Jackson County, Iowa. She married Peter Michael Koos at Holy Rosary Catholic Church in La Motte, Iowa on November 24, 1920, they became the parents of one daughter. Anna died August 22, 1970 and is buried at Holy Rosary Catholic Cemetery.

MANDERS, Mathias. The tenth of ten known children born to Nicholas Manders and Magdalena Capesius, Mathias was born June 6, 1796 in Sandweiler Luxembourg. On January 9, 1823 he was married to Elizabeth Hengen. Mathias, a stone mason, emigrated with his family in 1850 and bought a farm. He enjoyed farming and continued in that line until he passed away on June 13, 1869. Mathias is buried at the Saint Donatus Catholic Cemetery.

MANDERS, Mathias. The fourth of nine children, Mathias was born September 5, 1830 in Sandweiler, Luxembourg to Mathias Manders and Elizabeth Hengen. He emigrated with his family in 1850 and farmed with his parents until his marriage to Suzanne Meysenburg on September 14, 1864 in Saint Donatus, Iowa. They had five children, Suzanne died four days after the youngest was born. Mathias then married Elizabeth Gluden October 15, 1872. Mathias died January 3, 1902.

MANDERS, Peter Donatus. The fourth of five children of Mathias Manders and Suzanne Meysenburg was born July 6, 1870 in St. Donatus, Jackson County, Iowa. He married Margaret Schartz January 22, 1895 in Iowa. Their Jackson County, Iowa farm was located south of La Motte, it was there they raised ten children. Peter died September 16, 1931 at the age of 61. He is buried at Holy Rosary Catholic Cemetery in La Motte.

MEYSENBURG, Pierre Nicholas. The second of eight children born to Pierre Meysenburg (b. 1780) and Angelique Schuh, he was born March 27, 1810 in Sandweiler, Luxembourg. Around 1836 he married Catharina Thekes and the couple had ten children. Peter Nicholas (b. 1838, m. Mary Barbara Dehner 1869), Marguerite (b. 1840), Suzanne (b. 1842, m. Mathias Manders 1864), Mary Susanne (b. 1844, m. Bernard Schlentz, Sr. 1864), Anna (b. 1846, m. Michael Demuth), John Baptiste (b. 1849, m. Susan Reisdorff 1877), Auguste (b. 1851), Anne Marie (b. 1853), Anne Marie (b. 1856) and Pierre (b. 1859). The youngest child died at two days of age, Catharina died three days later. The patriarch emigrated with his surviving children in 1864; he died in Bellwood, Nebraska on August 1, 1888.

MEYSENBURG, Suzanne. The third of ten children, Suzanne was born April 10, 1842 to Pierre Nicholas Meysenburg and Catharina Thekes in Sandweiler, Luxembourg. In 1864 she emigrated with her father, two sisters and a brother, all joining her older brother in Cascade, Iowa. A couple months after arriving, September 14, 1864 she married Mathias Manders. The couple had five children, Nicholas (b. 1865, d. 1885), Catherine (b. 1867, m. Henry Piitz 1890), Rose (b. 1868, m. Theodore Wieseler 1894), Peter Donatus (b. 1870, m. Margaret Schartz 1895) and an infant (d. 1872). Suzanne died January 19, 1872, four days after her infant, she is buried at the Saint Donatus Catholic Cemetery.

MULLER, Marguerite. Marguerite was born in Bilsdorf, Luxembourg on November 23, 1799 to Jean Muller and Anne Catherine Duce. On July 12, 1826 she married Franz Koos. The couple had eight children, Johannes (b. 1827), Marie (b. 1828), Elizabeth (b. 1829, m. Nicholas Kayser 1855), Pierre (b. 1832, m. Anne Catherine Lech), Catherine (b. 1836), Infant (b. 1837, d. 1837), Nicholas (b. 1839, m. Catherine Reiland 1863), Nicholas Steven (b. 1843, m. Elizabeth Schill). Immigrants to America include her son Nicholas Steven and grandchildren that immigrated included one of Elizabeth's sons, and four of Nicholas's sons.

MULLIGAN, Bernard Anistasius. The fifth of fifteen children, Bernard was born October 2, 1886 in Vicksburg, Mississippi to John and Mary Ann Farrell. He married Francisca H. Ward. The couple's children included Franciscum Elaine, Bernard A., Jr. and Lloyd E. Their home was in Louisiana. Bernard died at Port Gibson, Mississippi April 15, 1935.

MULLIGAN, Clifford Aloysius. Born September 3, 1895 to John and Mary Ann Farrell. Clifford married Nellie E. Maples April 29, 1917 in Mississippi, his second wife was Mary Cefalu. Their children were Clifford and John. Clifford Sr. died around 1972.

MULLIGAN, Edward Francis. The third of fifteen children of John Jacob Mulligan and Mary Ann Farrell, born October 1879 in Vicksburg, Warren County, Mississippi. In 1891 he was a student at Saint Stanislaus Collage in Saint Louis where he excelled at debating, he later returned to Saint Louis where he studied law and in 1903 he was admitted to the bar in Missouri. He was then admitted to the Mississippi Bar and for one term was a member of the State House of Representatives in Mississippi. He later added real estate and oil leases to his specialties. November 28, 1905 marks the date of his marriage to Alma Zahner. Their married life began in Vicksburg, moved on to Kansas City, Missouri and finally to Wichita Falls, Texas. Six children blessed their family. Ed died in 1949 and is buried in Wichita Falls.

MULLIGAN, John Jacob. J. J. or John Mulligan was born in Illinois between 1844 and 1854. His father may have been Thomas Mulligan from

La Salle County, Illinois, no confirmation. He was a tinsmith who made his way to Vicksburg, working maintenance for a local railroad when he married Mary Ann Farrell on July 29, 1873. He was a business man and a plumber, father to fifteen children and devout member of the local Roman Catholic Church. John died March 14, 1919 at Vicksburg, Mississippi.

MULLENKAMP, Mary. The fifth of nine children born November 1865 in Petersburg, Iowa to Anton Müllenkamp and Anna Maria Elizabeth Ostwald. She married Frank Stuntebeck April 5, 1888 and the couple raised five daughters, Anna Mary (b. 1889, m. John Henry Krogman 1907), Mary (b. 1892, m. William Beckmann, Sr. 1913), Margaret (b. 1894, m. Peter Lanners 1917), Katherine (b. 1897, m. Theodore Hansen 1916, m. August Haack 1925) and Frances (b. 1898, m. Ferdinand Arens 1919). The girls were all born at the Stuntebeck farm home near Remsen. After their retirement, Mary lived with complications of diabetes until her death November 3, 1928; she is buried at Saint Mary's Catholic Cemetery in Remsen, Iowa.

NEMMERS, Caroline. The fifth of six children, Caroline was born to John Nicholas Nemmers and Catherine Weber, Caroline was born December 26, 1827 in Kehlen Luxembourg. She married Johann Theodor Haxmeier September 25, 1848 in Dubuque, Iowa. Their seven children were Henry P. (b. 1849, m. Elizabeth Maria Gilles 1871), Mary (b. 1853), Margaret (b. 1855), Anna (b. 1856, m. John Peter Herrig 1874), Johannes (b. 1859) and Michael T. (b. 1862, m. Louise Eggspuehler 1889). Caroline passed away on March 16, 1869 and is buried at the Saint Donatus Catholic Cemetery.

NEMMERS, John Nicholas. Nicholas was born March 5, 1783 in Tuntange, Luxembourg to Petrus Viduus Nemmers and Anna Marie Nessen. He married Catherine Weber November 27, 1811 in Kehlen, Luxembourg. They had a family of six children, five grew to adulthood. Nicholas immigrated to America in 1847 and spent ten years in the New World. He passed away March 7, 1857 in Jackson County, Iowa.

NIEMANN, Johann Heinrich. Henry Niemann was born September 1, 1817 to Herman H. Niemann and Margaret Klaphake, they were all natives of Hannover, Germany. Henry immigrated prior to 1846, his marriage to Anna Maria Elizabeth Schulte took place April 28, 1846 in Jo Daviess

County, Illinois. Henry worked a land claim near Spruce Creek in Jackson County, Iowa, next to his brother Theodore. He died at the age of 46, on March 30, 1864, Elizabeth continued on the farm after his death.

NIEMANN, Mary Ann. Mary Ann Niemann was the oldest of seven children, born to Henry Niemann and Elizabeth Schulte in Jackson County, Iowa on February 7, 1847. She married John Nicholas Flammang, a Luxembourg immigrant on November 21, 1866 in Jackson County. Nicholas and Mary Ann had two daughters and eleven sons, two sons died in childhood; the remaining children grew to adulthood. Their children were Michael (b. 1867, d. 1867), Elizabeth (b. 1868), Alois Francis (b. 1870, m. Anna Loewen 1894), Joseph (b. 1872, d. 1874), Joseph Walter (b. 1874, m. Mary Ann Eltz 1897), John Peter (b. 1876), Alphonse Clement (b. 1878, m. Christina Wolbers 1901), George (b. 1880, m. Louise Lennemann 1911), Rose Anna (b. 1881), Nicholas Leo (b. 1882, m. Christina Herrig 1910), Michael Joseph (b. 1884), Henry R. (b. 1887, Antoinette Streit 1917) and Theodore Joseph (b. 1890). Mary Ann lived to age 73, passing away on May 18, 1920, she is buried next to her husband at Mount Calvary Cemetery in Dubuque. Their daughter Rose rests in the same plot.

OLBERDING, Franz Henrich. Franz was the son of Herm Henrich Olberding and Maria Elisabeth Fortmann, sister to Maria Catharina. He was a witness to her marriage to Johann Heinrich Krogmann. On June 2, 1852 in Steinfeld, Germany he married Catharina Gertrud Froehle. Their children were Marie Josephine (b. 1853, m. Henry Hameier 1868), Mary Elisabeth (b. 1857), Catherine Bernadina (b. 1859, m. John Richels), Clemens August (b. 1863), Johanna Catherine (b. 1867) all born in Germany. In 1868 the family immigrated to America, Johanna Catherine died during the voyage. The family settled near Petersburg, Iowa where their youngest son Clemens was born in 1869. Franz died in 1874 and is buried in Delaware County, Iowa at St. Peter & Paul Cemetery.

OLBERDING, Herm Henrich. The oldest of five children born to Gerhard Henrich Olberding and Catherine Elisabeth Haskamp, Herm was born January 2, 1778 in Holthausen, Germany. He married Elisabeth Neeman January 21, 1806, she died in 1809, he then married Maria Elisabeth Fortmann August 1, 1809 at St. Johannas Church in Steinfeld. Their children include Joan Henrich (b 1810), Maria Elisabeth (b. 1812),

Franz Henrich (b. 1815, m. Catharina Gertrud Froehle) and Maria Catherina (b. 1818, m. Johann Heinrich Krogmann 1851). Herm died June 21, 1851.

OLBERDING, Maria Catharina. Born November 12, 1818 in Holthausen to Herm Henrich Olberding and Maria Elisabeth Fortmann, she married Johann Heinrich Krogmann February 17, 1851. Their children were Johann Heinrich (b. 1852), Franz (b. 1853), Catharina Josephina (b. 1856), Maria Anna (b. 1859) and Johann Heinrich (b. 1861, m. Christina Caroline Schmidt 1886). Catharina died around 1879.

OSTWALD, Anna Maria Elizabeth. Was the fifth of nine children born to Michael Ostwald and Anna Marie Gerken. She was born May 6, 1834 in Hegensdorf, Germany. On December 19, 1856 she married a fellow German native, Anton Müllenkamp. The couple raised their nine children in Petersburg, Delaware County, Iowa. Margaretta (b. 1858, m. Frank J. Bohnenkamp 1878), William (b. 1860, m. Mary Agnes Klosterman 1895) Herman (b. 1863, m. Mary Overman 1894), Philomena Antonetta (b. 1865), Mary (b. 1865, m. Frank Stuntebeck 1888), Katie (b. 1869), Elizabeth (b. 1873), Anna (b. 1875, m. Edward Budden) and Anton (b. 1880, m. Mary Ann Kruse 1906). Anna Maria Elizabeth died August 15, 1902 in Delaware County, Iowa.

PHILIPPS, Angelina. Angelina was the daughter of Nicolas Philipps and Catherine Molitor, she was born September 20, 1825 in Graulinster, Luxembourg. On January 29, 1856 she married widower Nicholas Welter (b. 1812) they had three Luxembourg-born children, Peter (b. 1859, m. Hannah Regan), Katharina (b. 1859, m. Adam Seiler 1877) and Catherine (b. 1861, m. Nicholas Ehlinger). Nicholas Welter died in 1865, Angelina emigrated to America with her three children, two of her brothers were living in Iowa. On January 21, 1869 she married Civil War veteran Peter Schartz, they had two children, Catherine Anna (b. 1869, d. 1874) and Margaret (b. 1871, m. Peter Donatus Manders 1895). Angelina's husband Peter died July 28, 1901, Angelina died December 20, 1907. They are both buried at Holy Rosary Catholic Cemetery in La Motte, Iowa but the marker only lists Peter.

PHILIPPS, Nicolas. Nicholas was the son (unconfirmed) of Carl Caspar Philipps and Margaretha Comes, born March 22, 1780 in Altrier,

Luxembourg. He married Catherine Molitor. The couple had three children that emigrated from Luxembourg, Johan Pierre (b. 1810, m. Margaret Schreiner, m. Barbe Groos 1839), Jean Pierre (b. 1821, m. Anna Huss, m. Anne Groos) and Angelina (b. 1825, m. Nicolas Welter 1856, m. Peter Schartz 1869). Nicolas died September 24, 1843 in Graulinster, Luxembourg, his wife died September 11, 1846, also in Graulinster.

REILAND, Catherine. The first of at least four children born to Jacques Reiland and Catherine Block, Catherine was born in Bilsdorf, Luxembourg, December 11, 1842. She was married to Nicholas Koos April 13, 1863 at Arsdorf, Luxembourg. Their nine children were Marguerite (b. 1864, m. Christopher Scheck), Peter (b. 1866, m. Margaret Banks 1885), Marie (b. 1867, m. Dominick Gehenge 1896), Nicholas (b. 1870), Henry (b. 1872, m. Anna Banks 1897), Anne (b. 1874), Francois (twin b. 1875), Jacques (twin b. 1875) and Joseph F. (b. 1878). Four of their sons, Peter, Henry, Nicholas and Joseph emigrated, all lived in Jackson County, Iowa at some point in time.

REILAND, Peter. The fourth of four children born to Jacques Reiland and Catherine Block, Peter was born in Bilsdorf, Luxembourg June 25, 1834. He emigrated from Luxembourg in 1870 and made his home in Chicago, Illinois. On May 10, 1885 he married Mary Heinen, she was born in Wisconsin in 1866. Their children include Lizzie (b. 1886), Matthew (b. 1886), Peter (b. 1891) and Mamie (b. 1895)

REILAND, Jacques. Jacques was born June 29, 1800 to Michel Reiland and Anne Marie Santer in Wolwelange, Luxembourg. He married Catherine Block February 6, 1828 in Bigonville, Luxembourg. Jacques died in Bilsdorf on August 16, 1855.

RIEBOLD, Frances Antonia. Fannie was born January 17, 1853 to Francis Xavier Riebold and Louisa Kraft in Franklin County, Missouri. She married William Ignasse Zahner around 1871 in Jackson County, Missouri. The couple had eight children, Louise (b. ~1872, m. Benjamin Allen Cantrell, Jr. 1895), Frank Louis (b. 1875, Anna Catherine Slichter 1916), Henry Fredrick (b. 1878, m. Marie Rosalia Bruening 1903), Edward Joseph (b. 1882, m. Frances Graf), Alma (b. 1884, m. Edward Francis Mulligan 1905), Margaret (b. 1886, m. David W. Newcomer 1910), Mary (b. 1888) and Karl William (b. 1894, m. Mary Gwendolyn Burns). Fannie died at the age of seventy-five, March 5, 1928 in Kansas City, Missouri.

RIEBOLD, Francis Xavier. Francis was born 1813 in Germany, he married widow Louisa (Kraft) Meis June 20, 1948 in Franklin County, Missouri. The couple had five children. Francis Xavier died December 14, 1858 and is buried at St. Francis Borgia Catholic Cemetery in Washington, Missouri. His ancestry is unknown, but census records and historical publications lead to the likelihood that five siblings immigrated. Three sisters Cordula (m. Ambrose Friedmann), Mary Antonia (m. Leo Kohler, m. Anton Yerger), Mary Anna (m. Xavier Arbeiter) and two brothers Anselm and Meinard.

SCHARTZ, Margaret. The second of two children, she was born March 12, 1871 near La Motte, Iowa to Peter Schartz and Angelina Philipps. Margaret married Peter Donatus Manders January 22, 1895, they farmed in Jackson County where they raised ten children. The oldest was Anna (b. 1895, m. Peter M. Koos 1920), Peter (b. 1896), George (b. 1898, m. Lena Till), Leo (b. 1900, m. Lavina Lidwina Herrig 1922), Mary (b. 1902, m. Leroy Manderscheid 1925), Catherine (b. 1904, m. John Kaiser), Mathew (b. 1906, m. Marie Arensdorf 1933), Christopher (b. 1907, m. Veronica Clasen 1934), Loretta (b. 1910, m. Louis J. Till) and Irvin (b. 1915, m. Vivian C. Junk) Margaret lived to the grand old age of 91, passing away November 27, 1874. She was buried beside her husband at Holy Rosary Catholic Cemetery in La Motte, Iowa.

SCHMIDT, Andres. Andrew was born to Johann Bernard Schmidt (son of Heinrich Schmitt and Anna Bruckmann) and Catharina Aleio Eilemann on November 3, 1817 in Lengerich, Germany. His emigration occurred in 1846 and he married Anna Maria Elisabeth Bonnekesel about three years later. He was a farmer near Saint Donatus, Iowa where the couple raised their nine children. Andrew died January 15, 1894.

SCHMIDT, Christina Caroline. Lena was the seventh of nine children born March 1866 in Tete des Mortes Township, Jackson County, Iowa to Andres Schmidt and Anna Maria Elisabeth Bonnekesel. She married Johann Heinrich Krogmann. Of their five children, only Henry (b. 1888, m. Anna Mary Stuntebeck) survived infancy, except for Elizabeth (b. 1892) the names of the other children are unknown. Lena died April 9, 1906 after complications of an appendicitis surgery. She is buried at Saint Mary's Catholic Cemetery in Remsen, Iowa.

SCHULTE, Anna Maria Elizabeth. Elizabeth was born January 30, 1825 in Hannover Germany to Theodore Schulte and Maria Elizabeth Heimann. On April 28, 1846 she was married to Henry Niemann in Jo Daviess County, Illinois. They had seven children before Elizabeth became a widow. The children were Mary Ann (b. 1847, m. John Nicholas Flammang 1866), John (b. 1850, m. Katharine Sieverding), Margaret Elizabeth (b. 1854, m. John Anton Koob 1874), Elizabeth (b. 1854, m. George Benninghouse 1886), Henry Herman (b. 1855, m. Catherine Carabena Schultz 1890), Theodore (b. 1858, m. Hope Walsh 1895) and Joseph M. (b. 1861). Her husband died in 1864 and Elizabeth lived another 47 years to August 16, 1911.

SCHULTE, Theodore. Theodore Schulte was born in Germany around 1796 to Theodor Christoph Shulte (1773-1836) and Eva Maria Thoene (1778-1852). He married Maria Elizabeth Heimann (b. ~1796), confirmed children include Anna Maria Elizabeth (b. 1825, m. John Henry Niemann 1846), Frances (b. ~1831, m. Henry Tobin), and (not confirmed) a brother Frank Schulte. Theodore and his wife relocated with their daughter Frances and family to Wabasha County, Minnesota. It appears they both passed away between the years 1870 and 1875.

STUNTEBECK, Anna Mary. The oldest of five daughters of Frank Ferdinand Stuntebeck and Mary Mullenkamp, she was born April 24, 1889 near Remsen in Plymouth County, Iowa. Mary grew up on her parents' farm. On October 8, 1907 she married a neighboring farmer John "Henry" Krogman. They began their life together joining Henry's father' household. There they raised a family of nine children, Clarence, Frank, Marie, Henry, Helen, Irene, Florence, Joseph and Jeanette. In her later years, Anna developed health issues and needed a pacemaker for her heart. She died November 30, 1975 and is buried at St. Mary's Catholic Cemetery in Remsen, Iowa.

STUNTEBECK, Carl. The twelfth of twelve children born to Johann Heinrich Stuntebeck and Maria Agnes Kruse, Carl was born February 8, 1841 in Lehmden. He married Thekla Maria Witte and they had four children, all born in Cloppenburg, Germany. Johann Herman (b. 1876, m.

Maria Elisabeth Backhaus), Anna Maria Bernadina (b. 1879, d. 1894), Henrich Hermann (b. 1882, d. 1883) and Georg (b. 1886, m. Franziska Dohm).

STUNTEBECK, Franz Ferdinand. Frank was the third of five children born to Franz Anton Stuntebeck and Anna Maria Behne, he was born on April 15, 1865 in Lehmden, Germany. He married Mary Mullenkamp April 5, 1888, their five daughters were all born in Plymouth County, Iowa. Frank lived to the age of 91, passing away on September 24, 1956.

STUNTEBECK, Franz Anton. The sixth of twelve children born to Johann Henrich Stuntebeck and Maria Agnes Kruse, Franz was born October 22, 1828 in Lehmden, Oldenburg, Germany. He married Anna Maria Behne (daughter of Johann Arend Behne and Maria Agnes Pepersack) on June 27, 1860 in Steinfeld, Germany. Their children include Hermann August (b. 1861, m. Anna Francisca Harwickhorst), Franz Heinrich (b. 1863, d. 1863), Franz Ferdinand, b. 1865, m. Mary Mullenkamp 1888), Henry (b. 1869, m. Mary Fritz 1901) and Leonard Bernard (b. 1872, m. Lottie Marie Drier 1911).

STUNTEBECK, Johann Heinrich. The oldest of six known children, Johann Henrich was born to Bernard Johann Stuntebeck and Anna Maria Sandman in Lehmden, Oldenburg, Germany on June 19, 1788. He married Maria Agnes Kruse November 21, 1822, she was the daughter of Johan Anton Kruse and Maria Agnes Bunger, her birth date was June 4, 1799. The couple had twelve children, all born in Lehmden, Johann Carl, Gerhard Heinrich, Johan Heinrich, Maria Bernardina, Maria Dorothea, Franz Anton (b. October 22, 1828, m. Anna Maria Behne), Johann Arend, Franz Ludwig, Franz Clemens, Maria Catharina (b. June 10, 1837, m. Ferdinand Bohlke), Maria Agnes and Carl (b. February 8, 1841, m. Thekla Maria Witte).

STUNTEBECK, Johann Herman. Born to Carl Stuntebeck and Thekla Maria Witte on March 17, 1876, Johann Hermann was married to Maria Elisabeth Backhaus April 29, 1909. Their children were Heinrich (b. 1910), Maria (b. 1911), Johann (b. 1913), Elisabeth (b. 1916), Alois (b. 1914), Engelbert (1919), Georg Hermann Josef (b. 1922), Johanna (b. 1924) and Agnes (b. 1926)

STUNTEBECK, Maria Catharina. The tenth of twelve children born June 10, 1837 to Johann Heinrich Stuntebeck and Maria Agnes Kruse. She married Ferdinand Bohlke July 29, 1857; he was the son of Henrich Friedrich Arend Bohlke and Maria Agnes Scherbring. Their children were all born in Germany, Henry, Joseph, Joseph M., August, Anna Elisabeth, Frank, Johann Martin, Herman, Johann Ferdinand, Bernard and Josephine. Once in America, they initially settled in Delaware County, Iowa, after a few years they relocated to the fertile land of Plymouth County, Iowa. Their nephew Frank later joined them in Remsen, working as their hired hand for a time before investing in his own farm.

THILL, Catherine. Catherine was born in Wormeldange on January 30, 1804 to Guillaume Thill and Anne Marie Metzel, the former born in Wormeldange, the latter in Wasserbillig, Luxembourg. She married Michael Herrig February 21, 1827. The couple had seven children, William (b. 1828, m. Catharine Nemmers 1861), Anna Maria (b. 1831, d. 1832), Mathias Michael (b. 1834, m. Joanna Arens 1863), Anna (b. 1836, m. Nicholas Ohms 1867), John (b. 1840, m. Helena Haxmeier 1868), Peter (b. 1843, m. Margaretha Reuter 1872) and John Peter (b. 1846, m. Anna Haxmeier 1874).

WEBER, Catherine. Born in Dondelange, Luxembourg February 2, 1790 to Nicholas and Catherine Weber. She married John Nicholas Nemmers on November 27, 1811 in Kehlen, Luxembourg, their children include Nicholas (b. 1816, m. Maria Catherina Freymann 1841), Catherine (b. 1820, m. John Kleitsch), Petrus (b. 1820, d. 1820), Michael Sr. (b. 1821, m. Anna Even), Caroline (b. 1827, m. Johann Theodore Haxmeier 1848) and Susanne (b. 1831, m. Johann Heinrich Haxmeier). Catherina died March 23, 1876; she is buried at the Saint Donatus Catholic Cemetery.

ZAHNER, Alma. The fifth of eight children, Alma was born July 1, 1884 in Kansas City, Jackson County, Missouri to William Ignasse Zahner and Frances Antonia Riebold. On November 28, 1905 she was married to Edward Francis Mulligan, a native of Vicksburg, Mississippi. Alma and Francis had one daughter Frances Mary (b. 1906) and five sons, Frank Zahner (b. 1909), John Edward (b. 1911), Edward David (b. 1914), Karl William (b. 1916) and William Ignatius (b. 1920). Ed died January 18, 1949, Alma remained in Wichita Falls until the death of her son Edward David in

1966 when she moved to Iowa for a time, then back to her native Missouri. She died in Kansas City, Missouri at the age of 91 on April 12, 1976. She is buried in Wichita Falls, Texas.

ZAHNER, Ludwig Louis. Ludwig was born to Ludwig (son of Franz) Zahner and Magdalena Spitz on June 8, 1809 in Liel, Germany. He married Josepha Lang June 8, 1837, she died in 1939. They had one son Maxmillian (b. 1838, m. Elizabeth Henbit). On February 11, 1841 Ludwig married Fredericka Meier, their son Fredrick Louis was born February 15, 1842, Fredericka died in childbirth. Ludwig then married Louisa Boehler June 30, 1842. Four children were born to Ludwig and Louisa. Ludwig died at 45 years of age on September 10, 1854, two years after immigrating to America.

ZAHNER, William Ignasse. William was born October 22, 1847 to Ludwig Louis Zahner and Louisa Boehler. Around 1871 he married Frances Antonia Riebold. He was a tinsmith and became a successful entrepreneur. The couple had eight children, all born in Kansas City, Missouri. Fannie passed away in 1928 and William married Martha Elizabeth Smith. William died June 25, 1935 and is buried at Calvary Catholic Cemetery.

Glossary

SELECT 18th and 19th CENTURY TERMS

Following is a limited collection of words you may encounter when reading historical documents, old news items or local histories. Among the terms, a smattering were regional and others were cultural.

&c. – Nineteenth Century abbreviation for "and et cetera" or "and Etc."

AEt. – An abbreviation for aetatis, used in 18th and 19th century obituaries, meaning "at the age of." For example AEt. 94. This abbreviation can also be found on 19th century tombstones.

AGUE – Symptoms including a high fever, chills and sweating, an illness like malaria.

ALMSHOUSE – Charitable housing often for older people, especially widows that can't afford to pay rent. Generally maintained by a religious or other charitable organization.

ANTEBELLUM – The period of time before a war, this term is most often used in reference to the time prior to the American Civil War.

APOPLECTIC FIT or APOPLEXY – A stroke.

BILIOUS FEVER – An eighteenth and nineteenth century description of a fever in conjunction with vomiting.

BLACKSMITH – A metal smith who forges and repairs tools, horseshoes, plows as well as smaller items like hinges, latches and nails.

BLUING – A laundry rinse additive used for centuries to help brighten whites that have been dulled by age or the effects of lye soap. Bluing is still available and used today.

BRACES – A term used during the Civil War, referring to suspenders. The term is of British origin and is still used today.

BRAIN FEVER – A term that was used to describe the symptoms of meningitis.

BRIMSTONE – Another term for sulphur.

CAISSON – In the Civil War this referred to a two wheeled horse-drawn cart carrying an ammunition box.

CALIFORNIA WIDOW– A wife separated by distance from her husband. A phrase that began during the time of the California Gold Rush when husbands left their families behind while they prospected for gold.

CALK – In northern and icy climates, providing horses or oxen with shoes with sharp points to prevent the animals from slipping on icy surfaces.

CARTWRIGHT – A maker of carts.

CASIMERE – A spelling of cashmere no longer in use, it was a product carried in eighteenth and nineteenth century general stores.

CHAPMAN – A peddler.

CHAUTAUQUA – During the early 20th century, this was a touring event, locals flocked to see their lecturers, musicians, plays and other displays. Topics ranged from temperance to prison reform and other social issues, often tailored to specific local interests.

CHINK – A crack or fissure, when relating to log cabins, a chink was the space between the logs.

CHINKING – When building a log cabin, chinking was the mixture used to fill the spaces or chinks between the logs, creating a draft-free cozy living area.

CISTERN – An underground rainwater storage container, water was then used for laundry or non-drinking purposes.

COAL OIL – An extract of a soft oily coal used as lamp oil. It was sometimes referred to as "kerosene oil" but a completely different product than the petroleum based product that became known as kerosene in the early twentieth century.

COMMON SCHOOL – 19th century public schools in the United States and Canada.

CONSCRIPTION – Compulsory enrollment of people in the military, a practice that dates back centuries, today in the United States it is more commonly called the draft.

CONSUMPTION – In days gone by, when cause of death was described as consumption, they were referring to tuberculosis or a bacterial infection involving the lungs.

CONESTOGA WAGON – A Heavy-duty canvas covered wagon that hauled freight or family possessions over rough terrain, it was pulled by oxen or large horses. These wagons were used before railroads were built, the larger wagons could carry a six ton load.

COOPER – A maker of wooden barrels, buckets and other vessels, a cooper also repairs these containers.

COPPERHEAD – During the Civil War, northerners who were opposed to the war or worked against the Union Army were called Copperheads.

CORDWAIN – A supple, luxury grade of leather.

CORDWAINER – A shoemaker that works with cordwain.

CRACKLINGS – The crispy pork bits that remain after rendering fat into lard.

CUCUMBER PUMP – A common form of water pump used by early settlers, where the main pipe was a hollowed length of cucumber wood.

DAUBING – A mixture of materials used to fill spaces between logs of a log cabin, like chinking.

DROPSEY – A term formerly used to describe edema or swelling from fluid retention, it also sometimes described congestive heart failure.

DRUGGET – A heavy woolen rug with a print design on one side often carried in upscale general stores.

EMBALMED BEEF – A term used by Union Soldiers to describe the canned beef they were issued. The name was given due to the color of the product, which was less than appealing.

ENCLAVE – This term was often used to describe a community of Germans living in America, but maintaining their German language, culture and habits.

ERYSIPELAS – A skin infection.

FARRIER – A person that cares for equine hooves, trimming, shaping and shoeing the hoof, a blacksmith often handled the role of a farrier.

FLAX SEED OIL – A non-petroleum based oil obtained from pressed dried flax seeds. Flax seed oil is the base from which linseed oil is extracted.

FLUX – Diarrhea.

FOUNDLING – Orphaned and abandoned infants and young children. Infants "found" with no adult to care for them.

FOURSCORE – Eighty.

FURBISH – Clean or polish a weapon.

GUNNING – An early reference to hunting with a gun.

HARDTACK – A hard flat dry biscuit or cracker made from flour, salt and water. Hardtack was a common traveling food and it was issued to Civil War Union Soldiers as their main food source. The Civil War soldiers applied the nickname "jawbreakers."

HEPATIC ABSCESS – A liver abscess, commonly caused by an appendicitis infection

HEUERLING – A German social class describing a tenant farmer that puts in a lifetime of hard work with little in return.

HYDROPHOBIA – A fear of water, this term is one of the symptoms of rabies.

INDENTURED SERVANT – A practice that was used during the 17th, 18th and early 19th centuries, where an emigrant without money would agree to work for a period of seven years in return for passage to America.

INMATE – In the 19th century and prior, an inmate referred to a resident of a home or other facility, it was referring to a fellow-resident (mate).

INSTANT or INST. – In or of the current month. This term is found in 18th and 19th century newspapers referring to the current month, "he left for Washington on the 1st inst."

JOURNALIER – When describing an occupation, this term refers to day laborer, researchers are most likely to encounter this term when looking at French or Luxembourgish birth or marriage records.

KEVEL – A stone mason's hammer.

KEY NIPPER – A burglary device, or an old time lock pick.

KINETOSCOPE – An early, stand-alone, motion picture device. One person at a time could view the film through a peephole on top of the device.

LA GRIPPE – A reference to Spanish Flu, an influenza that killed tens of millions of people worldwide in 1918 and 1919.

LAND GRANT – A grant of public land.

LAND PATENT – In respect to our pioneer ancestors it is the initial conveyance of title of a land grant, including the legal description, from the U. S. Government to a citizen.

LARDER – A pantry or cupboard for storing food before refrigerators were common, an area as cool as possible near the kitchen.

LAUDANUM – The dictionary describes laudanum as a tincture of opium, laudanum was easily available during the 19th century and it wasn't uncommon to see the cause of death, whether accident or suicide contributed to an overdose of laudanum.

LIMBER – During the Civil War this was a two wheeled vehicle often mounted with a large artillery piece.

LINSEED OIL – A non-petroleum based oil extracted from flax seed oil which is pressed from dried flax seeds. Linseed oil was used by pioneers for waterproofing cloth used for outer clothing, covered wagons, table cloths, mattress covers and more.

LOGGER – A person who harvests lumber, similar to a lumberjack but not as dedicated to the profession as a lumberjack.

LUNG FEVER – Pneumonia.

LUNGER – A person with tuberculosis.

MAN'S ESTATE – 18th and 19th Century meaning of reaching adulthood.

MANIA A POTU – Madness or delirium from drinking.

MILLER – A person that mills grain, or grinds wheat into flour.

MILLINER – A person involved in designing, creating or selling hats.

MILLWRIGHT – A person that builds or repairs mills or machinery that mills grain.

MOBOCRACY – Rule or domination by the masses. This was a term used in reference to a lynching.

MORIBUND – When this term is used in reference to a person, it means they are at death's door.

NORMAL SCHOOL – A noun describing a two-year school for the training of elementary teachers.

OLD STATES– The original or eastern states, for example "The Smith's move here from The Old States."

OLDERMOST– Simply refers to the oldest.

PALLET – A straw mattress or a crude bed.

PELT – The skin of an animal with the hair or fur still intact, fur trading was often used to supplement a farmer's income in the 19th century.

PHAETON – Sporty 19th century open carriage often with larger than normal wheels.

PICKET DUTY – When referring to the Civil War, it is classified as one of the most dangerous roles carried out by soldiers. They circled the encampment, acting as guards and watchmen, this made them first in line to be shot or captured.

PINERIES or PINERY – Forested areas. When a 19th century ancestor is said to have worked in the pineries he was a logger, performing the dangerous job of cutting down trees.

POCK or THE POCK – A slang word used for referring to Small Pox.

PRIMOGENITURE – A custom or law where the firstborn son inherits his parents entire estate or land rights. If no sons are living, there have been customs where daughters are still passed over in favor of brothers of the deceased. Most of these laws have been discontinued.

PROTHONOTARY – The head clerk in certain courts of law, generally an elected or appointed position.

PROMIMO or PROX. – In or of the following month. Terminology often used inn 18th and 19th century newspapers referring to the upcoming month.

RELICT – When used in an older obituary, this referred to a surviving widow or widower, a remnant of a species . . . the remaining person of the couple.

REPAST – A noun used to describe a meal or feast, the term is now obsolete.

ROCKAWAY – A 19th century horse-drawn carriage with curtained or windowed openings and a cover projecting over the driver's seat.

ROD – A unit of measurement 16.5 feet in length, used in the past for surveying land.

S.A.T.C. – A WWI abbreviation for Student Army Training Corp.

SALTPETER – Potassium nitrate. Not only used in gunpowder, settlers used to aid food preservation, medicinal concoctions as well as an aid for speeding the decay of tree trunks.

SAMP – Coarsely ground yellow corn. Pioneers made this economical long-time Native American staple into a porridge, sometimes adding beans.

SATURNISM – Lead poisoning.

SAWYER – A person who saws timber for a living.

SCRIP – When used in reference to land, the Federal Government would barter using land as cash with railroads and local governments, who would then sell the land or scrip to individuals or businesses. Land scrips were also given to soldiers for service to their country.

SCURVY – A vitamin C deficiency resulting in bleeding gums or the opening of healed sores, it was common among sailors. Once it was determined that limes are particularly effective in preventing the disease, the Royal Navy issued limes to their sailors, resulting in the British sometimes being referred to as "Limeys."

SHINPLASTERS – A term for early to mid-nineteenth century frontier paper money issued by wildcat banks or large local businesses due to a shortage of regular currency. It was common for this currency to experience a sudden loss of value, especially as the currency moved away from the location of the issuing bank.

SHOAT – A young piglet ready to be weaned or newly weaned.

SMUTTER – A machine used by farmers or grain handlers that separated debris from grain, resulting in a cleaner higher value collection of seeds and grain.

SPRING WAGON – A four wheeled horse drawn wagon with removable seats. The seat feature made it useful for travel as well as farm or business use. The wagon had spring suspension.

STAVE – A narrow strip of wood of varied uses such as the slats that form a barrel and rods that stabilize chair legs and ladder rungs, among other uses.

STONE MASON – A pioneer stone mason was a person who could take rocks and chisel them into shapes to build homes, churches and other structures.

SURTOUT – A man's loose fitting overcoat, a term used in the 18th and 19th centuries.

TEAMSTER – A teamster in the 19th century or earlier was a person that drove a team of horses for a living.

TINNER or TINSMITH – A person who makes things such as pails and coffee pots from lightweight metal. Young tinsmiths often peddled their wares, traveling from door to door until they accumulated the funds to open their own shop.

TONSORIAL ARTIST – A barber.

TOW SHIRT – Clothing made from a rough linen fabric, the term was often used as a description of clothing a runaway indentured person was wearing when last seen.

TURNKEY – A jailer.

TWAIN – A an archaic meaning of two, still used in the phase . . . never the twain shall meet.

QUINSY – Also listed as quinzy is a term for Peritonsillar Abscess, a complication of tonsillitis or an abscess around one or both tonsils.

WHEELWRIGHT – A talented craftsman that builds or repairs wooden wheels, a common occupation prior to the twenty-first century.

WHITE CAPS – A movement that began in Indiana, white males, often farmers, who delivered "justice" where the state failed; targets included men who neglected their family, women with children out of wedlock, etc. In the south the White Caps were similar to the KKK.

WILDCAT BANKS – An early to mid-nineteenth century description of frontier state licensed banks that issued shinplaster currency without adequate backing. The currency could quickly lose value, leaving depositors with a fraction of their original savings.

WRIGHT – A builder or maker of something, such as a wheelwright.

ULTIMO or ULT. – In or of the month preceding this one. It was often used in older newspapers as "died the 28th Ultimo."

Bibliography

Ash, Sister Mary Kay. Archivist. *Sisters of Notre Dame.*

Bellevue Herald Leader, Thursday November 30, 2006, Section A.

Biennial Report for The New York Foundling Hospital, New York, 1902.

Bohlke, Mrs. Mary. Remsen Bell-Enterprise. *Oldest Resident is Given to the Grave.* Remsen, Iowa, July 5, 1934.

Bohnenkamp, Frank. Dyersville Commercial. *Death of Frank Bohnenkamp.* Dyersville, Iowa, May 14, 1910.

Bohnenkamp, Margaret (Millenkamp). Dyersville Commercial. *Mrs. F. Bohnenkamp's Death Was Sudden.* Dyersville, Iowa, Sept. 17, 1920.

Census, 1843 Luxembourg. Manders Family. Sandweiler, Luxembourg Census of 1843, FHL Microfilm..

Census, 1849 Luxembourg. Flammang Family. Koerich, Luxembourg Census from 1849, FHL Microfilm.

Census, 1850 United States. Franklin County, Missouri; Tete Des Mort Twsp, Jackson County, Iowa; Bellevue Township, Jackson County, Iowa.

Census, 1860 United States. Tete Des Mort Twsp, Jackson County, Iowa. Carr Township, Clark County, Indiana. Franklin County, Missouri.

Census, 1870 United States. Jackson County, Iowa. Warren County, Mississippi. Jackson County, Missouri. Louisville, Jefferson County, Kentucky.

Census, 1880 United States. Warren County, Mississippi. Jackson County, Iowa. Jackson County, Missouri.

Census, 1900 United States. Nobles County, Minnesota. Warren County, Mississippi. Delaware County, Iowa. Plymouth County, Iowa. Jackson County, Iowa. Jackson County, Missouri.

Census, 1910 United States. Jackson County, Iowa. Plymouth County, Iowa. Jackson County, Missouri. Franklin County, Missouri. Warren County, Mississippi.

Census, 1925 Iowa State. Clinton, Jackson and Plymouth Counties.

Chambers, Vicki Jean. Associate Archivist. General information on Sister Mary Pulcheria Hoxmeier and Sister Mary Prosper Hoxmeier.

Chapman-Brothers. *Portrait and Biographical Album for Jackson County, Iowa.* Chicago. Biographies for N. A. Hoffmann, Theodore Niemann.

Charity, Sisters of. New York Foundling Hospital. New York, NY, 1902.

Civil-War. Battle of Fort Blakely. *My Civil War.* [Online] [Cited: November 25, 2008.] www.mycivilwar.com/battles/650402e.htm.
—. Benton Barracks. *Civil War.* [Online] [Cited: November 26, 2008.] www.mcwm.org/history_bentonbarracks.html.

Dame, Sisters of Notre. Obituaries, teaching history and family notes. Three Flammang Sisters - Irena, Agapia and Chionia.

Deltgen, Bob. Luxembourg Genealogist.

Dubuque, Archdiocese of. Archives and Historical Records.

Elting, Colonel John Robert. Commentary and historical consultant to PBS "Napoleon at War" .

Fallis, C., editor. The Encyclopedic Atlas of Wine pg 258-259 Global Book Publishing 2006.

Fisch. Hastings Conserver. Hastings, Minnesota, August 4, 1863.

Fisch, Eva (Manders). Luxemburger Gazette. [trans.] Mary Kay Krogman. November 12, 1907. Translated from German.

Fisher. Fisher Funeral Home Records For Mulligan, O'Neil and Farrell 1887-1919.

Fisher, Onieta. Life in a Log Home. *Frontier Life.* [Online] [Cited: November 2, 2009.] www.uni.edu/iowahist/Frontier_Life/Life_in_Log_Home.htm.

Flammang, Mary (Niemann). Obituary. *Dubuque Times-Journal.* May 18, 1920.

Flammang, Nicholas. Golden Anniversary. *Luxemburger Gazette.* August 17, 1916, Mr. and Mrs. Nicholas FLammang, translated from German.

Frevert, Ute. *A Nation in Barracks : Modern Germany, Military Conscription and Civil Society.* pp. 102-115, 138-140. Bloomsbury Publishing, 2004, London.

Gardini, Fausto. *Luxembourg On My Mind.* Jacksonville, Florida, 2011. History, Immigration, Background.

Geer, Captain J. J. 1863. *Beyond The Lines.* Philadelphia : J. W. Daughaday, 1863.

Gonner, Nicholas. *Luxembourgers in the New World, Volume I.* Dubuque, Iowa. Surnames - Manders, Flammang, Koos, Herrig, Hoffmann.

Graves, Judy. Archivist for St. Mary's Catholic Church in Hull, Iowa.

Halbach, Rev. Arthur A. *Dyersville - Its History and Its People.* pp. 288,382, 412 and 421. St. Joseph Press, Milwaukee, Wisconsin, 1939.

Hansen, Theodore. Remsen Bell-Enterprise. *Theo. Hansen is Dead.* Remsen, Iowa, November 21, 1918.

Herrig, Michael. Luxemburger Gazette. [trans.] Mary Kay Krogman. *A Double Celebration.* Dubuque, Iowa, March 6, 1877, translated from German.

History. Dust Bowl. *Living History Farm.* [Online] [Cited: December 10, 2008.] Living in the Dust Bowl Years. www.livinghistoryfarm.org/farminginthe30s.

Holls-Reibold. Certificate of Marriage -1860. *Franklin County Missouri Public Records.*

Hull, Isabel V. *Absolute Destruction, Cornell University Press .*

Illinois. Secretary of State. *Muster and Descriptive Rolls of Illinois Civil War Units.* Recruit listing (Peter Schartz).

Interior, Department of. *Bureau of Pensions.* Application dated May 16, 1898 .

—. *Bureau of Pensions.* Declaration for Widow's Pension. Application, stamped Aug. 26, 1901.

—. *Official Register of the United States.* September 30, 1867. Entry for Michael Manders.

Iowa, State Historical Society of. Iowa Territorial and State Legislators Collection. [Online] Nicholas B. Nemmers, Legislature Standard Form for Representatives.

Jackson, County of. *Farm Ownership Plat Book.* Stacy Map Publishers, Rockford, Ill, 1914. Prairie Springs, Tete des Morts, Richland and Bellevue Townships.

Jaeger, Betty (Manders). *Manders Farm.* Online postings of visit to Manders farm in Luxembourg, and history of the farm..

Kehlen, Luxembourg. Luxembourg Civil Records. Birth records of Marie Hoffmann, Nicholas Hoffmann, Michael Hoffmann, Nicholas Banks, Henry Banks, etc.

Keller, Catherine. Copies of Certificate of Birth, Foundling Hospital Letter.

Koerich, Luxemburg. *Civil Records - Birth Records on Microfilm 1750 - 1850.* Flammang and Gretan.

Krenzelok, Greg. The Steerage Experience. *Rootsweb.com.* [Online] [Cited: March 20, 2008.] freepages.family.rootsweb.com/~gregkrenzelok/.

Krieps, Roger. *Luxembourgers in America.* Luxembourg American Cultural Society, Belgium, Wisconsin, 2013.

Krogman, Henry. Certificate of Death, certified copy. Plymouth County : Iowa State Department of Health, 1942.
—. Obituary "Death Claims Pioneer Settler". *Remsen Bell-Enterprise.* November 20, 1942.

Krogmann, Heinrich. Passport Application. Plymouth County, Iowa : 1908.

Krogmann, Henrich. Naturalization Paper. Sioux County, Iowa : 1889.

Krogmann, Joh. Passenger List. *Bremen Germany to Baltimore Maryland, Sep 1882.* S. S. Ohio.

Krogmann, John Henry. Chattell Mortgage. (for a brown mule) 1886, Sioux County, Iowa.

Krogmann, Lena. Certificate of Death, certified copy. Meadow Township, Plymouth County : Iowa State Board of Health, 1906.

Krogmann-Olberding. Germany Civil Records. *1851 Holthausen Marriage Documents.* FHL Microfilm.

Labor, US Department of. *Wages and Earnings in the United States.* 1881 - Chapter 5 Wages by Industry and Region.

Land Patents. *Bureau of Land Management.* [Online] Certificates: Haxmier #39313;Riebold #16867, 16238; Mees #17499; Manders #11469; Niemann #5268, 5269, 12,537. www.glorecords.blm.gov.

Lanners. Family Tree. *Rootsweb.* [Online] [Cited: January 24, 2002.] www.worldconnect.rootsweb.com/.

Larson, Tom. Gerken-Larson Heritage. [Online] Extensive research including sources and transcribed news articles. http://freepages.genealogy.rootsweb.ancestry.com/~tdlarson/.

Manders, Elizabeth. Jackson Sentinel, Maquoketa, Iowa. *Obituary.* December 7, 1893.

Manders, Mathias. *Grand-Duchy of Luxembourg.* 1851 Government Document detailing militia call-up and deserters.

Manders, Michael. Our Civil War Veterans. *Minnesota Lake Tribune.* June 9, 2011.

Manders, Veronica.
—. Iowa City Press-Citizen. *Mystery of Missing Twain is Cleared.* Iowa City, Iowa, 1922.
—. Rockford Republic. *Girl, 15, and Cousin, 22, Found Dead.* March 31, 1922.

Manders-Family-Tree. Tree created circa 1975, accompanied by a listing of birth dates of people on the tree.

Michael L. Nemmers, A Centennial Appreciation. **Nemmers, Erwin Esser. 1955.** July - August 1955, Caecilia.

Mississippi. *Biographical and Historical Memoirs of Mississippi, Vol. II.* s.l. : The Goodspeed Publishing Company, Chicago 1891. 483.
—. *The Official and Statistical Register of the State of Mississippi Centennial Edition.* 1917, page 254.

Muehlenkamp, William. Death Takes Old Remsen Resident. *Remsen Bell-Enterprise.* March 31, 1932.
—. Verdict For Plaintiff. *Remsen Bell-Enterprise.* October 12, 1916.

Mulligan. Mississippi State Board of Health. *Certificate of Death, certified copies.* For John J. Mulligan dated March 14, 1919. For Mary A. Mulligan dated September 10, 1917.
—. Various News Articles. *Daily Herald.* Vicksburg, Mississippi. September 3, 1877, February 7, 1878, May 20, 1878, February 7, 1879, April 30, 1880, August 29, 1882, June 11, 1901, November 15, 1903, September 9, 1917, September 11, 1917 and March 15, 1919.

Mulligan, John J. 1896. *Car Door. 554,078* Mississippi, February 4, 1896.
—. 1894. *Freight Car Door. 513,336* Mississippi, January 23, 1894.
—. Last Will and Testament. Signed Mar. 3, 1919.

Mulligan-Farrell. *Marriage Certificate.* Warren County, Mississippi, Jno. J. Mulligan and Mary Ann Farrell - July 29th, 1875.

Mulligan-Zahner. Married. *Kansas City Star.* Marriage news article dated November 29, 1905.

Nebraska. Harlan County History. *USACE.* [Online] [Cited: December 10, 2008.] Republican River Valley (Nebraska). www.nwk.usace.army.mil/hc/History.cfm.
—. Republican River Flood of 1935. *Nebraska History.* [Online] [Cited: December 10, 2008.] www.nebraskahistory.org/publish/markers/texts/republican_river_floo do_1935.htm.

Nemmers, Michael P. 1873. *Hand Corn-Planter. 144,919* St. Donatus, Iowa, November 25, 1873.

Ostwald, Mich. Passenger Manifest. Le Havre to New Orleans on the Ship "New Orleans".

Otting, Rev. Loras C. Director of the Archives and Historical Records, Dubuque, Iowa.

Prince, Richard E. *Nashville, Chattanooga & St Louis Railway History and Steam Locomotives.* - 2001. (Rail Service During the Civil War).

Ragland, Mary Lois S. *Fisher Funeral Home Records - Vicksburg Mississippi 1854-1867.* Bowie Maryland : Heritage Books - 1992.

Redemptorist Church. Kansas City, Missouri. Church and burial records of Zahner parishioners.

Riebold, Xavier. Naturalization Papers. March 28, 1848.

Riles, Charles. Former owner of the Fisher-Riles Funeral home in Vicksburg, old records and obits of Mulligan, Farrell and O'Neil families.

Sacred Heart Church. Wichita Falls, Texas, Mulligan - Church, Burial and Cemetery Records.

Schartz, Angeline. Luxemburger Gazette. [trans.] Mary Kay Krogman. Dec. 31, 1907. Obituary of Mrs Peter Schartz, translated from German.

Schartz, Peter. Declaration for Widow's Pension. Pension office stamp August 26, 1901.
—. Philadelphia Inquirer Dec. 15, 1890, Omaha World Herald Aug. 16, 1898 Pension Announcements.

Schoone-Jonjen, Robert. 2008. *Historian at Calvin College.* 2008. Information related to Northwest Iowa and Dutch Calvinists.

Schott, Larry E. Volunteer at the Franklin County Missouri Historical Society. Cemetery and Church Information.

Sobczynski, Sister Suzanne Rene. Archivist for Sisters of Notre Dame.

SS Peter & Paul Church. Dyersville, Iowa. Muehlenkamp and Bohnenkamp baptismal, marriage, burial records.

St. Nicholaus Catholic Church. Spruce Creek, Iowa; Church baptism records of the Niemann Family.

St. Paul Catholic Church. Vicksburg, Mississippi; Mulligan and Farrell birth, marriage and death records from 1853-1919.

Steinfeld, Germany. Public Records of Birth. Krogmann births, marriages and deaths shared by Linda Edwards via email from her transcript of Steinfeld, Germany records.

Stevens, Missy. Via email, information on the history of the Missouri Bar Association - 2008.

Stuntebeck. *Certificate of Death.* State of Iowa, Certified Copies for Frank Stuntebeck 1956 and Mary Stuntebeck 1928.

Stuntebeck, Frank. Remsen Bell-Enterprise. *Funeral Here Today for Frank Stuntebeck.* September 27, 1956, Remsen, Iowa.

Stuntebeck, Mrs. Frank. Remsen Bell-Enterprise. *Death Takes Mrs. Frank Stuntebeck.* Remsen, Iowa, November 8, 1928.

Stuntebeck-Behne. Luxembourg Civil Records. Steinfeld, Germany Marriage records from mid 1800's on FHL Microfilm.

Swenson, G. A. *Soil Survey, Jackson County, Iowa.* United States Department of Agriculture Charge.

Tritz, Mary Cleo. *St. Donatus: A Settlement of Luxemburgers in Northeast Iowa.* Thesis written in 1954.

Tuntingen, Village of. Luxemburg Marriage Records FHL Film# 1981105. 1751 - 1800. Surnames include Nemmers, Mullhentgen, Cepesius, Maur and Meysenburg.

Vicksburg. *City Directories of Vicksburg and Port Gibson, Mississippi.* pp. 22, 30, 34, 39. 1879.

—. *City Directory.* pp. 44, 99, 102, 197, 205. Press of the Vicksburg Printing & Publishing Co. - 1895.
—. *City Directory of Vicksburg.* pp. 231, 232, R. L. Polk & Co. Publishers, 1911-12.
—. First Victim of Memphis Yellow-Fever Epidemic Dies. *This Day in History.* [Online] [Cited: November 7, 2008.] August 13 1878. www.history.com/this-day-in-history.
Vollor, Circuit Court Judge Frank. Warren County, Mississippi..

War, Department of. *Commissioner of Pensions Report for Peter Schultz aka Peter Schartz.* Washington D. C. : Adjutant General's Office, 1883.

Wilder, Frank A. *Iowa Geological Survey, Vol. XVI.* Des Moines : 1905.

Wildt, Sister Carol Marie. Sisters of Notre Dame Archivist. Obituary, teaching history and family background of Sister Irene Flammang .

Yeager, Lt. John Lynn. *Wrapped In Flames.* Vicksburg, Mississippi : 1976.

Zahner. Certificate of Death (certified copies). *Missouri State Board of Health.* Louisa Zahner August 12, 1880, Frances Zahner March 3, 1928 and William Zahner June 27, 1935.
—. Grow Your Factory Here. *Kansas City Star.* September 15, 1913. The Zahners' Metal Plant an Object Lesson to Manufacturers.
—. Various News Articles. *Kansas City Star.* Including September 1, 1894, November 15, 1903, February 25, 1906, June 27, 1919.

Zahner, Anton. Passenger Manifest. From Le Havre to New York on the Ship "Charlemagne".

Zahner, Louisa. Record of Death - Kansas City, Missouri (certified copy). August 12, 1880.

Index

A

B

C

D

E

F

G

H

J

K

L

M

N

O

P

Q

R

S

T

V

W

Y

Z

Made in the USA
Lexington, KY
12 December 2018